The Creation of Evil

Casting light into the purposes of darkness

JOHN NOĒ, Ph.D.

A Scholarly Review

This book has the potential to significantly reinforce a crucial trend in today's world—the correction of longstanding errors of biblical understanding. It is Noē's contention, with which I totally agree, that traditions of interpretation that have evolved from the faulty presuppositions of prominent theologians—some of whom lived long ago—have often overridden what the Bible actually teaches, with the consequence that popular Christian beliefs about God's role in the world and the destiny of humanity have often been led astray. It is Noē's mission in this book to dispel faulty beliefs about what the Bible teaches regarding evil and to offer suggestions as to how these misunderstandings can be rectified.

That a benevolent and all-powerful God has chosen to allow evil to befall even righteous people is an idea that troubles a great many Christians. The most popular rationale for explaining this dilemma has followed the Augustinian belief that humankind has free will and brings evil on itself because of its rebellion against God's will. Ultimately, many Christians believe, Satan and the demonic forces that perpetrate evil will be overcome, and a kind of heaven on earth will be established in which evil has been banished. It is Noē's well-argued contention, however, that a "Second Coming" of Christ that establishes this heaven on earth result is simply not to be found in the Bible. What is there is a new covenantal order as indicated in Revelation 21-22.

In dealing with the problem of evil, leading Christian authorities have tended to argue that to a great extent, God allows evil in order to bring good. Thus, without the presence of evil, humans tend to behave like spoiled children and fail to develop the moral character and depth of understanding of the world that results from coping with evil while doggedly maintaining the faith that God is in control. While Noe provides an impressive analysis of how evil can lead to good, he does not claim that God's intended purposes in allowing evil are fully comprehensible to us humans. We can, however, be confident that God knows what He is doing.

This book is written in easy to understand prose and is laid out so as to make it easy to grasp what is being presented. It also offers, however, an enormous quantity of scholarly references to both the Bible and to the works of leading biblical authorities. While Noe treats those authorities with whom he disagrees with respect, he does not hesitate to suggest when they are wrong. Especially appealing to me are his accounts of how some prominent Christian authorities who have suffered tragic losses have dealt with their situations.

In short, this book is powerful stuff, very meaningful to this 84-year-old seeker of Christ. It's well worth your attention.

John S. Evans, Ph.D.

<u>Pre-publication Comments
from Facebook Friends:</u>

"This is a scary topic!
Most folks don't want to think about it
or venture into it – at least not Christians anyways."
– Lori Edwards

"Looks awesome!"
– Deborah Brenner

"I am looking forward to getting this one. I have read a few of
John Noe's other books, and have learned so much from them.
He has such a great way of writing that is not only full of detail and
'meat,' but is simple enough for anyone to understand."
– Cindy DeGroot

"Looking forward to reading this one, Dr. Noē. I enjoyed
Hell Yes / Hell No and am also looking forward to your work on
Kingdom Christianity. I have listened to the podcasts; it is book worthy!"
Good stuff."
– Navon Lindo, Jr.

The Creation of Evil

By John Noē, Ph.D.

Published by:

East2West Press
Publishing arm of the Prophecy Reformation Institute

5236 East 72nd Street
Indianapolis, IN 46250 USA
(317)-842-3411

Cover: Tom Haulter

ISBN: 978-0-9834303-6-0

Library of Congress Control Number: 2015901365

Evil. Creation. Bible. Old Testament Revelation. New Testament
Revelation

Dedication

To my many readers over the years.
You have afforded me the honor and privilege
to serve as a writer and a teacher.
Without you, my efforts would be in vain.

To those who may stand on my shoulders one day.
May God "give you his Spirit of wisdom and revelation,
so that you may know him better" (Eph. 1:17).

To Tom Haulter, my friend and graphic designer,
for your incredible talent and perseverance in working with me.
This cover may be our best yet.

To John S. Evans, my 84-year-old friend and colleague.
Thank you for your many contributions and encouragements.
May this book specially bless, comfort, and encourage you.

CONTACT US:

Prophecy Reformation Institute
5236 East 72nd Street
Indianapolis, IN 46250
www.prophecyrefi.org
jnoe@prophecyrefi.org
Ph. # 317-842-3411

Contents

Introduction

No Evil, No Christianity

We live in a violent and dangerous world in which evil is inevitable. We also live in a world filled with good and plenty. Why is this so?

The fact is, sooner or later, evil strikes everyone. At different times, in different forms, and in differing degrees, it variously produces pain, suffering, disease, disaster, tragedy, and loss. If evil hasn't yet stricken you or someone you know or love, turn on your television news or glance at a newspaper and you shall see many manifestations thereof from the previous day, locally and internationally.

Some of us, of course, accept the eventuality of evil as a fact of life. Most of us, however, aren't so sure how to explain or handle it, especially when it crosses our path and hits home. Again, why is this so?

On the other hand, evil is a fascinating subject. Multiple millions are mesmerized by it. That's why, for instance, the most popular programs on the History Channel are about Hitler and the Nazis, not to mention the evil content of most movies and other television programs. For others, however, the mere mention of evil prompts a quick change of subject. By contrast, good seems dull and boring. But both good and evil, and their resultant blessings or sufferings, are universal realities of human life on this planet called Earth. Why so?

Sadly, in my study of this subject of good and evil over many years, it has become increasingly amazing to me how many unscriptural notions have evolved and appeal to most Christians, as well as to the world at large. Therefore, let's begin our discussion of the creation of evil by seriously considering the title of this Introduction. Do you find its theological proposition of "No Evil, No Christianity" startling, perhaps shocking? It was for me the first time I considered it. So did evil make Christianity possible, indeed necessary? Consider this.

True or False? Agree or disagree?

- Without evil, there would have been no need for a progression of covenants or grounds for the Law and the Prophets?
- Without evil, no reason for Israel or its animal-sacrifice-Temple system?
- Without evil, no rationale for Christ lowering Himself to be born into this world as a human being?
- Without evil, no justification for the cross?
- Without evil, no basis for redemption or resurrection?
- Without evil, no purpose in pouring out the Holy Spirit?
- Without evil, no churches, no pastors, no Bible, no gospel, no Christians?
- No evil, no Christianity?

Few in Church history have seriously contemplated this possible interconnectedness or recognized this conundrum. That is why theologians, philosophers, pastors, and even atheists have traditionally become accustomed to referring to and treating evil as "the problem of evil." Hence, they persistently pose this question—"Why evil?" Ironically, few have ever questioned, "Why good?"

One scholar who recognizes evil's interrelationship with Christianity and its necessity is Gregory E. Ganssle. He ardently declares with succinctness:

Christianity *requires* there to be evil. If no evil existed, we would know that Christianity is false. Furthermore, Christianity requires a great deal more than a superficial amount of evil. The evil has to be so significant that the highest sacrifice is warranted. Christianity is the story of God entering the world and paying the highest price to deal with the root of evil.[1]

Consequently, throughout history, untold numbers of human beings, as well as animals, have been haunted by and suffered from a wide variety of evil manifestations, even horrendous evil. Today, seven billion of us live in a world engulfed with evil and its devastating, intense, and insidious nature. Moreover, it's produced from a variety of sources: human beings, animals, nature, and perhaps supernatural beings and one other source as well, as we shall discover later on in this book. Then there is death, which many regard as the greatest evil of all. The Bible terms death the "last enemy" (1 Cor. 15:26a).

But the greater good news is, we are also surrounded by a lot of good—human good, animal good, natural good, and perhaps supernatural good. Hence, our world is filled with the dualities of pleasure yet pain, joy yet suffering, wellness yet disease, natural wonders yet natural disasters, justice yet injustice, prosperity yet poverty, opportunity yet misfortune, and life yet death. And no one is exempt from these polar opposites.

Paradoxically, however, evil seems to be unequally distributed. And while some evil seems fair; some seems blatantly unfair. Why is this so? Human speculations abound and opinions vary. But one thing is sure. Tragedy, pain, suffering, misery, anguish, loss, and death are part of being born into this world, living here, and getting out of it. Sooner or later, every person alive on planet Earth will suffer from evil and its inherent loss.

. . . theologians, philosophers, pastors, and even atheists have traditionally become accustomed to referring to and treating evil as "the problem of evil." Hence they persistently pose this question— "Why evil?"

---

[1] Gregory E. Ganssle, "Evil as Evidence for Christianity" in Chad Meister and James K. Dew, Jr., eds., *God and Evil: The Case for God in a World Filled with Pain* (Downers Grove, IL: IVP Books, 2013), 221.

Ironically, when the worst happens, people respond differently. Some triumph; others succumb; some become victors; others victims; some are made stronger; others are broken. Either way, evil awaits us all, and from a wide variety of circumstances which none of us would choose or can control. And when it happens to you, or those close to you, you cannot remain the same as before.

In his book *Walking with God though Pain and Suffering*, which I recommend, Timothy Keller lays out the unavoidable reality of evil this way:

> The loss of loved ones, debilitating and fatal illnesses, personal betrayals, financial reversals, and moral failures—all of these will eventually come upon you if you live out a normal life span. No one is immune.
>
> Therefore, no matter what precautions we take, no matter how well we have put together a good life, no matter how hard we have worked to be healthy, wealthy, comfortable with friends and family, and successful with our career—something will inevitably ruin it. No amount of money, power, and planning can prevent bereavement, dire illness, relationship betrayal, financial disaster, or a host of other troubles from entering your life. Human life is fatally fragile and subject to forces beyond our power to mange. Life is tragic.
>
> We all know this intuitively, and those who face the challenge of suffering and pain learn all too well that it is impossible to do so using only our own resources.[2]

So what do we do? We try not to think about these things as we live reasonably well and expect the best. Philip Yancey, in his book *The Question That Never Goes Away: Why?*, characterizes evil's ultimate inevitableness and our earthly dilemma, thusly:

> We all die, some old, some tragically young. God provides support and solidarity, yes, but not protection—at least not the kind of protection we desperately long for. On this cursed planet, even God suffered the loss of a Son.[3]

---

[2] Timothy Keller, *Walking with God through Pain and Suffering* (New York, NY: Dutton, 2013), 3.
[3] Philip Yancey, *The Question That Never Goes Away: Why?* (Grand Rapids, MI: Zondervan, 2013), 137.

The Purpose of This Book

So is there a point, a purpose, or purposes in all this evil adversity? Is there any rhyme or reason for the overwhelming amount of evil, pain, and suffering that exists? Is our planet truly cursed as Yancey maintains? If so, who's responsible? Today, as we truly wish our world was not this way, humankind still seeks for more satisfying answers and explanations than have been offered in the past. Few, on the other hand, have seriously contemplated the possibility that our world, indeed, may have been designed and created to be this way on purpose.

In this book we shall systematically readdress the dualistic reality and dynamic of the presence of good and evil. Our twofold focus will be to dispel faulty beliefs and to cast better light on the mystery of evil. This we shall do for the purpose of better preparing ourselves to more effectively and graciously respond when evil crosses our path in life and hits us squarely in the face—which it will. All this we shall also do explicitly within the framework of the evangelical and conservative Christian faith—and perhaps more carefully and clearly than many others have done. As you shall see, many others have fallen far short because the traditions of men, which they readily employ, have overridden Scripture and nullified the Word of God, making it of little or no effect (see Matt. 15:6; Mark 7:13). This same tendency is also evident in other theological areas and endeavors.[4]

My prayer for you is that this book will provide a much-needed corrective and an improved scriptural foundation for a greater understanding and a more factual basis for responding when (not if) you and/or those you know and love come face to face with one or more of evil's many manifestations.

My hope is that this book's title and content will enter into the lexicon of theological conversation, find its way onto college and seminary reading lists, and move the discussion of God, good and evil forward utilizing its more scriptural paradigm of reckoning. And yet I have endeavored to write a book that is easily accessible to Christian laypeople who normally do not venture into biblical or theological studies—but without dumbing anything down.

---

[4] See my other books and future books listed in the back, pp. 277-288.

> **. . . for the purpose of better preparing ourselves to more effectively and graciously respond when evil crosses our path in life and hits us squarely in the face—which it will.**

My caveat, however, must be that we humans in our limited ability can never fully or perfectly know or comprehend all the answers in this field of inquiry, at least not in this life. But I'm also convinced we can know much more than we have been led to believe.

Therefore, in this book you will discover, perhaps anew:

- Why evil made Christianity necessary
- The perplexing problems of evil
- The perpetuating problems of evil
- The ordained origin of evil
- The dualistic dynamic of evil
- The confounding confusion of natural evil
- The planned purposes of evil
- Our rehearsed responses to evil

Caution/Warning: this book is not for the faint-hearted or those comfortable with traditional explanations. Nor should this book be considered a work of pastoral comfort to help anyone get over or through a current or recent attack of evil. If this is you, my heart goes out to you. But I recommend the comfort of friends, not the counsel of scholars. I also wholeheartedly recommend Jerry Sittser's book, *A Grace Disguised,*[5] from which I shall be drawing. And though I have experienced some evil in my life, I have not experienced the depth or degree of evil as Jerry Sittser. Therefore, I pastorally yield to him.

For those who might try to label me as a Calvinist or Arminianist, I'm neither. I find strengths and weaknesses in both of those positions. Rather, and as I've shared with readers of my other books, I'm simply a follower of Jesus Christ on a quest for truth and understanding.

---

[5] Jerry Sittser, *A Grace Disguised* (Grand Rapids, MI: Zondervan, 1995, 2004).

This book, however, may be my most adventurous, challenging, and reformational one yet. That's because it will be intensely personal for many readers. Yet I believe that the incredible story of the creation and purposes of evil, pain, and suffering has not been adequately or fully told—i.e., Who actually put evil on planet Earth in the first place, how, and why. Consequently, much is amiss with what we've been told and taught on this subject. Nevertheless, massive volumes of books have been written.

Thus, I shall be quoting, referencing, and interacting with quite a few Christian scholars, authors, and popular spokespeople, and to a much greater extent than I have in any of my other books. Only a few of them will be in general agreement with me. The vast majority will not be. Literarily, however, I will be standing on all their shoulders as I often use their own words to present their positions rather than rephrasing them into my own. I do this for three reasons: (1) to honor them and their scholarship; (2) to enable you to see, first-hand, the spectrum of different beliefs and opinions on this subject and (3) for you to realize that I am not the first to bring up some of these rather "unsettling" and "radical" ideas.

It is also my desire is to keep this book as succinct and to the point as possible. This is why I have frequently utilized footnotes to reference particular sections from some of my other books and avoid repeating them. These references are provided for those readers interested in a fuller presentation on a particular issue or argument than the brief mention or excerpt I provide.

This book, however, may be my most adventurous and challenging one yet. That's because it will be intensely personal for many readers.
Yet I believe that the incredible story of the creation and purposes of evil, pain, and suffering has not been adequately or fully told . . .

But please be assured that during this re-exploratory process, and as we blaze a critical but hopefully refreshing trail through the morass of the problem and problems of good and evil:

This is my Father's world,
and to my listening ears
all nature sings, and round me rings
the music of the spheres.

This is my Father's world:
I rest me in the thought
of rocks and trees, of skies and seas;
his hand the wonders wrought.[6]

So if you are ready for an adventure of this magnitude, willing to engage with me in critical thinking, and have "listening ears" to hear—read on. I promise you that this book will offer a different paradigm of thinking, understanding, hoping, and responding than many of you are accustomed to reading or hearing. Thank you for reading this book.

Lastly, as I have asked readers of my other books, please question and test everything written herein with the Scriptures—i.e. what do the Scriptures say and not say, period. That is our one-and-only plumb line, standard, and hermeneutic as we venture out into some deep waters of God's word. I hope you are thirsty and willing to come into the water and drink with me (Rev. 22:17).

To reset the stage, let's begin by reconsidering the perplexing problems (plural) of evil.

---

[6] 1st stanza: "This Is My Father's World," hymn, **Text:** Maltbie D. Babcock, 1901 **Music:** Trad. English melody; adapt. by Franklin L. Sheppard, 1915.

Part I – The Problems

Chapter 1

The Perplexing Problems of Evil

It's the quintessential question and matchless problem of the ages. Philosophically, theologically, and emotionally it pierces heart and soul. Why would an all-powerful, all-knowing, all-just, all-good, and all-loving God allow, permit, and use evil, pain, and suffering in our world?

Ever since Adam and Eve ate the forbidden fruit and were cast out of the Garden of Eden, the pervasive presence of these insidious realities have vexed and perplexed the greatest minds of history. Both inside and outside the Christian Church, scholars, theologians, philosophers, atheists, and skeptics alike have grappled with this issue and its many other associated problems.

Hence, N.T. Wright characterizes "the history of European philosophy" as one that "can best be told as the history of people trying to come to terms with evil."[1] Randy Alcorn labels the reality of evil "the single greatest dilemma in human existence."[2] Paul Copan describes it as "the most troubling question we human beings face, both intellectually

---

[1] N.T. Wright, *Evil and the Justice of God* (Downers Grove, IL: InterVarsity Press, 2006), 20— in referencing Susan Neiman's book, *Evil in Modern Thought*.

[2] Randy Alcorn, *If God Is Good: Faith in the Midst of Suffering and Evil* (Colorado Springs, CO: Multnomah Books, 2009), front flap.

and emotionally."[3] Norman Geisler insists that it's "perhaps the most difficult question the Christian must face."[4]

The existence of evil, in many diverse forms (moral evil, natural evil, supernatural evil, animal evil,[5] even horrendous evil) is arguably the greatest conundrum of redemptive history. And much of it appears to be gratuitous—i.e., unnecessary, unreasonable, unjustified.

Of course, evil is not merely a theological or philosophical problem. It's a highly practical one. It forces each and every inhabitant of planet Earth to struggle with "how to survive in such a seemingly hostile environment"[6]—some are more forced than others.

Not surprisingly, countless books have been written trying to explain why bad things happen to good people and why suffering often seems unjust and disproportionate.[7] Predictably, a wide variety of speculative answers and explanations abound. But the age-old problem of evil, as well as its many other associated problems and perplexities, persist. Most, if not all, politicians, the media, governmental bureaucrats, and the Church as well truly don't know why evil, pain, and suffering are here or what can be done about them. And yet it is widely recognized that "the Bible . . . is about suffering as much as it is about anything."[8]

Therefore, the purpose of this first chapter will be to reassess these six perplexing problems of evil. As we shall see, most Christians, and the rest of the world as well, have largely and biblically been led astray on these issues:

---

[3] Paul Copan in endorsement of Jeremy A. Evans, *The Problem of Evil: The Challenge to Essential Christian Beliefs* (Nashville, TN: Broadman & Holman Publishing Group, 2013), i.

[4] Norman L. Geisler, *If God, Why Evil?* (Bloomington, MN: Bethany House Publishers, 2011), back cover.

[5] Carnivorous animals eat other animals, each other, and sometimes attack human beings.

[6] Marilyn McCord Adams and Robert Merrihew Adams, "Problems of Evil" in *The Problem of Evil* (New York, NY: Oxford University Press, 1990), 1.

[7] Harold Kushner's book, *When Bad Things Happen to Good People*, published in 1981, has sold over four million copies and continues to influence many people.

[8] Keller, *Walking with God through Pain and Suffering*, 6.

The Classic Problem of Evil

(Used with permission)

Evil is also considered the most ancient, persistent, single strongest objection, biggest obstacle, and gravest of all challenges to belief in the existence of God. It's the number one argument and primary tactic employed by those who want to discredit the Bible and the plausibility of Christianity in particular. It's been termed "the most important philosophical question of *any* era."[9]

The classic problem of evil was put forth three centuries before Christ by Epicurus, a Greek philosopher (341-270 B.C.). Ever since, it has fueled and empowered the atheistic assumption that "God does not exist." Thus, Norman L. Geisler acknowledges that "more skepticism, agnosticism, and atheism have sprung from an inability to answer various aspects of the problem of evil than from any other single issue."[10]

Dinesh D'Souza, who has publicly debated leading atheists, insightfully claims that "many of them aren't real unbelievers. . . . rather, they are angry and disappointed with God. Many . . . are wounded theists. And their main complaint is that God . . . seems to be uncaring and even malicious. They fault God for allowing so much evil and suffering in the world. Christians, too, can be wounded theists, cherishing God when things are going well but feeling godforsaken when there is tragedy."[11]

More than any other issue or challenge, this classic problem of evil has caused countless Christians to stumble and abandon their faith. Consequently, few topics in the history of Christianity and Western civilization have been discussed, debated, and written about more than the existence of evil, pain, and suffering in our world.

Sadly, however, the history of orthodox Christian thought on this matter has been one of evasion, depreciation, overt protection, and deflection. Some have simply dismissed the problem of evil as an enigma and ever-present challenge to biblical faith that is unanswerable, insoluble, and hopelessly inconclusive. All of which has only produced

---

[9] John G. Stackhouse, Jr., "Mind Over Skepticism," *Christianity Today* June 11, 1001, 74.

[10] Geisler, *If God, Why Evil*, 10.

[11] Dinesh D'Souza, *Godforsaken: Bad Things Happen. Is there a God who cares? Yes. Here's Proof* (Carol Stream, IL: Tyndale House Publishers, 2012), front flap.

more confusion and contributed to an array of other problems. Certainly, the burden to construct more responsible answers and a solution must lie with us Christians who take a high view of the Bible, and not with those who take a low view.

For these reasons and more, the classic problem of evil has been termed the "awkward trilemma" and "inconsistent triad." Over the centuries various people have expressed it in both short and amplified ways. These attempts are based on a deductive and intellectual argument that confirms a traditional evangelical understanding of three divine attributes of the God of the Bible and conjoins them with the existence of evil. Here is this classic problem of evil in a nutshell:

1. There is an omnipotent (all powerful) God who created and sustains our world.
2. He is omni-benevolent (all good) and omniscient (all knowing).
3. Evil exists and its amount is staggering.

The problem that arises within this set of three propositions seems to be an inconsistency, contradiction, or conflict. James K. Dew explains, "since no one can [realistically] question the existence of evil in the world, advocates of the logical problem of evil suggest that (1) or (2), or both (1) and (2) must be false."[12] But if they aren't false or in conflict, how do we make sense of them?

Alcorn expounds upon this tension thusly: "If God is all good, then he would want to prevent evil and suffering. If he is all knowing, then he would know how to prevent it. If God is all powerful, then he is able to prevent it. And yet . . . a great deal of evil and suffering exists. Why?"[13] Later on, he adds that "the problem of extreme evil, however, usually takes center stage. It's the most frequently cited argument against God, and many consider it the most devastating."[14]

Most people, however, accept the existence of God, *a priori*—it's a settled matter and not subject to challenge or review. But skeptics and critics disagree. They insist that this "awkward trilemma" is incompatible

---

[12] James K. Dew, Jr., "The Logical Problem of Evil" in Meister and Dew, Jr., eds., *God and Evil*, 27-28.
[13] Alcorn, *If God Is Good*, 18.
[14] Ibid., 131.

and irreconcilable and must be challenged. So they raise a series of follow-up questions: If God really exists, why is there evil? Where did it come from? Why isn't He doing something about it, like eliminating it? And if He does not want to eliminate it, why not? Is He unable, uninterested, or is He evil Himself?

In response, R.C. Sproul, Jr. defends God, declaring that "this argument . . . is fallacious. It presents a false dilemma." He maintains, "there are other options." Yet he also relents that "the church has, by and large, opted for a good God who cannot stop suffering."[15]

In retort to Sproul, Jr.'s response, Dew recounts the assertions of the 18th century Scottish philosopher and skeptic David Hume "that evil cannot be reconciled with the notions of divine power and goodness. If God is all-good, then he would eliminate evil. If he were all-powerful, then he could eliminate evil. If all this were true, then it seems that evil simply would not exist. . . . According to Hume . . . . one idea or the other must be rejected. Now, since evil obviously exists, God must not exist."[16] Dew next quotes Hume directly. "There is evil in the world; yet the world is said to be the creation of a good, omnipotent God. How is this possible? Surely a good, omnipotent being would have made a world that is free of evil of any kind?"[17]

. . . the classic problem of evil has been termed the "awkward trilemma" and "inconsistent triad."

Tellingly, however, Dew also observes that Hume, like most other critics, skeptics, and atheists, "merely *states* that these two propositions are logically contradictory, without actually showing that they are."[18] Meanwhile, Wright simply concedes the issue, lifts his hands in

---

[15] R.C. Sproul, Jr., *Almighty Over All: Understanding the Sovereignty of God* (Grand Rapids, MI: Baker Books, 1999), 141.
[16] Dew, Jr., "The Logical Problem of Evil" in Meister and Dew, Jr., eds., *God and Evil*, 29.
[17] Ibid., 30.
[18] Ibid., 29.

surrender, and confesses that "the problem of evil as classically conceived within philosophy is not soluble as it stands."[19]

The Atheist Problem

Atheists nail down their anti-God position by claiming that "the probability that such a God exists is inversely proportional to the amount of suffering there is in the world."[20] In apt and perspective reply, Alcorn wisely counsels that "non-Christians often raise concerns about evil and suffering as if they present a problem exclusively for the Christian worldview. But *every* worldview must attempt to account for them. . . . [even] worldviews that don't recognize God"[21]

The fact is, the presence and pervasiveness of evil, pain, and suffering pose a daunting challenge for atheists as well. Alcorn then turns the atheist argument—"since evil exists, there *can't* be a God"—on its head. He counters that "if evil exists, there *must* be a God, since evil could not exist without good, and good could not exist without God."[22]

In stark contrast, evil, pain, and suffering do not pose a problem for Hinduism or Buddhism. D'Souza responsively clarifies that "Hindus believe your suffering in this life is the consequence of your actions in a previous life. Buddhism holds that suffering is the product of egocentric desire and can be overcome through a dissolution of the self that has those desires."[23] Hence, and based on these two views, the existence of evil, pain, and suffering has not "established that God does not exist. . . . all it has shown is that evil and suffering have no explanation that we can figure out." Or do they?

Nonetheless, D'Souza affirms that "religion works . . . it speaks to human longings and needs in a way that no secular language can." Consequently, "God seems indispensable when life goes badly or when

---

[19] Wright, *Evil and the Justice of God*, 164.

[20] John W. Loftus, "Christianity Is Wildly Improbable," in John W. Lotus, ed., *The End of Christianity* (Amherst, NY: Prometheus Book, 2011), 85).

[21] Alcorn, *If God Is Good*, 93.

[22] Ibid., 112.

[23] Dinesh D'Souza, *What's So Great About Christianity* (Washington, D.C.: Regnery Publishing, 2007), 274.

we are staring death in the face."[24]He also agrees that it's a mistake to think that abandoning belief in the existence of God solves the problem of evil, or somehow makes it easier to handle. For if there is no God "everything becomes dark and meaningless . . . and evil is not a problem, because evil does not exist." Critically, D'Souza concludes that "life in this view is indeed a tale told by an idiot, full of sound and fury, signifying nothing. . . . Atheism offers only extinction. . . . atheism provides neither consolation nor understanding in the face of evil or tragedy."[25]

Accordingly, Keller fires back at atheists with these indicting questions, "What if evil and suffering in the world actually make the existence of God *more* likely? What if our awareness of absolute evil is a clue that we know unavoidably at some level within ourselves that God actually does exist?"[26]

The bottom line for the atheists—and nowadays "neo-atheists" with their bestselling authors, such as Richard Dawkins (*The God Delusion*), Christopher Hitchens (*god* [sic] *Is Not Great*), and Sam Harris (*The End of Faith*)—is, they don't know what to do with evil because they have no frame of reference. After all, upon what basis or moral standard can they say to anyone, "What you have done is evil?" Keller succinctly summarizes this atheist problem with this to-the-point statement. "The problem of senseless suffering does not go away if you abandon belief in God. If there is no God, why have a sense of outrage and horror when unjust suffering occurs . . . ?"[27]

Likewise, Sittser challenges atheists for having "no grounding in a greater, objective reality outside the self." Therefore, "it becomes all but impossible to establish the absoluteness of truth and falsehood, or good and evil, or right and wrong. Hence, there seems to be no objective reason why we should view catastrophic loss as bad and why we should feel bad about it."[28] The bottom line is, atheism "deprives us of the objective view of reality."[29]

---

[24] Ibid., 276.
[25] Ibid., 275.
[26] Keller, *Walking with God through Pain and Suffering*, 105.
[27] Ibid., 106-107.
[28] Sittser, *A Grace Disguised*, 155.
[29] Ibid., 156.

Appropriately then, Alcorn queries atheists who routinely speak of the problem of evil. "From a non-theistic viewpoint, what is evil? Isn't it just nature at work? In a strictly natural, physical world, shouldn't everything be neither good nor evil?"[30] He then scoffs at the atheistic assumption, claiming instead that "extreme evil may actually be seen as evidence *for* God's existence, not against it."[31] How can this be so?

A strong, if not stronger, case can actually be made that the existence, nature, and severity of evil provides evidence *for* the existence of God—and a good God. Ganssle responds by quoting philosopher R. Douglas Geivett:

> It is difficult to give even a rough characterization of what evil is without implying God's existence. When we call something evil . . . we mean something like, "things ought not be this way". . . . the fact that there is a way things ought to be, and evil is a deviation from this way, means that goodness is primary and evil or badness is a corruption of what is good. . . . each of these lines of thought fits better with the idea that a good God exists than they fit with the idea that there is no God. . . . Therefore, *there is a way things ought to be*. . . . One implication of there being a way things ought to be is that there must be some purposes or end to which things are directed. . . . Such purposes make little sense if there is no God, but it fits neatly within the idea that God exists and made the world for his own reasons. If there is no God, reality simply is what it is. There is no basis to think it ought to be otherwise.[32]

D'Souza picks up on this point in noting that "evil and suffering pose no less of a problem for unbelievers." In their invoking of evil to undermine the existence of God, "this implies that there are objective standards by which we identify good and evil. Well, where do those standards come from? What is the source of the moral law that enables us to distinguish good and evil?"[33]

This atheistic weakness causes Ganssle to deduce that "the very challenge that evil brings to God's existence relies on concepts and

---

[30] Alcorn, *If God Is Good*, 119.

[31] Ibid., 131.

[32] Ganssle, "Evil as Evidence for Christianity" in Meister and Dew, Jr., eds., *God and Evil*, 218.

[33] D'Souza, *Godforsaken*, 66.

perspectives that fit better with theism than with atheism." He admits, however, that "this support is not decisive, but it is stronger than many people realize. . . . Evil, it turns out, poses a problem for atheism as well"[34] and "points strongly in the direction of God's reality."[35]

Strategically speaking, Jeremy A. Evans suggests that Christians "turn the table on the atheist objector" with this new set of propositions *for* the existence of God, which he takes from William Lane Craig:

1. If God does not exist, objective moral values do not exist.
2. Evil exists.
3. Therefore, objective moral values exist—namely, some things are evil!
4. Therefore, God exists.[36]

Geisler concurs and chimes in by emphasizing that the presence of evil "actually presupposes the existence of God, for there is no way to know there is injustice in the world unless one has an objective standard of justice beyond the world by which he knows the world is not just. . . . So atheism's 'best' argument against God turns out to be an argument for God."[37]

In my opinion, however, the best counterargument against the atheists' purely materialist worldview and argument of evil against the existence of God is this argument from analogy, which certainly could be enhanced with more poignant examples.

Where life is viewed by some as nothing more than complex assemblages of molecules, what obligation does one molecule assemblage have for another? We don't scold the tree for using all the sunlight and withering the bush struggling in the shade beneath it. Why

---

[34] Ganssle, "Evil as Evidence for Christianity" in Meister and Dew, Jr., eds., *God and Evil*, 220-221.

[35] Ibid., 223.

[36] Evans, *The Problem of Evil*, 156 – in footnote: "See William Lane Craig and Walter Sinnott-Armstrong, *God: A Debate between a Christian and an Atheist*, Point/Counterpoint series, ed. James Sterba (Oxford: Oxford University Press, 2004), 126.

[37] Geisler, *If God, Why Evil?*, 131.

should we scold the fat-cat banker for having an abundance of resources when homeless children have none?[38]

Nevertheless, with evil so manifestly rampant, some wonder if it makes any sense to believe that God is in control, governing, or reigning in a world gone crazy like this? Moreover, how can we make any sense of our human predicament or possibly reconcile the classic problem of evil with a God who is all-powerful, all-knowing, all-just, all-good, and all-loving? Throughout Church history several theories have been offered. Unfortunately, they have created more problems than solutions. But once again the burden of reconciliation here rests on us Christian theists, who have a high regard for the Bible, and not on those who take a low view.

All of which brings us to our next perplexing problem.

The Degradation Problem

In attempting to deal with the classic problem of evil, some liberal scholars (who do not have a high view of the Bible) are forced to degrade one or more of God's omni attributes and character qualities—despite what Scripture reveals about Him, clearly and emphatically. Or they must deny the concept and reality of evil itself. Here it is in a nutshell:

- God is not wholly good, because He allows bad things to happen and will not eliminate evil.
- God is not totally omnipotent, preferring the concept of a good God Who cannot intervene.
- God is not all knowing, in that God does not and cannot know in advance the future choices of the free-will creatures He has created (this is termed "open theism").
- Evil does not exist. It's only an abstraction and not real.

The result of this degradation or redefining of God is, as Arthur W. Pink laments, "the Creator is reduced to the level of the creature; His

---

[38] Karl W. Giberson and Francis S. Collins, "Evil, Creation, and Evolution" in Meister and Dew, Jr., eds., *God and Evil*, 283.

omniscience is called into question, His omnipotency is no longer believed in, and His absolute sovereignty is flatly denied."[39]

But the acceptance of a finite god is an idea incompatible with Christianity and the Bible and has far-reaching consequences. It's also a conclusion arrived at more by emotion than by exegetical reasoning. What we end up with is a far-different god than we find in the Scriptures. A. E. Knock depicts this degradation procedure this way: "Men have whittled Him down to a second or third rate deity who *does not,* and *cannot* carry out His own counsel. In making man 'divine,' they have made God human."[40]

Below are four degradation examples from liberal scholars. Paradoxically, however, liberal theologians write more about evil, pain, and suffering than do most conservatives.[41]

Example #1 – In answer to the fundamental question of "why did God let this happen or that happen?" one liberal book reviewer writes that it's because "God does not have the power to insure that this happens in every situation." He further notes that while God doesn't choose, will, or want bad things to happen, some things are out of his control. He "is not able to prevent them. . . . They just happen." He also cites the "misuse of human freedom" and "existence of laws of nature." Not surprisingly from this liberal perspective, prayer is also of limited and mostly self-talking value. Consequently, he advises that we must be willing to "forgive the imperfections in God."[42]

---

[39] Arthur W. Pink, *The Sovereignty of God* (Blacksbury, VA: Wilder Publications, 1918, 2008), 185.

[40] A. H. Knoch, *The Problem of Evil and the Judgments of God* (Santa Clarita, CA: Concordant Publishing Concern, 2008 new edition), 224.

[41] The following examples are taken from a paper I wrote as part of my course work during my doctoral program. It was titled "The Origin of Evil." As part of the assignment, I surveyed articles in two academic journals and one major Christian magazine. They were:

    Journal of ETS – (conservative) (a 23-year period)

    Encounter – the journal of (liberal seminary) Christian Theological Seminary (a 19-year period)

    Christianity Today magazine (conservative) (a 32-year period)

[42] Rufus Burrow, Jr., in book review essay: "When Bad Things Happen to Good People by Harold S. Kushner," *Encounter* (theological journal of Christian Theological Seminary), (Vol. 55: 69-76 Winter 1994).

Example #2 – Another liberal also attacks God's omnipotence in her attempt to address the question of, "How are God's power and goodness to be understood in the face of tragedy?" In order to explain "why suffering was so pervasive and evil so powerful in a world that God has created and governs," she calls for "a reconstructed doctrine of omnipotence based upon a new meaning for power" and terms this "both desirable and possible." She suggests that this should be "along the lines of . . . feminist-process proposal—i.e. changing the kind of power we attribute to God from that of 'God as king' to that of 'God as mother.'" Surprisingly, she does admit, however, that "there are problems with this image. . . and I do not cherish any illusion of having conclusively settled the problems surrounding divine power."[43]

Example #3 – This liberal attempts to resolve the problem of evil by promoting God as Self-limiting. He writes that God lets us be because He emptied and limited Himself (*kenosis*), just as Christ did. Hence, God's divine omnipotence is redefined to mean that He chose to limit Himself because of his love for us, which is his "defining characteristic" and overrides all else. Hence, evil "ultimately results from the freedom given by God in the creative process." Evil becomes a byproduct of that freedom—the more freedom, the more evil; the more evil, the more suffering—and all this from a loving God. He then summarizes that "God is responsible for . . . evil because he created the kind of world in which, for example, wars and tornadoes can occur" and "Kenotic love refuses to intervene." So, "the origin of evil is due to God's self-limitation of divine power and the freedom of all creatures."

A good question to ask, once again, is, why pray if God never intervenes? This liberal answers, it will "show us ways of coping and sustains us in our efforts to cope . . . rather than to enlist God's direct, magical intervention in the situation." In other words, we serve a "laissez-faire" and "deistic God" – a "God totally non-involved in the course of history."[44]

Of course, the application of *kenosis* to the totality of God's nature and behavior is without biblical support. Also interestingly,

---

[43] Anna Case-Winters, "What Do We Mean When We Affirm That God Is 'All-Powerful'?" *Encounter*, (Vol. 57: 215-230 Summer 1996).
[44] Warren McWilliams, "A Kenotic God and the Problem of Evil," *Encounter* (Vol. 42: 15-17 Winter 1981).

eschatological aspects of a future resolution of the problem of evil are rarely, if ever, mentioned in liberal articles on this subject.

Example #4 – Another liberal simply throws up his hands and concludes that "there is no completely satisfying answer."[45] Or is there?

The Distancing Problem

Another approach to solving the classic problem of evil employed by conservative theologians is to distance God from any and all involvement or association with evil.

Consequently, scholars of this persuasion have tried almost everything imaginable to absolve, isolate, protect, exonerate, disassociate, and defend God from any blame or responsibility for creating or causing evil. Their goal is to relieve God from being tarnished by evil in any way. However, they are forced to acknowledge that God allows, permits, tolerates, and sometimes even uses evil to further his purposes.

For support, they cite various verses such as: "God is light; in him there is no darkness. . . (1 John 1:5), "For God cannot be tempted by evil, nor does he tempt anyone" (Jas. 1:13), and "Your eyes are too pure to look on evil; you cannot tolerate wrong" (Hab. 1:13).

Other conservatives take a more proactive stance. They insist that since God is good, He could not have had any part in the creation or perpetration of evil. For instance, one conservative emphatically remarks that "God did not originate evil – this would be incompatible with his holiness."[46]

On the other hand, the Rev. Billy Graham, while addressing the memorial service in Washington's National Cathedral after the terrorist attacks of September 11, 2001 admitted: "I have been asked hundreds of times in my life why God allows tragedy and suffering. I have to confess

---

[45] Peter Wyatt, "Human Suffering and Faith In God," *Encounter* (Vol. 57: 245-265 Summer 1996).

[46] Hubert P. Black, "The Problem of Evil," *Christianity Today* (April 23, 1971, Vol. 15; 9, 12-14.)

that I really do not know the answer totally, even to my own satisfaction."[47]

On the whole, and mostly as a result of this distancing tactic, conservative writers, pastors, teachers, theologians, etc. have been largely at a loss to explain why God allows, permits, tolerates, or even sometimes uses a crime like the Sandy Hook school shooting, or 9/11, the Holocaust, or any number of genocides committed throughout our world over the centuries. The best they can offer, in humble assurance to victims and others, is to quote Romans 8:28 KJV – "And we know that all things work together for good to them that love God, to them who are the called according to his purpose." How effective and soothing do you think the citing of this verse is for those going through the anguish of a tragedy, suffering, and pain?[48] Sad to report, it often comes across as shallow, trite, or insensitive, at best.

Lastly, some conservative scholars resort to referring to God's so-called "permissive will" or his "secretive will" (a la Deut. 29:29) for absolving God of any guilt in his allowing or using of evil, pain, and suffering. But do any of these distancing notions solve the problem of evil or absolve a sovereign God of any blame or responsibility in this matter? Practically speaking, they merely kick the proverbial can down the road or move the problem backwards one step. So where do these distancing tactics leave us?

The Culprit Problem

When we distance God from and absolve Him of any blame or responsibility for creating or perpetrating evil, we must come up with other culprits. And so we have. Here are the top four culprits from the literature, and in order of their prominence, for being the origin—i.e., the first-cause source—that created evil and brought it into our world.

---

[47] Quoted by David Kupelian, "God and Sandy Hook: Where is the Almighty when children are murdered?" *Whistleblower*, December 2013, 6.

[48] D'Souza claims that *pain* and *suffering* "are not the same. Pain is physical, whereas suffering is mental. Pain is the sensation of hurting, while suffering is the consciousness of pain. Suffering also involves the anticipation of pain." (D'Souza, *Godforsaken*, 153).

#1 Culprit – Human Free Will and Sin

The overwhelming choice as the number one culprit for the creation and cause of evil is human free will. Since most Christians presume that God could not have created anything evil, they believe, like Augustine, that evil exists because human beings chose to rebel against God. Hence, evil was a non-existent entity and outside of God's original program until sin entered from human beings making free will choices in mismanagement or misuse of their God-given freedom. And it all started with Adam and Eve in the Garden of Eden.

For example, in his textbook on systematic theology, James Montgomery Boice blames evil on we humans: "But one thing we can say is that evil is our fault, whatever reasons God may have for tolerating it."[49] Like so many others, Boice is saying that God designed a perfect world in which we could live and enjoy Him forever, but something went wrong. That is the essence, the totality, and the shallowness of his treatment. Never once does he address the actual origin of evil.

Many side with Boice's position that the "Scriptures make it plain that God did not create the world in the state in which it is now, but evil came as a result of the selfishness of man . . . . God is neither evil nor did He create evil. Man brought evil upon himself by selfishly choosing his own way apart from God's way."[50]

Likewise, Bob Sorge first notes that "the suffering all around us tells us there's something terribly wrong with our world." He then asks, "How did things get this way?" He promptly answers: "the problem, in a nutshell, is sin. Mankind became subject to death through Adam's sin (see Rom. 5:17). When Adam bowed to Satan's temptation, Satan became 'the ruler of this world' (John 12:31). Things haven't been working right ever since."[51]

William A. Dembski also labors somewhat inconsistently in offering up his defense: that "all evil in the world ultimately traces back to human

---

[49] James Montgomery Boice, *Foundations of the Christian Faith* (Downers Grove, IL: InterVarsity Press, 1986), 195.

[50] "Why Does a Good God Allow Evil to Exist" – www.josh.org/resources/study-reascher/answers-to-skeptics-questions/why-does-a-good-god-allow-evil-to exist/, 7/19/2014).

[51] Bob Sorge, "It's OK to Ask God Why," *Charisma*, September 2009, 27.

sin." Then later he tactfully disclaims that he "is not attributing to humanity an absolute origin of evil." Rather, he asserts, "human sin is the immediate or proximate cause of evil in the world. . . . the fall of humanity presupposes the fall of angelic beings. And the fall of angelic beings may presuppose some still deeper features of reality that bring about evil. In any case, the crucial question is not the ultimate origin of evil but whether all evil in the world traces back to humanity and its sin."[52]

One self-proclaimed "theologian" on a Facebook group explained it to me this way: "Free choice was a factor that God of course foresaw, and He took a huge chance. Love is always risky, and God took a risk with creation . . . however the action was played out by free moral agents."[53] Therefore, as Dembski further elaborates, "God writes our story and, when we fall, rewrites it—but with the engine running and thus with no break in the action. . . . The Fall represents the entry of evil into the world."[54]

The simple logic and basic rationale behind the so-called free-will defense is this. Since God desired to have creatures who would truly love Him, He could not create robots or zombies. Real love has to be a real choice. To have a real choice He had to allow his creatures total freedom to love or not love, and to choose good or evil. God knew all this because He is omniscient. Therefore, God foreknew that in a world of much love there would also be much evil. But the potential for love outweighed the existence of much evil, especially if evil would only exist for a temporary period of time (our next perplexing problem to address).

Gordon H. Clark puts it this way: God "has adopted a hands-off policy and allows men to act apart from divine influence. We choose, and we choose evil, of our own free wills; God does not make us do so; therefore, we alone are responsible, and not God."[55]

In other words, we must live in a world in which evil greatly abounds if our freedom is to be truly real, the argument goes. We must

---

[52] William A. Dembski, *The End of Christianity: Finding a Good God in an Evil World* (Nashville, TN: B&H Publishing Group, 2009), 8-9.

[53] Posted, 3/19/14.

[54] Dembski, *The End of Christianity*, 110, 144.

[55] Gordon H. Clark, *God and Evil: The Problem Solved* (Hobbs, NM: The Trinity Foundation, 1961, 1996), 12.

be free to turn our backs on God and to choose evil over good. Hence, evil is simply the consequence of free will gone awry. And since "God gave us free will so it's our fault."[56] Ironically, or perhaps paradoxically, Gary A. Haugen terms this God-given freedom, "the terrible gift of free will."[57]

Chuck Colson, defensively, conceives this about this terrible gift:

> In the beginning we were created by God in His image, which meant that we have free will. Free will presupposes that you can choose to obey God or to disobey God. If you didn't have that right, you wouldn't have free will. . . . It doesn't mean that God created evil. God did not create sin. He told us how to behave, and had we obeyed Him, there would never be evil or sin in the world . . . . that non-good choice caused evil.[58]

Fox News' Bill O'Reilly certainly believes that human free will is the #1 culprit. In commenting on a recent shooting at Fort Hood in Texas that left three people dead and sixteen others wounded before the shooter committed suicide, he told his viewers: "What this is really all about is freedom. . . . Evil human beings armed with freedom make that terrible scenario inevitable."[59]

Since most Christians presume that God could not have created anything evil, they believe, like Augustine, that evil exists because human beings chose to rebel against God.

Similarly, Geisler frames evil as a conundrum in proclaiming that "the only way God could literally destroy all evil is to destroy all

---

[56] Wright, *Evil and the Justice of God*, 73.

[57] Gary A. Haugen, *Good News About Injustice* (Downers Grove, IL: IVP Books, 2009), 118.

[58] "A Conversation With Charles W. [Chuck] Colson," *Decision*, 01.2002, 15.

[59] Bill O'Reilly, The O'Reilly Factor, April 3, 2014.

freedom. However, to destroy all freedom is to destroy the possibility of all moral good. *All moral choices are free choices.*"[60] Or are they?

Assuming for a moment that this number one consensus-culprit notion is correct, here are a few hard and follow-up questions to ponder.

1. If human free will is responsible for creating and causing evil in our world, are we human beings then being elevated from creature to a co-Creator with God? Of course, "this claim is quite heretical from a technical point of view."[61]

2. How free is free will? Christians differ greatly on this issue. There are verses that support both sides. For verses supporting the sovereignty of God and not human free will see: John 6:44, 65; 12:38-40; 15:16; Rom. 9:10-21; 11:5-24; Phil. 2:13; 2 Thess. 2:10-11. For verses supporting the sovereignty of human free will and choice see: Deut. 1:13; 11:26-8; 30:19b; Rev. 22:17. Therefore, human free will may not be as free as some think. Nevertheless, and based on our limited view from below (down here on Earth), we perceive our choices as free—at least free enough that we don't think things are being forced on us, but not so free that we are not subject to God's sovereignty and will. Rightly, Alcorn concludes that our "our theological position on sovereignty and free will depends on which scriptures we include and which we ignore . . . ."[62] But Knoch portrays the free-will notion in this manner:

> The so-called 'freedom' consists merely in the lack of *conscious* coercion. Being ignorant of the constraining or restraining influences which determine his conduct, and altogether unaware of ulterior forces, he subconsciously *yields* at the very time that he imagines he is most independent. His freedom of will is simply ignorant unconsciousness or submission to environment or heredity. In relation to the will of God, men are consciously independent. . . . [but they are]

[60] Geisler, *If God, Why Evil?*, 38.
[61] Giberson and Collins, "Evil, Creation, and Evolution" in Meister and Dew, Jr., eds., *God and Evil*, 277.
[62] Alcorn, *If God Is Good*, 221.

no more masters of their fate than they were of the date and
details of their birth.[63]

3.   If all evil is created by the will of free agents, how do we explain
     other types of evil not caused by humans but by animals, nature,
     or supernatural beings? Knoch further proposes that "the
     possession of a free, untrammeled, unconquerable will is the
     exclusive attribute of deity. Only One God can possess it. Our
     blessed Lord Himself did not claim it. He came, not to do His
     own will, but the will of Him Who had sent Him."[64]

Entering into a lengthy discussion of human free will versus the
sovereignty of God, however, is beyond the scope and purposes of this
book. Notably in this regard, William Barclay in his commentary on the
Book of Romans maintains that "there is no resolution of it. It is a
dilemma of human experience. We know that God is behind everything;
and yet, at the same time, we know that we have free will . . . . It is the
paradox of the human situation that God is in control and yet the human
will is free."[65] Or is it really?

#2 Culprit – Satan and Fallen Angels (Demons)

Our #2 consensus culprit to blame for the creation of evil is Satan
and his fallen angels (his demonic cohorts). A classic example of this
notion are Billy Graham's comments to this effect that frequently appear
in his nationally syndicated newspaper column.

In a column answering a reader's question, "Where does evil come
from?" Dr. Graham replied: "Evil is real . . . . Although there is much we
can't understand about evil this side of heaven, the Bible does make it
clear that evil comes from Satan, not from God. Evil came into the world
because Satan rebelled against God and his will."[66]

---

[63] Knoch, *The Problem of Evil*, 185.
[64] Ibid., 186.
[65] William Barclay, *The Letter to the Romans* (Philadelphia, PA: The
Westminster Press, res. ed. 1975, 1955), 143.
[66] Billy Graham, "My Answer," *The Indianapolis Star* (Indianapolis, IN), 7
August 2000, B-6.

In two other columns he writes: "The world was perfect when God created it, but sin intervened and now this world is in the grip of sin and Satan. God now permits evil things to happen – but that doesn't mean he causes them. Instead, Satan must bear the ultimate blame[67] . . . Evil is real, and so is Satan, for ultimately all evil can be traced back to him.[68]

Numerous scholars support Dr. Graham's notion that "evil came from a single rebellious act of a one-time great angel of God, Lucifer. . . . Satan and his demons are clearly fallen angels. . . . Through them sin and rebellion entered into the human race and the rest of creation."[69] Some, such as Gregory A. Boyd, attribute evil to both "Satan and/or other free agents"—i.e., human free will and Satan's fallen angels.[70]

Jonathan Kirsch, however, introduces another possible culprit into the mix. While he first maintains that "the author of Revelation, of course, sets up 'that old serpent, called the Devil and Satan' as the source of all evil in the world," he also maintains that "by contrast . . . the Hebrew prophets do not seem to know or care much about Satan, and they embrace the simple if also harsh idea that everything, good *or* bad, begins and ends with God."[71]

Following up on this "harsh idea," Pink raises a poignant question and makes a most relevant observation: "Who is regulating affairs on this earth today—God or the Devil? That God reigns supreme in Heaven, is generally conceded; that He does so over this world, is almost universally denied—if not directly, then indirectly. . . . relegating God to the background."[72] We'll have more to say on this issue later in this chapter.

---

[67] Billy Graham, "My Answer," *The Indianapolis Star* (Indianapolis, IN), 8 February 2001, E-5.
[68] Billy Graham, "My Answer," *The Indianapolis Star* (Indianapolis, IN), 25 May 2013, E-4.
[69] John H. Sailhamer, *Biblical Prophecy* (Grand Rapids, MI: Zondervan, 1998), 53.
[70] Gregory A. Boyd, *Satan and the Problem of Evil* (Downers Grove, IL: InterVarsity Press, 2001), 411.
[71] Jonathan Kirsch, *A History of the End of the World* (New York, NY: HarperSanFranscico, 2006), 27.
[72] Pink, *The Sovereignty of God*, 8.

But once again, if Satan and his fallen angels (his demonic cohorts) is/are responsible for the creation of evil in our world, is he/are they being elevated from creature to a co-Creator status with God?

#3 Culprit – Pre-creation Chaos

In the "believe it or not" category, some liberal scholars think that evil existed long before creation. They believe that God did not create *ex nihilo*, but creation was "the result of a dynamic victory of God over the forces of chaos."[73] Hence, these evil forces predated creation, still survive, and must be subdued. They are the source of evil.

In this vein, Rabbi Harold S. Kushner in his bestselling book, *When Bad Things Happen to Good People*, assumed that God did not create the world from nothing, but from chaos. And "pockets of chaos remain." They are the source of the random and arbitrary occurrences of much human suffering—people struck with cancer, earthquakes, airplane crashes, etc. And yet he also believes that human lawlessness is another source. While Kushner feels that these occurrences pain God, he insists that God is unable to prevent all of them. The forces of chaos are too powerful for a good God.[74]

Of course, these culprit #3 conclusions lack scriptural support. As J. Richard Middleton accurately states: "it is clear in Genesis 1 that God creates without vanquishing any primordial forces of chaos."[75] But if Kushner et al. are right, why bother with prayer or why worship a God who will not or cannot help us?

---

[73] J. Gerald Janzen, review of John D. Levenson, *Creation and the Persistence of Evil: The Jewish Drama of Divine Omnipotence*, Encounter (Vol. 50: 101-103 Winter 1989).

[74] Summarized from: Michael J. Latzer, in book review, "'My God Is Not Cruel': The Theodicy of Harold S. Kushner," *Encounter* (Vol. 57: 139-147 Spring 1996).

[75] J. Richard Middleton, *A New Heaven and a New Earth* (Grand Rapids, MI: Baker Academic, 2014), 50.

#4 Culprit – All the Above and a Mystery

In what we might term the "catch all" culprit category, Timothy Keller reasons: "evil is neither simply the result of flawed individuals nor merely of a single powerful being like the devil. It stems from both as well as from the effects of a corrupted created order. And ultimately we can't see all the roots and sources of evil—it is a mystery."[76] Keller, however, does have some scriptural support for his claim (see 2 Thess. 2:7, KJV).

We also must mention that a few fringe writers look to outer space aliens from other galaxies as the origin of evil. However, we shall not devote any space in this book to that bit of speculation. But next we shall address a widely held, fantasy belief.

The Fantasy Problem

"Imagine there's no heaven. It's easy if you try." These are the opening lines of the Beatles' popular 1970's song written by John Lennon and titled, "Imagine."

Similarly, "imagine there's no evil. It's easy if you try." Sound ridiculous? But that's exactly what most Christians have been imagining God someday will do. On that day, we've been told and taught, everything will change when God rescues our evil-filled, sin-stained world by making an end of all evil and restoring our world to its originally created, pristine, pre-Fall perfection. But this time, the utopian paradise of the veritable Garden of Eden will cover the entire earth.

It's a theological school of thought that collapses redemption back into physical creation—i.e., "paradise restored." It has also been variously termed:

- "God's rescue plan" for our "broken planet."[77]
- "Christianity's ultimate victory."[78]
- "The final fulfillment of God's purposes."[79]

---

[76] Keller, *Walking with God through Pain and Suffering*, 157.
[77] Yancey, *The Question That Never Goes Away*, 151.
[78] Frank Turek's endorsement in Evans, *The Problem of Evil*, i.

- "The full establishment of God's Kingdom."[80]
- "God's ultimate purpose . . . to rid the world of evil altogether and to establish his new creation of justice, beauty, and peace."[81]
- The "final showdown between God and evil."[82]

In this section we will test this popular futuristic belief with the Scriptures and by utilizing an easy-to-follow, point-counterpoint format.

Point – Away with all evil: Here's the latest version (as I write) of a long line of comments in support of this fantasy problem, straight from the nationally syndicated newspaper column of Dr. Billy Graham:

From the first verse of Genesis to the last verse in Revelation, the central theme of the Bible is God, He made this world – and someday, the Bible says, he will do away with all the evil that spoils it and bring about a perfect world of peace and justice.[83]

This present world is not the way God wants it to be. All creation, including humanity, has been scarred by sin, and that is why we have suffering and evil in our world. Even the physical creation is not what God intended it to be. But one day God will change all that.[84]

All evil will be destroyed, and even this earth will be renewed and become part of our heavenly experience.[85]

Our world will never be perfect – not until Jesus comes back to destroy all evil and injustice, and usher in his rule of perfect justice and peace."[86]

[79] John Hick, *Evil and the God of Love* (England: Palgrave Macmillan, 1966, 2010), 193.
[80] Ibid., 358.
[81] Wright, *Evil and the Justice of God*, 102.
[82] Ibid., 106.
[83] Billy Graham, "My Answer," *The Indianapolis Star* (Indianapolis, IN), 11 August 2014, E-4.
[84] Billy Graham, "My Answer," *The Indianapolis Star* (Indianapolis, IN), 11 October 2000, B-2.
[85] Billy Graham, "My Answer," *The Indianapolis Star* (Indianapolis, IN), 8 November 2012, E-4.

N.T. Wright concurs and adds:

> What the New Testament does in two or three key passages is to point instead to the ultimate future, to the promise of a world set free from evil altogether, and to invite us to hold that in our minds and hearts so that we know where we're going. . . . to *anticipate* God's eventual world.[87]

Counterpoint: I know of nowhere in the Bible—from Genesis to the last verse in Revelation—that says this. Nowhere! So are Drs. Graham's and Wright's claims based on fact or fantasy? Let's explore further.

Point – Encompasses the whole cosmos: "Deliver us from evil" we pray every time we recite or sing the Lord's Prayer. But how will this deliverance happen? According to Alcorn: "I revel in God's emphatic promise that he will make a New Earth where he will come down to live with us, and on which 'he will wipe every tear from their eyes. There will be no more death or mourning or crying or pain' (Revelation 21:4)."[88] Hence, "one day" God will "conquer evil and eliminate suffering[89] . . . . on a resurrected Earth in a redeemed universe." Alcorn further believes that without this hope "the biblical case for evil being defeated and suffering being redeemed does not stand up."[90] For him, then, "Christ's redemptive work . . . encompasses the whole cosmos."[91]

Middleton adds this ringer to this futuristic scenario that "we will discover that eschatological redemption consists in the renewal of human cultural life on earth rather than our removal from earth to heaven. . . . there is simply no role for heaven as the final destiny of the righteous."[92]

Counterpoint: "Something most Bible readers and many scholars *do not know* is—*three different entities* in the Bible are called 'heaven

[86] Billy Graham, "My Answer," *The Indianapolis Star* (Indianapolis, IN), 17 November 2011, E-4.
[87] Wright, *Evil and the Justice of God*, 104.
[88] Alcorn, *If God Is Good*, 2.
[89] Ibid., 26.
[90] Ibid., 100.
[91] Ibid., 375.
[92] Middleton, *A New Heaven and a New Earth*, 58.

and earth.' One entity would never pass away. Another had already passed away. A third would soon pass away and be made new. If this sounds like a riddle, perhaps, it is. It is also a biblical and historical fact and truth. . . . The 'heaven and earth' that would never pass away is *the physical creation* [Gen. 1:1]. The one that had already passed away was *Babylon in the 6th century B.C.*[Isa. 13:1, 13]. The third one that would soon pass away and be made new was *Old Covenant biblical Judaism* [Deut. 32:1; Isa. 1:2-3; 51:13-16 KJV]. Thus, the Bible's new heaven and new earth is not a re-creation of the physical universe. It's the complete arrival of the new covenantal order on Planet Earth. And its Holy City, the New Jerusalem, is its ultimate reality, ultimate joy, and the beloved community for God's overcoming people here on this earth! I suggest you read about it, anew, in Revelation 21 and 22."[93]

On the other hand, Wright rightly puts this futuristic belief into a more relevant, here-and-now perspective by proclaiming "it's not enough to say that God will eventually make a new world in which there will be no more pain and crying; that does scant justice to all the evil that has gone before."[94]

Point – Heal the planet of pain and death: In a similar manner, Yancey emphatically asserts and yet laments: "God will one day heal the planet of pain and death. Until that day arrives, the case against God must rely on incomplete evidence. We cannot really reconcile our pain-wracked world with a loving God because what we experience now is not the same as what God intends[95] . . . . I need reminders of God's promise to heal creation permanently of the twin enemies, evil and death. Otherwise, what hope do any of us have?"[96]

Dr. Graham concurs in writing: "but some day Christ's victory over evil and death will be complete."[97]

---

[93] Excerpt from and for the biblical references and support, see: John Noē, *The Perfect Ending for the World* (Indianapolis, IN: East2West Press, 2011), 279, 319. For a complete presentation and scriptural documentation of these three entities, see pages 279 through 319.

[94] Wright, *Evil and the Justice of God*, 96.

[95] Yancey, *The Question That Never Goes Away*, 94.

[96] Ibid., 140.

[97] Billy Graham, "My Answer," *The Indianapolis Star* (Indianapolis, IN), 7 March 2011, E-4.

Counterpoint: Then how much victory over evil and death do we have currently? Before you answer, please consider the following four propositions:

1. Jesus came to destroy death ("who has destroyed/abolished death" – 2 Tim. 1:10 – past tense). Did He fail? Then why do we still see people dying?
2. Jesus came "to destroy the devil's work" (1 John 3:8). Did He fail? Then why do we still see works of the devil on this earth?
3. Jesus came "to do away with sin" (Heb. 9:26). Did He fail? Then why do we and others still sin?
4. The Bible says that in Christ "there is neither Jew nor Greek, slave nor free, male nor female, for you are all one in Christ Jesus" (Gal. 3:28). Did He fail here, too? Then why do we still see Christians who are Jews, Greeks, slaves, free, and men and women?

Obviously, Jesus did not terminate these ongoing earthly realities by putting an end to them. Perhaps we are the ones who have failed to understand how these words and finished works of Jesus (i.e., the nature of fulfillment) were actually accomplished—past tense.

For instance, since we still see people physically expiring, we conclude that death has not been destroyed or abolished yet, in spite of what Scripture says. But please notice that Paul in 2 Timothy 1:10 didn't say "was being" or "someday will be." By inspiration, he used the aorist active tense—"has destroyed" (NIV) or "hath abolished death" (KJV). The Greek verb here is *katargeo*. But it does not mean destroyed in the sense of eliminated. It means destroyed in the sense of "to render inoperative, powerless, idle, useless, to disable." Furthermore, the aorist active tense conveys a completed action with ongoing implications and significance.

Every Christmas, Christians sing: "Born that man no more may die" (3rd verse, 3rd line of *Hark, the Herald Angels Sing*). Do we really mean it or know what we're singing? Then what kind of abolishment of what kind of death was Paul talking about and do we sing about every year? Wouldn't it be far better that we adjust our understanding of the nature of Jesus' victory over death and what this means for us today rather than adjusting the time factor to some yet-future occurrence?

The fact is, Jesus did not conquer death by not dying. He died. But He overcame, destroyed, and abolished death by resurrection. Thusly, death has been destroyed/abolished for us.[98] Even Dr. Graham agrees with this fulfillment as he writes: "God sees death as an enemy, an enemy that has now been conquered through the death and resurrection of Christ."[99]

Unfortunately, so many have bought into the sleight-of-hand deception of a future utopian paradise on planet Earth that the promised death-free, mourning-free, crying-free, pain-free, new life in Christ, which already has been made everlastingly available for us (past tense), does not seem plausible or possible. But please be assured that this type of life and all these aspects are available, here and now, if we chose to enter and dwell in God's new city. That's the only way to experience and enjoy this previously delivered and fulfilled blessing.[100]

Point – When it will arrive: Alcorn interprets that this supposed New Earth will arrive at "the final judgment[101] . . . . when Christ sets up his eternal kingdom[102] . . . . at "Christ's triumphant return."[103] Ganssle places this arrival at "the last judgment" that's when "God will make all things right."[104] Graham agrees that "when Christ returns, he will destroy

---

[98] For more, see "Resurrection Reality," in John Noē, *Unraveling the End: A balanced scholarly synthesis of four competing and conflicting end-time views* (Indianapolis, IN: East2West Press, 2014), 379-414. Also, "He 'Raptures' a Remnant" and "He Wants You to Live in the City, in John Noē, *The Greater Jesus: His glorious unveiling* (Indianapolis, IN: East2West Press, 2012), 291-389.

[99] Billy Graham, "My Answer," *The Indianapolis Star* (Indianapolis, IN), 23 August 2014, E-4.

[100] See Jude 3, and for a fuller discussion see: Noē, *The Perfect Ending for the World*, 279-319. Also, Noē, *The Greater Jesus*, 339-389.

[101] Alcorn, *If God Is Good*, 282.

[102] Ibid., 297.

[103] Ibid., 339.

[104] Ganssle, "Evil as Evidence for Christianity" in Meister and Dew, Jr., eds., *God and Evil*, 223.

all evil and rule the world in perfect righteousness and justice. This is why the Bible calls his return 'the blessed hope' . . . (Titus 2:13)"[105]

Counterpoint: Several scriptural difficulties arise from these assertions. First, what does the Bible say about a "final judgment" or "last judgment." The answer is, NOTHING! Neither expression is used in Scripture, and for a good reason.

Secondly, judgment is an intrinsic component of Christ's kingdom—as are love, grace, and mercy, etc. Affixing the adjectives "final" or "last" to the noun of "judgment" means that after that event, there will be no more judgment. The problem is, you cannot have a "final" or "last" anything of any intrinsic component of his kingdom. Why not? It's because his kingdom is not only everlasting, but to its increase there is no end (see Dan. 2:44; Isa. 9:7; Luke 1:33). Likewise, there is no such thing as "last love" or "final grace"—after which there will be no more. This reality is the factual reason why Scripture never uses these expressions, and neither should we.

Thirdly, Christ set up his everlasting kingdom in the 1st century during the "days of those kings" (Dan. 2:44)—which ended in A.D. 476. It arrived fully established at his birth and in the form of his human flesh (Col. 2:9). And "from that time on and forever" it has only been increasing (Isa. 9:7; Luke 1:33). From what time on and forever? "For unto us a child is born, to us a son is given" (Isa. 9:6). That time![106]

Fourthly, what does the Bible say about Christ's "return?" NOTHING and for some other good reasons. Here's one of them, excerpted from my book, *The Greater Jesus*:

> Most everyone recognizes that words matter and wording is important. With this in mind, the late-great theologian, George Eldon Ladd, in his highly acclaimed book, *The Blessed Hope*, acknowledged something very important: "The words 'return' and 'second coming' are not properly speaking Biblical words in that the two words do not represent any equivalent Greek words."[107] This is a major admission with huge

[105] Billy Graham, "My Answer," *The Indianapolis Star* (Indianapolis, IN), 17 July 2014, E-4.

[106] For more, see: John Noē, *Off Target: 18 bull's-eye exposés* (Indianapolis, IN: East2West Press, 2012), 37-51.

[107] George Eldon Ladd, *The Blessed Hope* (Grand Rapids, MI: Eerdmans, 1956),

implications. Another fact is, we Christians have been hamstrung for centuries with these two non-scriptural expressions and unscriptural mindsets. As we shall soon discover, biblically, the idea that Jesus is off somewhere waiting to come back at some future time, as well as the idea of limiting the comings of Jesus to only two or three times, or to any at all, is man's idea and not God's.[108]

Point – The delay: Why has God been delaying his creation of this supposed evil-less and sin-less New Earth for all these centuries and made it a distant goal? Why hasn't He done it already or doing it right now? Alcorn offers this explanation: "God postpones his judgment upon sin, allowing evil and suffering to continue . . . . the suffering of further delay so that others may obtain the mercy God extended to us."[109]

Dr. Graham agrees and in answer to the question of "Why is Christ's coming delayed?" he responds, "One reason, the Bible says, is because God wants to give as many people as possible an opportunity to repent and believe."[110]

Counterpoint: – In theological circles this speculative idea is called the "delay theory." The *Dictionary of Biblical Prophecy and End Times*, in a section titled "Delay of the Parousia," defines and explains this theory thusly:

> The term *Parousia* refers to the second coming of Christ. The delay of the Parousia refers to the assumption by some New Testament scholars that the first generation of Christians (A.D. 30-70) believed that Christ would return before their deaths. When that didn't happen (i.e., when the Parousia was delayed), the early believers were supposedly thrown into a crisis of faith . . . . Thus it appears that in both Luke and Matthew Jesus provides strong hints that there could indeed be a delay between some of the immediate, partial fulfillment of his prophecies and the

---

69. Unfortunately, Ladd ignored his own and valid biblical insight by continuing to use these non-scriptural expressions and unscriptural concepts.

[108] Noē, *The Greater Jesus*, 24.

[109] Alcorn, *If God Is Good*, 335.

[110] Billy Graham, "My Answer," *The Indianapolis Star* (Indianapolis, IN), 3 April 2013, E-4.

ultimate final fulfillment of this prophecies, particularly in regard to the Parousia.[111]

Later, in its section on the "Second Coming," and in agreement with Alcorn and Graham above, this dictionary provides the reason for this delay: "[It] reveals God's patience and desire that many will come to repentance and faith."[112]

The problem here, however, is that Scriptures reveal something far more weighty on this topic of delay than mere "hints." Here's an excerpt from my book, *Unraveling the End*. It lays out three of those instances:

> Below are three significant scriptural problems for this "invented" delay theory, which—as we saw in Chapter 1, p. 32—was probably first espoused "around the middle of the second century by the Shepherd of Hermas."[113]
>
> Problem #1 – If God's plan of redemption was, indeed, delayed, you would hope and expect that this "delay" would show up somewhere in the Bible, if for no other reason than this revealed truth: "Surely the Sovereign Lord does nothing without revealing his plan to his servants the prophets" (Amos 3:7). So where did God ever reveal a "delay" of something as big as his plan of redemption to one of his prophets, to Jesus, or to any New Testament writer?
>
> Problem #2 – In three places the Bible emphatically declares there would be no delay. (Bold and italics emphasis mine.)
>
> - "For the revelation awaits an appointed time; it speaks of the end and will not prove false. Though it linger, wait for it; it will certainly come and will ***not delay***" (Hab. 2:3).
> - "The word of the Lord came to me: 'Son of man, what is this proverb you have in the land of Israel: 'The days go by and every vision comes to nothing'? Say to them 'This is what the Sovereign Lord says: I am going to put an end to this proverb, and they will no longer quote it in Israel.' Say to them, 'The

---

[111] J. Daniel Hays, J. Scott Duvall, and C. Marvin Pate, *Dictionary of Biblical Prophecy and End Times* (Grand Rapids, MI: Zondervan, 2007), 114-115.

[112] Ibid., 410.

[113] Kurt Aland, *A History of Christianity* (Philadelphia, PA: Fortress Press, 1980), 91-92.

days are near when every vision will be fulfilled. For there will be no more false visions or flattering divinations among the people of Israel. But I the Lord will speak what I will, and it shall be fulfilled ***without delay***. For in your days, you rebellious house, I will fulfill whatever I say, declares the Sovereign Lord'" (Ezek. 12:21-25).

- "For in just a very [very] little while, 'He who is coming will come and will ***not delay***'" (Heb. 10:37).

Sadly, the Church has been preaching delay for nineteen centuries and counting. Whom should we believe—the uninspired Church or the inspired writers of Scripture?

Problem #3 – It was the "wicked" or "evil" servant in Jesus' parable in Matthew 24:42-51 who said, "My lord delayeth his coming" (Matt. 24:48, *KJV* – also see: Matt. 18:32; 25:26; Luke 19:22).

First, let's notice that this "delay" in the parable was only within that servant's lifetime, and not 1,900 years and counting. Secondly, let's ask this question – Has the Church become a "wicked servant" for inventing, preaching, and teaching "delay theory" for 19 some centuries and in blatant contradiction of Scripture? I'll let you contemplate the answer to that question.[114]

Point – Gradual redemption, incomplete salvation: Wayne Grudem, in his textbook on *Systematic Theology*, further tries to justify "delay theory" with this argument:

In his great wisdom, God decided that he would not apply to us the benefits of Christ's redemptive work all at once. Rather, he has chosen to apply the benefits of salvation to us gradually over time. . . . Similarly, he has not chosen to remove all evil from the world immediately, but to wait until the final judgment and the establishment of the new heaven and new earth . . . . In short we still live in a fallen world and our experience of salvation is still incomplete.[115]

---

[114] Noē, *Unraveling the End*, 126-127.
[115] Wayne Grudem, *Systematic Theology* (Grand Rapids, MI: Zondervan, 1994), 810.

Counterpoint: There are several problems with Grudem's theological defense that we've already counterpointed. So here I'll simply raise three follow-up questions for you to ponder: 1) How much salvation do we currently have? 2) What's currently lacking? 3) If it's still "incomplete," how is the New Covenant system any different from the Old Covenant in this important regard?[116]

Point – Who rules our world—God or Satan?: Yancey, and many others, see our world as "enemy territory, a spoiled planet ruled by the father of lies, the wizard of woe. What else should we expect from Satan's lair?"[117] Interestingly, the Gnostics of the 1st century, with whom the early Church and New Testament writers contended, also viewed our world as evil (see 1 Tim. 4; Gal. 1-2).

Counterpoint: Once again, whom should we trust and believe— inspired Scripture or uninspired theorists? Psalm 24:1 tells us—"The earth is the Lord's, and everything in it, the world, and all who live in it." Jesus told his disciples that "all authority in heaven and earth has been given to me" (Matt. 28:18). The writer of Hebrews further revealed that Jesus is "sustaining all things by his powerful word" (Heb. 1:3). All this is just as true after the Fall as before the Fall. God never relinquished any of his sovereignty and control to Satan to do whatever he wanted with the whole creation. Nothing could be further from the biblical truth. Then what do we do with verses that appear to the contrary and seem to support Satan being in control, such as:

- "the whole world is under control of the evil one" (1 John 5:19).
- Satan being called "the god of this age/world" (2 Cor. 4:4a – NIV/KJV).
- Satan being called "the prince/ruler of this world" (John 12:31b – NIV-KJV/NAS)
- Satan being called "the ruler of the kingdom of the air" / "prince of the power of the air" (Eph. 2:2 – NIV/KJV)?

---

[116] For an extensive discussion on this issue, see: "How much salvation do we currently have?" in Noē, *Unraveling the End*, 18-23.

[117] Yancey, *The Question That Never Goes Away*, 44.

First, in the original Greek, 1 John 5:19 reads, "the world whole in the evil one lies." It says nothing about control.

Secondly, in an earthy human kingdom a prince has only limited and minimal power, if any, and only as the king allows. The king is the one in charge.

Thirdly, "god/ruler of this world" only indicates that Satan has influence on the majority of people through philosophies, education, commerce, thoughts, ideas, false religions, etc. But this does not contradict or conflict with God's sovereignty. For reasons we'll explore later in this book, God allows Satan and his demonic cohorts to operate in this world within boundaries that God sets. As far back as the book of Job, the Bible reveals that Satan was bound—i.e. limited—in what he could do (see Job 2:1-7).

Jesus and his disciples demonstrated that Satan was bound by casting out demons from A.D. 26 through the early 60s (Matt. 12:28-29; John 12:31; Rev. 12:10-12). Jesus further bound him at the cross (Col. 2:15; Heb. 2:14). Hence, Satan has always been bound. Binding, however, does not mean the elimination of his person, power, or activity. Again, it only means a limitation, reduction, or lessening of his reach.

Fourthly, Satan is a created being. God is his Creator. And God rules and reigns over all things He created. Many other scriptures and passages expound upon God's sovereignty and supremacy over all things He has created in heaven and on earth.[118]

Point – The Antichrist is coming: Dr. Graham casts the Antichrist as "the embodiment or fulfillment of all evil." In answer to a reader's question about whether "the Antichrist is alive today," he responds: "The Antichrist refers to a specific person who will appear at the end of the current age (just before Christ returns). . . . Although the Bible doesn't go into detail, it's clear the Antichrist will be part of Satan's final attempt to stop God's plan for the world."[119]

---

[118] See: Psa. 9:7; 22:28; 47:8; 59:13; 66:7; 97:1; 103:19; 146:10, and passages such as Gen. 1-2; Job 1-2; John 1; Col. 1; Rom. 9-11; Rev. 19-22.
[119] Billy Graham, "My Answer," *The Indianapolis Star* (Indianapolis, IN), 22 January 2010, C-6.

Counterpoint: Once again, with all due respect for Dr. Graham, this is not what the Bible says or teaches. In retort, below are two excerpts from my book, *Off Target*, on this topic:

> It's almost unbelievable how some Christians speculate that some future and final Antichrist is the one who confirms the covenant in Daniel's 70th week. What is their textual proof? There is none.
>
> First, in Scripture, there is no such thing as a "final Antichrist." [Rather] "Many antichrists" (note the plural, see 1 John 2:18) were present in the midst of 1st-century saints, and have been present ever since (see 1 John 2:22; 2 John 7). Moreover, they don't confirm covenants. Only God makes and confirms covenants. If anything, antichrists break them. Speculation about some future, final Antichrist is just that—pure speculation that has been read into prophecy. . . .
>
> Fourthly and finally, John defines who and what an "antichrist" was and is. "It is the man who denies that Jesus is the Christ . . . . Many deceivers, who do not acknowledge Jesus Christ as coming in the flesh, have gone out into the world. *Any such person is the deceiver and the antichrist*' (1 John 2:22; 2 John 7 – bold emphasis mine). Facts are, there were many antichrists back in that 1st century, have been many since, are many today, and will be many in the future. This is the whole teaching of Scripture on this topic of "antichrist."[120]

Point – At the end of time: Yet many mistakenly persist in their belief that evil is provisional for some strange but ultimate good purpose until God eventually decides He's had enough of it. Hence, Keller assures his readers that "evil and suffering are not God's original intent for the world, and therefore only a temporary condition until its renewal."[121] And this "renewal of the world" will happen "at the end of time. . . . at the end of history."[122]

Counterpoint: Once again, what does the Bible say about an "end of time" or "end of history?" NOTHING! "The biblical expression is the 'time of the end' (Dan. 12:4, 9; 11:35; 8:19; also see Hab. 2:3), not the 'end of time.' Big difference! . . . "Changing the order of these words

---

[120] Noē, *Off Target*, 114-115.

[121] Keller, *Walking with God through Pain and Suffering*, 276.

[122] Ibid., 92, 116, 155, 158.

has led many into gross error, such as numerous end-of-the-world misconceptions."[123]

Point – The climax of the Book of Revelation: This is exactly how it's billed by Keller and many others as "the climax of the book of Revelation[124] . . . . Here at the end of the Bible is the ultimate hope—a material world in which all suffering is gone[125] [in] a new heavens and a new earth[126] . . . . the future-perfect world"[127]

Wright agrees and affirms that "when God eventually makes the new heavens and new earth promised in Revelation 21; when God eventually sets creation free from its bondage to decay to share the freedom of the glory of God's children as promised in Romans 8; when God is eventually 'all in all,' having defeated all enemies including death itself as proclaimed in 1 Corinthians 15—when all this comes to pass . . . in this new world there will not only be no evil but no residual anger or resentment, no burden of guilt still to bear . . . ."[128]

Yancey concurs that "the last book in the Bible spells out what that will look like."[129] According to Middleton, the intent of this "final judgment" is "to purge the world of evil so that it might be renewed and, ultimately, saved. . . . but we do not presently see all things redeemed."[130]

Our Capstone Counterpoint: Problem is, that's not how my Bible reads. I've read the last page of the Bible, the page before that, and before that, and all of the Book of Revelation, including chapters 21 and 22. No removal of evil from planet Earth is ever mentioned. Even more troublesome for Keller, Wright, and Yancey's above proclamations, is that evil is still present on earth throughout the Bible's last chapter. Here's what we actually find when we go to the text. I recommend you

[123] Noē, *The Perfect Ending for the World*, 127. Also see 127-133 and Noē, *Unraveling the End*, 213-236.
[124] Keller, *Walking with God through Pain and Suffering*, 159.
[125] Ibid., 313.
[126] Ibid., 314.
[127] Ibid., 321.
[128] Wright, *Evil and the Justice of God*, 136.
[129] Yancey, *The Question That Never Goes Away*, 142.
[130] Middleton, *A New Heaven and a New Earth*, 196, 212.

check out these verses for yourself in your own Bible to see what they actually say.

Revelation 22:11 – One of the last commands given to John in Revelation (and for anyone else reading this prophecy) was to "let him who is unjust, be unjust still; let him who is filthy, be filthy still; let him who is righteous, be righteous still; and let him who is holy, be holy still." Whatever this means, the reality is clear. Evil is still present on planet Earth at that point.

Revelation 22:15 – Outside of the New Jerusalem, which comes down from heaven to earth (Rev. 21:2, 10) are bunches of evil people. Regardless of whether you believe this New Jerusalem has already come down to earth (as I do) or is yet to come down someday in the future, it's irrelevant to our discussion here. Either way, evil is still present on earth, just outside the gates of this earthly city. Here's what this verse actually says: "Outside are the dogs, those who practice magic arts, the sexually immoral, the murderers, the idolaters and everyone who loves and practices falsehood." This is evil still on planet Earth on the last page of the Bible, folks! What do you do with that?

It simply does not follow from this last chapter of the Book of Revelation (or anywhere else in the Bible) that evil is ever banished from the earth. Those who perpetuate this belief are simply indulging in wishful thinking (perhaps deception) without any biblical authority. Where am I wrong on this? If I'm not, then let's call this misplaced hope for what it truly is, "fantasy Christianity."[131] And the fact is that this fantasy will not hold up to an honest and sincere test of Scripture.

Not surprisingly, liberal scholars, who read the same Bible, often scold evangelicals for coming up with a "comfortable notion of God as our warm protector" and thinking that God will someday "make all things right . . . When this, our world, shall be no more."[132]

So what can and should we conclude from our above point and counterpoint exposés? Most likely, Yancey and others will continue

---

[131] For more, see my chapter, "The New Heaven and New Earth—Are Thy Really a Sequel?" in Noë, *The Perfect Ending for the World*, 279-319. Also, my chapter, "He Wants You to Live in the City" in Noë, *The Greater Jesus*, 339-389.

[132] Frederick Sontag, "Master of the Universe, Why?," *Encounter* (Vol. 50: 141-149 Spring 1989).

clinging to their hope "that creation will be transformed. Until then, God evidently prefers not to intervene in every instance of evil or natural disaster, no matter how grievous."[133] Others might take on a defeatist attitude and continue wondering if even praying for vague things like world peace is a waste of time?

It simply does not follow from this last chapter of the Book of Revelation (or anywhere else in the Bible) that evil is ever banished from the earth.

But here is what I believe we can scripturally and confidently conclude. The Bible clearly demonstrates that the existence of sin and evil in this world will never end. Furthermore, Christian hope for an evil-free, sinless, better world, will only be realized in heaven, not on a re-made or all-new earth. Would you now agree?

Practically speaking, but sad to say, Geisler hits the proverbial nail on the head in recognizing and lamenting that "sometimes error seems more comforting than truth—at least for a time."[134] In our next chapter, we'll see how the problems of evil keep perpetuating themselves.

---

[133] Yancey, *The Question That Never Goes Away*, 47.
[134] Geisler, *If God, Why Evil?*, 153.

Chapter 2

The Perpetuating Problems of Evil

Caution: Some readers may want to skip this chapter if they find it too taxing or confusing. Others, I'm sure, will find it further illuminating as we explore three more problems of evil perpetuated by this confusion. Either way, I have included this chapter because it is necessary to complete laying out the problems of evil. Therefore, the three additional problems we'll address herein are:

The definition problem
The theodicy problem
The "hell" problem

The Definition Problem

Great care has not been used by many writers in defining the terms of good, evil, and sin. Hence, readers are left to guess what these words mean. This deficiency also makes differentiating among these words difficult and confusing. So what do we mean when we call something evil or bad? Truly, what is evil? And how can we define evil without first defining good? Then what is good? And what's the difference between evil and sin? Moreover, how does one go about defining these terms when they are supposedly embedded in the midst of "the mystery of iniquity" (2 Thess. 2:7 KJV)?

Let's take a brief look at a mixed bag of confused and confusing definitional attempts.

An Absence of Good: Some claim evil is the absence of good. If that is true, how can the absence of something be a created reality, an entity, or a tangible and relevant force?

One Internet site tries to explain this definition of absence to its visitors this way."Evil is not a 'thing' like a rock or electricity. You cannot have a jar of evil. Evil has no existence of its own; it is really the absence of good." Next, it offers this argument from analogy. "For example, holes are real but they only exist in something else. We call the absence of dirt a hole, but it cannot be separated from the dirt. . . . When a bad relationship exists between two good things we call that evil, but it does not become a 'thing' that required God to create it."

Sensing that their point may not have been adequately made, this site provides these additional illustrations: "If a person is asked, 'Does cold exist?' the answer would likely be 'yes.' However, this is incorrect. Cold does not exist. Cold is the absence of heat. Similarly, darkness does not exist; it is the absence of light. Evil is the absence of good, or better, evil is the absence of God." Consequently, "God did not have to create evil, but rather only allow for the absence of good."[1]

Another akin website adds that since "evil is not really a created thing. You can't see, touch, feel, smell or hear evil. It is not one of the fundamental forces of physics, nor does it consist of matter, energy, or the spatial dimensions of the universe."[2]

A Privation: In a similar but equally confusing manner, Augustine defined evil as "the corruption of a good"[3] and its nature as "a

---

[1] "Did God create evil?" – www.gotquestions.org/did-God-create-evil.html, 7/19/14.

[2] Rich Deem, "Did God Create Evil – Does the Bible Say so?," www.godandscience.org/apologetics/evil.html, 7/19/14)

[3] R. Douglas Geivett, "Augustine and the Problem of Evil" in Meister and Dew, Jr., eds., *God and Evil*, 69.

privation."[4] Hence, evil is "not a substance as such. Rather it is a privation in a substance."[5] But how is this a solid definition? What does "not a substance" mean?

Evans, who agrees that evil is not "a substance or a thing but instead a privation of a good thing that God made," answers that a privation is the "corruption or twisting" of a good thing, but "not a thing in itself."[6] Copan also terms "evil . . . not a thing but a privation" and elaborates that a privation means "a defect, and lack of what ought to be there."[7] But he also defines sin as "a privation—not a substance/thing or creation of God. Sin or evil is a corruption or privation of God's good creation. Evil is parasitic upon the good, and goodness can exist without evil" and "the definition of goodness doesn't require any reference to evil."[8]

Geisler absolutely disagrees with both of these confusing definitional attempts of absence or privation. He categorizes them as "misunderstandings" that "have arisen from this explanation of evil's nature." Instead, he contends that "evil is not a mere absence of good" and advises that "viewing evil as a privation does not imply that evil is unreal."[9]

A Loss: Some define evil as a loss and good as a gain. But this delimited definition is also highly problematic. Why so? One reason is because some losses are good and some gains are not good, right? Others further limit this definition of evil to being only a catastrophic loss of whatever kind and something terrible that cannot be reversed.

Real: Most inhabitants of planet Earth intuitively know that both good and evil are real and evil is wrong. Dr. Graham frequently assures the readers of his newspaper column that "evil is real" and "Satan is still at work."[10] Others agree that "evil is a reality and not an illusion." But

---

[4] Ibid., 73-74.

[5] Ibid., 70.

[6] Evans, *The Problem of Evil*, 1.

[7] Paul Copan, "How Evil Emerged in a Very Good Creation" in Meister and Dew, Jr., eds., *God and Evil*, 116.

[8] Ibid., 118.

[9] Geisler, *If God, Why Evil?*, 20-21.

[10] Billy Graham, "My Answer," *The Indianapolis Star* (Indianapolis, IN), 1 May 2014, E-4.

they also declaim that "it cannot be a substance because all substances are created by God and are therefore inherently good, evil must be a privation of some kind."[11] Hick suggests that "evil must ultimately be defined as that which thwarts God's purpose for His creation"[12] and "the going wrong of something good."[13] But who determines and decides what God's purpose and "something good" are?

Loath to Say: "Atheists and agnostics have generally been loath to say what evil is."[14] Why is that? As we discussed in our last chapter, atheists don't know what to do with evil because they have no frame of reference, nor do they recognize any moral order or objective standard in the universe. Consequently, they can provide no workable definitions of good, evil, or sin.

Bad: Others retort that "evil is whatever is intrinsically bad." But again, who determines what's "bad"? Some suggest it's the "departure from the way things ought to be."[15] But who determines and decides "the way things ought to be?"

An Illusion: Some dismiss evil as an illusion and thus "deny that evil is any kind of reality."[16] If this is true, how could it have a cause, been created, or be perpetrated?

Mysterious: Some others chalk evil off as merely "mysterious matter." But Hick cites "the theodicy-tradition, which has descended from Augustine" and claims Augustine did not find evil mysterious. Rather, he wrote that all evil that indwells or afflicts mankind is "either

---

[11] Geivett, "Augustine and the Problem of Evil" in Meister and Dew, Jr., eds., *God and Evil*, 75.

[12] Hick, *Evil and the God of Love*, 363.

[13] Ibid., 180.

[14] Geivett, "Augustine and the Problem of Evil" in Meister and Dew, Jr., eds., *God and Evil*, 77.

[15] ibid.

[16] ibid.

sin or punishment for sin."[17] So given this definition, is evil sin and sin evil? Are they the same? Or is evil the entity that causes the human race to sin. Or does sin create evil? Mysterious and confusing, isn't it? Let's see what some experts are saying about sin. Maybe they can help us out of this confusion.

Sin: John MacArthur says: "sin is not itself a thing created. Sin is neither substance, being, spirit, nor matter. So it is not proper to think of sin as something that was created. Sin is simply *a lack of moral perfection in a fallen creature.* Fallen creatures themselves bear full responsibility for their sin. And all evil in the universe emanates from the sins of fallen creatures."[18] So is sin simply a lack that creates and perpetuates evil?

The Westminster Confession of Faith defines sin as "any lack of conformity to or transgression of the law of God."[19]

Billy Graham maintains that sin is "anything that isn't pleasing to God. It may be something we do or say, or an evil thought or selfish motive."[20]

Hick believes "the essence of all sin is selfishness."[21]

Middleton simply reckons that sin is "our culpable mismanagement of our human calling."[22]

Joe Kovacs defines iniquity by lumping together "evil, sin, lawlessness, unrighteousness, and perversity" and claiming that all this is "anything that goes against the laws or instructions of God."[23]

The World Book Dictionary broadly and variously defines the noun sin as: "**1a** – a breaking of the law of God on purpose. **b** the state or condition resulting from this. **2** –wrongdoing of any kind; immoral act.

---

[17] Hick, *Evil and the God of Love*, 173, from *De Genesi Ad Litteram, Imperfectus liber,* chap. i, para. 3.

[18] John MacArthur, "Is God Responsible for Evil?" www.gty.org/resources/articles/A189/Is-God-Responsible-for-Evil, 7/19/2014.

[19] Quoted in Sproul, Jr. *Almighty Over All,* 54.

[20] Billy Graham, "My Answer," *The Indianapolis Star* (Indianapolis, IN), 10 July 2014, E4.

[21] Hick, *Evil and the God of Love,* 382.

[22] Middleton, *A New Heaven and a New Earth,* 48.

[23] Joe Kovacs, *Shocked by the Bible: The Most Astonishing Facts You've Never Been Told* (Nashville, TN: Thomas Nelson, 2008), 167.

Lying, stealing, dishonesty, and cruelty are all sins. **3** – a violation of any rule or standard, as of taste or propriety." It also broadly, variously, and vaguely defines the noun evil as "**1** something bad; sin; wickedness; evil quality or act. . . **syn:** iniquity, depravity, unrighteousness. **2** a thing that does harm. **3** misfortune; harm; mischief; damage . . . **syn:** disaster, calamity."[24]

. . . is evil sin and sin evil? Are they the same? Or is evil the entity that causes the human race to sin. Or does sin create evil?

Once again, how do we succinctly define good, evil, and sin and differentiate among them when even the *World Book Dictionary* equates evil and sin? I've been advised that when in doubt, Google Search is your friend. So let's go there. Google Search defines evil and sin in a board and vague manner as well. Interestingly, however, it also provides a revealing graph that tracks the "use over time mentions" of these two words from the 1800s to 2010 (see in *italics* below).

Google Search – definition of evil (adjective)

- profoundly immoral and malevolent.
- (of a force or spirit) embodying or associated with the forces of the devil.
- harmful or tending to harm.
- (of something seen or smelled) extremely unpleasant.

Google Search – definition of evil (noun)

- profound immorality, wickedness, and depravity, especially when regarding it as a supernatural force.
- a manifestation of this, especially in people's actions.
- something that is harmful or undesirable.

---

[24] *The World Book Dictionary*, 1982 Edition, Doubleday & Company.

Their graph of "use over time mentions" of the word "evil" in 2010 shows that its use is about 1/3 of what it was at its height in the 1840s.

Google Search – definition of sin (noun)

- an immoral act considered to be a transgression against divine law.
- an act regarded as a serious or regrettable fault, offense, or omission.

Google Search – definition of sin (verb)

- commit a sin.
- offend against (God, a person, or a principle).

Their graph of "use over time mentions" of the word "sin" in 2010 also shows that its use is less than 1/3 of what it was at its height in the 1840s.

What might we glean from this dramatic drop in mentions of these two words over the past one hundred and seventy years? Perhaps, less sin and evil are happening today compared to back then. Or, our definitions and meanings of these two words have changed in our modern-day cultures and we are simply calling (defining) less things as being sin and evil today. I'll let you decide which scenario you think is more probable. But Todd Wilson explains this dramatic and downward change this way:

> It's not that people sin less today than they did in previous generations. Rather it's that we as a society no longer use the word *sin* for much of anything—other than a sumptuous piece of chocolate cake on the dessert menu. Because of the ingenious devilry of modern society, we've invented a thousand ways to talk about the bad things we do without ever having to mention the dreadful "s-word." Nowadays we're prepared to label bad behavior a thousand things—criminal, unhealthy, self-destructive, intolerant, politically incorrect, dysfunctional, but *not* sinful. . . . We live in a therapeutic age in which the real offense of

sin—if anything is even identifiable as sin anymore—is that it's not
good for you . . . . not healthy for us. [25]

But one thing I believe we can safely surmise is this. More and more,
it appears that "we are left with simple intuitive definitions of good and
especially evil" and we downgrade evil to being "just a natural
phenomenon, to some extent innate, and its being evil consists precisely
in its being undesirable, not conducive to well-being."[26] And then there
are others, like Leon Morris, who mix words together, for example
terming the cross "the evil of sin."[27]

In our next chapter we'll attempt to break through this ongoing
confusion by looking at a more biblical way of defining the meaning of
good, evil, and sin and differentiating among them.

The Theodicy Problem

Since Scripture never offers a direct or comprehensive explanation
for why God allows, permits, and uses so much evil and suffering—even
Job was given no explanation—we humans have attempted to provide
our own. In theological circles that explanation is called a "theodicy."[28]
The word "theodicy" is derived from the Latin, *theo*, meaning god and
the Greek, *dikē*, meaning justice, judgment, right. It is variously defined
as:

- A vindication of the justice and holiness of God in establishing a
  world in which evil exits.
- A vindication of divine goodness and providence in view of the
  existence of evil.

---

[25] Todd Wilson, *Real Christian: Bearing the Marks of Authentic Faith* (Grand
Rapids, MI: Zondervan, 2014), 98-100.

[26] David Beck, "Evil and the New Atheism" in Meister and Dew, Jr., eds., *God
and Evil*, 206.

[27] Leon Morris, *The Epistle to the Romans* (Grand Rapids, MI: Eerdmans, 1988),
191.

[28] This term was coined by the German philosopher and mathematician Gottfried
Wilhelm Leibniz (1646-1716).

- "A defense of God's goodness and omnipotence in view of the existence of evil."[29]
- An "argument for the justification of God, concerned with reconciling God's goodness and justice with the observable facts of evil and suffering in the world."[30]
- A "defense of the righteousness of God in face of the fact of evil."[31]
- "An explanation of the justice of God in the face of counterevidence."[32]
- Gottfried Leibniz, the philosopher who coined the term, more broadly defined it as "a justification of God's ways to human beings."[33]

Keller elaborates that "a theodicy seeks to give an answer to the big 'Why?' question. Its goal is to explain why a just God allows evil to come into existence and to continue. It attempts to reveal the reasons and purposes of God for suffering so listeners will be satisfied that his actions regarding evil and suffering are justified."[34] Hence, a theodicy is a human attempt to reconcile the problem of evil—i.e., "the apparent contradiction between the experience of suffering and the existence of a good and powerful God."[35] It's also a necessitated by-product of distancing God from any involvement in the creation and ongoing presence of evil.

Another way of looking at a theodicy is in its serving a somewhat negative function as a deductive defense of the honor or character of God in the face of the existence of evil. But theodicies do not an attempt to prove God's existence. As D'Souza points out, "the Bible doesn't attempt to *prove* anything; it merely asserts things, such as, 'In the beginning God made the heavens and earth.'"[36]

---

[29] http://www.merriam-webster.com/dictionary/theodicy, 8/13/14.
[30] http://www.merriam-webster.com/dictionary/theodicy, 8/13/14.
[31] Hick, *Evil and the God of Love*, 94.
[32] Wright, *Evil and the Justice of God*, 45.
[33] Keller, *Walking with God . . .*, 89.
[34] Keller, *Walking with God . . .*, 89
[35] Sittser, *A Grace Disguised*, 150.
[36] D'Souza, *Godforsaken*, 41.

Practically speaking, therefore, a theodicy is an attempt to get God off the proverbial hook. It's put forth "to deflect the charge of inconsistency or incoherence of the claims that both God and evil exist." Furthermore, a theodicy "attempts to demonstrate that for every evil that exists, there is a morally sufficient reason for God's allowing it to exist. So evil is completely justified in a world God created."[37]

And yet no theodicy of the many developed by scholars across the centuries has ever answered all questions or satisfied all the evidential problems of the reality and extent of evil and the intense suffering it produces. Instead, all theologians have been able to offer is the caveat that somehow "God allows evils to happen in order to bring a greater good therefrom."[38]

Another way of looking at a theodicy is in its serving a somewhat negative function as a deductive defense of the honor or character of God in the face of the existence of evil.?

As a consequence, theodicy attempts have been labeled "the most formidable theological challenge Christians face as we begin the twenty-first century." No doubt this is because of the "many atheistic philosophers" who now boldly "argue that the presence of evil and suffering give powerful evidence that God does not exist."[39] The practical fact of the matter is, however, that on this side of heaven we shall never be able to account for all suffering and evil with a single model.

But one of the more troubling models being offered today is an open view of God, termed "open theism." This theodicy tries to defend a supposed "risk-taking God who does not control creation. Thus evil and suffering are gratuitous byproducts of a world containing freedom." According to Steven R. Tracy, "the open view theodicy has its strengths.

---

[37] Introduction in Meister and Dew, Jr., eds., *God and Evil*, 9.

[38] Hick, *Evil and the God of Love*, 97.

[39] Steven R. Tracy, "Theodicy, Eschatology, and the Open View of God," in David W. Baker, ed., *Looking into the Future: Evangelical Studies in Eschatology* (Grand Rapids, MI: Baker Academic, 2001), 295.

It takes suffering and evil seriously, does not make God the author of evil, and affirms the eschatological triumph of God. Unfortunately, however the open view reformulation of the nature of God undercuts the very basis for God's ultimate triumph over evil and suffering . . . . [for] a God who cannot foresee or control evil in history cannot necessarily do so at the end of history."[40]

On the other hand, one of the first, if not the first, theodicy ever presented has been labeled "soul-making." Its influence throughout church history has been considerable. Keller recaps this model thusly:

> One of the first theodicies was that of "soul-making," formulated by the second-century theologian Irenaeus and promoted in contemporary form by author John Hick. This view says that the evils of life can be justified if we recognize that the world was primarily created to be a place where people find God and grow spiritually into all they were designed to be. This happens through "meeting and eventually mastering temptation . . . rightly making responsible choices in concrete situations," which results in "a positive and responsible character that comes from the investment of costly personal effort."[41] Hick argues that this kind of soul-making is an infinite good and cannot be achieved by simply being created in a state of innocence or virtue. . . . So the unfairness and difficulty of life in the world is a means by which we grow into something more than behaviorally conditioned animals."[42]

Hick further stipulates that soul-making is "an inevitable result of God's creation of man as an immature creature, at the beginning of a long process of moral and spiritual development." And that "the harsh features of the world, which we call natural evil, are integral to its being an environment in which a morally and spiritually immature creature can begin to grow towards his perfection."[43] Hick also supports the notion that the "eternal future good . . . justifies and redeems all the pain and suffering, sin and sorrow, which has occurred on the way to

---

[40] Ibid., 312.

[41] Keller, *Walking with God through Pain and Suffering*, 89-90. From: John Hick, *Evil and the God of Love*, (rev. ed.; Harper, 1978), 255-256, quoting John Hick.

[42] ibid.

[43] Hick, *Evil and the God of Love*, 369.

it."[44] Assuredly, Irenaeus' soul-making theodicy has merit. Yet others recognize that "the soul-making theodicy suffers from some glaring weaknesses." Keller cites these two weaknesses: (1) "pain and evil do not appear in any way to be distributed according to soul-making need" and (2) "This theodicy does not speak to or account for the suffering of little children or infants who die in pain, or even for the suffering of animals."[45]

Hick himself adds five more weaknesses. (3) "At best it can only account for a small amount of evil and cannot account at all for the maiming of character which too much evil often produces." (4) It "must still show us how all the suffering in this world is the most efficient way of achieving God's goal."[46] And in response to a challenge from critics, Hick insists that the soul-making process "continues far beyond this earthly life." (5) "The price that is paid for spiritual growth even when it does occur is often too high to be justly exacted." (6) "It is not clear why God, if he is all-powerful, could not have created spiritually significant people in the first place." Hick rebuts "that God is creating, not perfect automata, but 'children' who will eventually have come to Him by their own free responses of faith and love." (7) If "moral and spiritual growth occur through overcoming evil and that evil therefore contributes to good by being overcome by it . . . . then the evil conditions which foster them should not be mitigated."[47] Most significantly, Hick concludes—and contrary to most other theodicies—that with "such a theodicy" that "sees moral and natural evil as necessary features of the present stage of God's creating of perfected finite persons," then "the ultimate responsibility for the existence of evil belongs to the Creator."[48] We shall have much more to discuss on this possibility in our next chapter.

Another prominent theodicy revolves around the free-will defense and dates back to Augustine, an early Christian theologian and philosopher of the 4th and 5th centuries whose writings have been most influential. Keller lays out Augustine's theodicy this way.

---

[44] Ibid., 375.
[45] Keller, *Walking with God through Pain and Suffering.*, 90.
[46] Hick, *Evil and the God of Love*, 375, in quoting Maddan and Hare.
[47] Ibid., 376.
[48] Ibid., 385.

In its simplest form . . . God created us not to be robots or animals of instinct but free, rational agents with the ability to choose and therefore to love. But if God was to make us able to choose the good freely, then he had to make us capable of also choosing evil. So our free will can be abused and that is the reason for evil. But this greater good—for us, of having a rational soul, and for God, of having real loving sons and daughters rather than some kind of 'pets'—is worth the evil that inevitably also comes.[49]

But, once again, how can human free will, or demonic free will, explain the violence of nature? Another problem is, if in heaven God's will transformed us into agents capable of love without being capable of evil, why didn't He create us this way from the beginning?

. . . one of the first, if not the first, theodicy ever presented has been labeled "soul-making." Its influence throughout church history has been considerable.

Of course, there are other theodicies, some even more complex and difficult to grasp. But all have the same problem, as Keller pinpoints. "Taken all together, the various theodicies can account for a great deal of human suffering—each theodicy provides some plausible explanations for some of the evil in the world—but they always fall short, in the end, of explaining all suffering." He winds up quoting theologian Alvin Plantinga, who is most critical: "I must say that most attempts to explain *why* God permits evil—*theodicies* . . . strike me as tepid, shallow and ultimately frivolous."[50] Likewise, Marilyn McCord Adams critically concludes that the "standard strategies for 'solving' the problem of evil are powerless in the face of horrendous evils."[51] Atheists, like John W. Loftus, also strike back hard in denouncing that "there is no cogent

---

[49] Keller, *Walking with God through Pain and Suffering*, 90-91.
[50] Ibid., 95.
[51] Marilyn McCord Adams, "Horrendous Evils and the Goodness of God" in Adams and Adams, *The Problem of Evil*, 212.

theodicy that can explain why there is such ubiquitous and massive human and animal suffering . . . ."[52]

But, and once again as Bruce Little retorts, "the burden of proof rests on the theist. . . . the atheist only says it *seems* that certain evils appear to be gratuitous, while the theist denies that as a possibility." And yet he laments that "the idea that God can 'bring more good out of their evil than he could without' is 'traditional, but problematic.'"[53] All of which brings us to our biggest perpetuation problem of all.

The 'Hell' Problem

Many believe that "hell" ultimately solves the problem of evil and sin and suffering. Hence, the traditional view of "hell" is considered to be God's "final solution"[54] and the dichotomy of heaven and hell as "the final fulfillment of the divine purpose."[55] Why is this? It's supposedly because "heaven and hell will set the record straight."[56] But also under this traditional scenario sin and evil "will continue without end, accompanied by unending punishment."[57] Therefore, Sharon L. Baker maintains that hell's existence and continuance "exacerbates evil by keeping the wicked perpetually in existence. If hell exists eternally, so does evil, and so does the suffering of untold numbers of people whom God supposedly loves and desires to redeem."[58]

This continual perpetuation of sin and evil prompts Blanchette and Walls to term "the problem of hell . . . arguably the thorniest aspect of

---

[52] Loftus, "Christianity Is Wildly Improbable," *The End of Christianity*, 99.

[53] Bruce Little, "God and Gratuitous Evil" in Meister and Dew, Jr., eds., *God and Evil*, 40.

[54] For instance, see Steve Gregg, *All You Want to Know About Hell: Three Christian Views of God's Final Solution to the Problem of Sin* (Nashville, TN: Thomas Nelson, 2013).

[55] Hick, *Evil and the God of Love*, 147.

[56] Keller, *Walking with God through Pain and Suffering*, 201 in quoting theologian Don Carson.

[57] Hick, *Evil and the God of Love*, 177.

[58] Sharon L. Baker, *Razing Hell: Rethinking Everything You've Been Taught about God's Wrath and Judgment* (Louisville, KY: Westminster John Knox Press, 2010), 12.

the problem of evil" because "the presence of suffering, and perhaps evil, may stretch everlastingly into the future."[59] Evans labels this unending aspect of evil as "without a doubt, the most troubling belief affirmed in traditional Christian doctrine"[60] and "the pinnacle of suffering both for its intensity and for its duration."[61]

Not surprisingly, critics of Christianity characterize "hell" as, "Christianity's most damnable doctrine"[62] because it employs "naive forms of Christian moral motivation—bare threats of hell and the bribery of heaven."[63] They also make special note that "recent surveys" indicate "more and more Evangelicals are questioning or rejecting the doctrine of an eternal hell as well as the idea that non-Christians will not be saved in the afterlife."[64]

Alcorn, like most Christians, recoils at such suggestion and fires back in support of "hell" claiming that "hell exists precisely because God has committed himself to solving the problem of evil." What is more, he adamantly assures us that "Hell is not evil; it's a place where evil gets punished." Therefore, "Hell is morally good, because a good God must punish evil. . . . It is justice. . . . [and] to argue against Hell is to argue against justice."[65]

Hick just as adamantly disagrees and charges that "hell," as it is traditionally understood, is the place where "the great majority of mankind" is destined "eternally to suffer torment. . . . Thus hell . . . must be accounted a major part of the problem of evil."[66]

D'Souza agrees with Hick and terms hell, "the greatest evil of all" and to which "the vast majority of humanity is headed."[67] Nevertheless,

---

[59] Kyle Blanchette and Jerry L. Walls, "God and Hell Reconciled" in Meister and Dew, Jr., eds., *God and Evil*, 243.

[60] Evans, *The Problem of Evil*, 81.

[61] Ibid., 217.

[62] Keith Parsons, "Hell: Christianity's Most Damnable Doctrine" in Loftus, ed., *The End of Christianity*, 233.

[63] Richard Carrier, "Moral Facts Naturally Exist (And Science Could Find them)" in Ibid., 339.

[64] Robert M. Price, " Changing Morals and the Fate of Evangelicalism" in Ibid., 365.

[65] Alcorn, *If God Is Good*, 309.

[66] Hick, *Evil and the God of Love*, 89.

[67] D'Souza, *Godforsaken*, 224.

he is encouraged that "a strenuous effort" has been put forth by many scholars and theologians to "rescue theodicy from the apparently insurmountable problem of hell." And while he embraces the traditional doctrine of "hell," he quotes C.S. Lewis' lament: "There is no doctrine which I would more willingly remove from Christianity than this, if it lay in my power."[68] Hick, on the other hand, simply calls the very idea of hell "morally intolerable."[69]

Notably, as with the other problems of evil we've addressed in this and the previous chapter, the doctrine of "hell" is also plagued with significant biblical problems. Therefore, many Christians throughout the history of the Church have sensed that there might be something wrong with this doctrine. And since I have written extensively on this topic in another book—99 pages worth—I shall only mention one of those problems here.[70] That problem is this. What does the Bible actually say about an afterlife place called "hell?" And the biblically correct answer is: NOTHING! Absolutely, nothing.

Notably, as with the other problems of evil we've addressed in this and the previous chapter, the doctrine of "hell" is also plagued with significant biblical problems

---

An easy way to demonstrate this conspicuous absence is to look at the number of matches in various translations of the Bible for the word "hell." A match occurs whenever an original language word (Hebrew or Greek in the Bible) is translated into a specific English word. In this regard, below is an excerpt taken from my book, *Hell Yes / Hell No: What really is the extent of God's grace . . . and wrath?*

****

---

[68] Ibid., 226 in quoting C.S. Lewis, *The Problem of Pain* (New York, NY: Macmillan, 1940), 119.

[69] Ibid., 225 in quoting John Hick.

[70] I refer interested readers to: John Noē, *Hell Yes / Hell No: What really is the extent of God's grace . . . and wrath?* (Indianapolis, IN: East2West Press, 2011), 1-99.

A Bit of Hard-core Reality

If you are a Bible-reading and -believing Christian like me, you may be a little shocked by this bit of hard-core reality. I was the first time I discovered it. Here's how I introduced this dose of hard-core reality to my aforementioned weekly Bible study and discussion group.

I showed them one of Reverend Billy Graham's recent, nationally syndicated newspaper columns in which a reader inquired of the much-revered evangelist, "After we die will God give us a second chance to believe in Jesus and go to heaven?" In his response, Dr. Graham first assured the reader that "not one word in the Bible suggests that there will be a second chance after death . . . ." He then affirmed that "once this life is over, you will go into eternity – either to that place of eternal joy the Bible calls heaven, or that place of eternal sorrow and separation from God that the Bible calls hell."[71]

Next, I gave them this short numerical exercise. I asked each one to write down this series of numbers on a piece of paper: 570, 54, 32, 14, 13, and 0. Then I asked two questions:

1) *Does the Bible ever "call" or literally mention "heaven?"*

Correct answer: YES! There are **570 matches** in the original King James Version for original language words translated as "heaven."[72] And Scripture takes us to heaven—describing it in Isaiah 6, Daniel 7, and Revelation 4, 5, 6, for instance. The Apostle Paul also talks about a man he knew who was caught up to the "third heaven." There is no disagreement about any of this.

2) *Do you know what the Bible "calls," says, or literally mentions about "hell"?*
Correct answer: **NOTHING! ZERO!** And Scripture never takes us to hell by describing it to us. My group stared at me like a tree full of owls. Moreover, not everyone agreed. After all, many

---

[71] Billy Graham, "My Answer," (*The Indianapolis Star*, 4 December 2009), C-5.
[72] *Strong's Exhaustive Concordance of the Bible*, Reference Library Edition (Iowa Falls, IA: World Bible Publishers, n.d.), 474-475.

scholars confidently assure us that "Hell is vividly described in the pages of the New Testament."[73]

Next, I shared this tidbit and explained this absence with my group this way. The Italians have a saying, "traduttore, traditore." It literally means, **"translator, traitor."** Or more freely, "all translators are traitors." In this vein, I showed them a revealing statistic in the form of a graphic illustration regarding translation matches for the word "hell" throughout both the Old and New Testaments in a few notable translations, along with their original publication dates:

54 matches in the original King James Version (1611)
32 matches in the New King James Version (1982)
14 matches in the New International Version (1978)
13 matches in the New American Standard Bible (1971) and
    American Standard Version (1901)
0 matches in Young's Literal Translation (1862)—i.e., the word
    "hell" is not found once.

What's going on? I asked. Why such great discrepancy among Bible translations? Do you see a trend here or sense a problem? Clearly, in my opinion, these differences indicate something is wrong, or at least changing. So are any of these translators traitors, as the Italian saying goes?

As we will soon see, the reason for this variance from 54 to zero is . . . there are no equivalent Hebrew words in the Old Testament or Greek words in the New Testament for the present-day term, concept, and eternal place of damnation variously and differently translated (or perhaps mistranslated) as "hell."

One hell critic explains this disparity this way:

If 150 scholars swear to a statement of faith that there is a Hell of everlasting punishment before they are allowed to work on a translation which they will be paid to produce, what are the odds that the translation will contain a Hell of everlasting punishment? (That is the

---

[73] Christopher W. Morgan and Robert A. Peterson, general editors, *Hell Under Fire* (Grand Rapids, MI: Zondervan, 2004), 226.

case with the NIV, and most other Bible translations produced by committees.)[74]

Yes, this major inconsistency is a huge and troubling problem. It is ignored or denied by most scholars. Clearly, however, something is wrong—very wrong.[75]

****

As revealing a bit of information as is this above excerpt, it's just the proverbial "tip of the iceberg" of many other problems associated with the traditional doctrine and belief in an afterlife place of called "hell." But please do not jump to a quick (and wrong) conclusion. The Bible contains numerous mentions of fire, God's judgment, wrath, anger, punishment and loss even for believers in this life and the afterlife, as well as other associated phraseology and terminology, such as: "weeping and gnashing of teeth," "fire and brimstone," "outer darkness," "the abyss or bottomless pit," and "the lake of fire." However, none of these mentions is ever translated as or linked in the text to "hell" in any Bible version that I am aware of.

Let's also note that "the Christian tradition has been far from unanimous over the kinds and lengths of punishment of the bad."[76] Those who are condemned to "hell" to suffer extreme torment for their persistent rejection of Jesus Christ and participations in evil are sometimes called "the damned" and are considered by most Christians to be beyond redemption. What happens to those who have never heard of Christ or the gospel of Christ—estimated to be "between 15-25% of the world's [current] population"[77]—has been for many centuries and currently still a greatly disputed issue in Christian circles.[78]

---

[74] Gary Amirault, "The Hell Test," www.tentmaker.org/articles/hell_test. html, 12/1/10, p-13.

[75] Noē, *Hell Yes / Hell No*, 22-23. For more see pp. 1-99.

[76] Richard Swinburne, *Providence and the Problem of Evil* (Oxford: Oxford University Press, 2011), 200-201.

[77] William Lane Craig, "Diversity, Evil and Hell" in Meister and Dew, Jr., eds., *God and Evil*, 228.

[78] Noē, *Hell Yes / Hell Noe,* my chapter titled, "The 'All' Controversy," 103-125 and "How Long Is 'Eternal' in Eternal Punishment?" 209-234.

Nevertheless, we are told and taught that the concept and reality of an afterlife place called "hell' is shrouded in mystery. But, once again, what does the Bible actually say about this terrifying and mystifying place called "hell"? The biblically correct answer is NOTHING! A literal and plain-faced reading of the text finds no "hell." What we find are four original, biblical-language words that have been variously translated in different versions of the Bible as "hell." They are: the Hebrew word, *Sheol* and three Greek words: *Gehenna, Hades, and Tartarus.* So does translating any of these words as "hell" make sense? I devote two chapters in my aforementioned book to re-exploring that question and another chapter to revealing "Shocking Etymology and Other Hellish Problems."[79] And, yes, I recommend these chapters to your further attention.

For me, I believe the biblically correct answer for this above biblical question is succinctly provided by Hick with his insightful assessment that hell . . .

> . . . is totally without biblical warrant, and can be connected with the teaching of our Lord only by long speculative and theoretical extensions and constructions. Not only are these theoretical constructions the work of the human mind . . . . There is no reason why they should not be subjected to uninhibited Christian scrutiny; and . . . may well have to be rejected as products of a sinful imagination. . . . [and] projections of our own darkened hatreds, resentments, and fears. . . . It has been suggested that the theology implied by the title of Jonathan Edwards' famous sermon, 'Sinners in the Hands of an Angry God,' reflects God in the hands of angry sinners!"[80]

Hick thus concludes about this problem of "hell" that "the contrast between the bad news of a God who deliberately makes creatures for whom He must also make a hell, and the good news of the God of Love heard in the parables and sayings of Jesus, is so great that I cannot regard them both as true."[81] Christian Universalist Gregory MacDonald concurs and further argues that "Hell, as traditionally conceived, removes any possibility of God's overcoming the evils participated in by any

---

[79] See again: Noē, *Hell Yes / Hell No*, 39-99.
[80] Hick, *Evil and the God of Love*, 92-93.
[81] Ibid., 114.

individuals sent there and must surely represent the eternal frustration of his loving purposes for them." Instead, he posits that "the post-mortem state in which most turn to God is vastly better suited for the conversion of the unregenerate."[82]

But, once again, what does the Bible actually say about this terrifying and mystifying place called "hell"? The biblically correct answer is NOTHING!

In other words, and arguably, "hell" is an extra-biblical concept that has been and is used to control the masses. And so Sproul traditionally summarizes in a lamenting manner that "if there is any teaching of Jesus that the church does not believe, it is His teaching about this dreadful calamity that awaits an impenitent world."[83]

Then what are we Christians saved from if it's not being saved from "hell?" In short, we are saved from our sins and from God and his wrath (as we shall see in our next chapter). Make no mistake, "It is a dreadful thing to fall into the hands of the living God" (Heb. 10:31). But we are also saved into God and a right relationship with Him, his blessings, and for his service, here and now, and for which there are both great rewards or losses (more on this in Chapter 6).

Furthermore, once the traditionally mistranslated and misconstrued doctrine of "hell" and eternal separation from God is scripturally taken off the table, intellectually honest and scripturally grounded theologians, scholars, pastors, and laypeople, alike, will have to rethink and reformulate this aspect of their faith called "Christianity."

---

[82] Gregory MacDonald, *The Evangelical Universalist* (London: Society for Promoting Christian Knowledge/Wipf & Stock, 2008, 2006), 160-161.
[83] R.C. Sproul, *When Worlds Collide* (Wheaton, IL: Crossway Books, 2002), 76.

Conclusion

With all due respects to Drs. Graham, Wright, Kushner, Geisler, Boice, and others (but not all) that I have quoted and interacted with in this and the last chapter, I believe they are biblically inaccurate on their treatments of the many problems of evil and especially with their various sidestepping techniques to distance God from any responsibility thereof.

In our next chapter we shall turn to what I believe you will find to be a more biblical and accurate accounting for the ordained origin of evil in our world. This important realization will reset the stage for reconsidering its outworking in our last four chapters.

Part II – The Solution

Chapter 3

The Ordained Origin of Evil

*"If we get the 'first things' wrong,
'last things' will also turn out wrong."*[1]

No consensus exists in the literature for a solution to the classic problem and other associated problems of evil covered in our last two chapters. Instead, we find a vast array of confusing and conflicting human speculations. In this author's opinion, this lack of consensus results from the failure to biblically and properly account for the ordained origin of evil. Consequently, the whole subject area of evil is characterized by compromising and equivocating language.

The goal of this chapter will be to better address and answer this question: "What does the Bible actually say and teach about God and the origin of evil?" I believe that bringing this biblical realization into sharper focus will produce a new paradigm of thought and belief for how we deal with the so-called classic problem and its other associated problems. This refinement will also reset the table for a more effective discussion of the purposes of and our responses to evil, which we'll cover in our last two chapters.

---

[1] Gordon J. Spykman, *Reformational Theology: A New Paradigm for Doing Dogmatics* (Grand Rapids, MI: Eerdmans, 1992), 152.

Let us begin by reviewing key portions of the two creation accounts in Genesis 1 and 2. I consider these accounts to be accurate and historical, and not metaphorical or allegorical. Various disputes over the length of the six days of creation or the age of the earth will not have a bearing on our goal in this chapter and will not be discussed.

The Creation of the World Revisited

So where did evil come from in the first place? N.T. Wright maintains that "the origin of evil itself remains a mystery."[2] But the biblically correct answer and sole solution to the problem of evil is— God, first and foremost, put evil on this planet. And He did this before the creation of Adam and Eve, before the serpent was cast into the garden paradise to tempt them, and before the Fall. Yes, God placed evil in our world on "the third day" of creation week.

Do you find this biblically revealed fact hard to believe? Below is a bulleted presentation from the opening two chapters of the Book of Genesis highlighting when and how all this occurred.

- Clearly, the Bible tells us that "In the beginning God created the heavens and the earth" (Gen. 1:1).
- On "the third day" of creation week, God created all the "seed-bearing plants and trees" and "saw that it was good" (Gen. 1:11-13).
- A small portion of his original, pre-Fall creation was the Garden of Eden (Gen. 2:8).
- One of the trees located "in the middle of the garden" contained both good and *evil* in some form. Hence, it was called "the tree of the knowledge of good and evil" (Gen. 2:9, 17).

Who created that tree, along with all the other trees, and placed it in the garden? Certainly, it was not human free will, Satan, his fallen angels, pre-creation chaos, or any mysterious entity, force, or other deity. Sad to say, this literal and biblical fact of the presence of evil in God's

---

[2] Wright, *Evil and the Justice of God*, 71.

original pre-Fall garden is the crucial point missed or ignored by most writers on the subject.

Critical Objection: But "God only created the potential for . . . evil, not the actuality."[3]

My Response: Not only was that tree an actual tree, but there is more to highlight:

- Who placed Adam and Eve in the garden where this tree was located? It was God.
- Who gave them permission to eat from all the other trees (Gen. 2:16)? It was God.
- Who placed the prohibition of not eating from "the tree of the knowledge of good and evil" on Adam and Eve (Gen. 2:17)? It was God.
- Who turned the devil or Satan into a serpent (perhaps on "the sixth day") (Gen. 3:1f)? It was God.
- Who placed "that ancient serpent called the devil or Satan" (Rev. 12:9) into that garden and gave him access to tempt Adam and Eve? It was God. Certainly, God could have cast Satan elsewhere in his newly formed creation —to Pluto, Uranus, the moon, to a different galaxy altogether, even to the other side of the world in what would one day become Australia or America.[4] But He did not.
- Who gave Adam and Eve access to "the tree of the knowledge of good and evil" so they would have the opportunity to disobey and partake of its forbidden fruit? It was God. Obviously, God could have put an angel with "a flaming sword flashing back and forth" (see Gen. 3:24) in front of or a ring of angels around it to guard that tree. Or, far simpler, He could have never planted that tree there in the first place. But He did.
- Who created Adam and Eve with the capacity to be susceptible to temptation and to sin? It was God.

---

[3] Garry DeWeese, "Natural Evil: A 'Free Process' Defense" in Meister and Dew, Jr., eds., *God and Evil*, 61.

[4] Pink suggests that "between the first two verses of Genesis 1 some awful catastrophe had occurred [the Gap Theory-ed.]—possibly the fall of Satan." (Pink, *The Sovereignty of God*, 58-59.)

- Of course, God could have arranged things differently so Adam and Eve would not have been tempted. Or, He could have created them differently so they could not have succumbed to temptation and been capable of sinning. Rather, they would have remained steadfast in a state of holiness. After all, He created the holy angels in this way and Satan in another way (see John 8:44; 1 John 3:8). Or, He could have turned the other cheek and pretended not to have noticed their disobedience. But He did not.
- Yes, God could have created the world differently, if He had so desired. He could have made it free of evil, sin, and suffering as many Christians erroneously think He will do someday. But He did not.
- And "God saw all that he had made, and it was very good" (Gen. 1:31).
- In this creation, God acted freely and in his sovereignty.
- The only thing pronounced "not good" before the Fall was for Adam "to be alone" (Gen. 2:18).

Critical Objection: God didn't cause the Fall to happen. He only knew it would happen.

My Response: Of course, God knew Adam and Eve would disobey. He's omniscient. But He also created an environment conducive for disobedience, created the players susceptible, placed them in the garden vulnerable, and arranged the circumstances so that the Fall could happen. Thus, He both enabled and allowed the events to happen. Did He not?

Critical Objection: "This isn't the way God meant for the world to be. When God created it, it was good and free from all evil. . . . But someday God will intervene; Christ will return, and the whole world will be restored to what it once was: perfect and good."[5]

Critical Objection: Likewise, Alcorn insists but also equivocates that "though evil had no part in God's original creation, it was part of his original plan. . . . Evil didn't take him by surprise. God isn't the author of evil, but he is the author of a story that includes evil. He intended from the beginning to permit evil, then to turn evil on its head . . . . God

---

[5] Billy Graham, "My Answer," *The Indianapolis Star* (Indianapolis, IN), 19 August 2013, E-4.

originally planned that human beings live unswervingly happy, fulfilled, righteous, and God-centered lives on Earth."[6]

My Response: If we truly and seriously subscribe to the sovereignty of an omnipotent and omniscient God and the authority of his Word, then we must also submit to the realization that God through Christ is the Creator and Sustainer of *all* that is—i.e. the First Cause behind *everything* that exists (see Gen. 1:1; Deut. 10:14; Psa. 24:1-2; 89:11; 103:19; 115:3; 135:6; Prov. 16:4; Isa. 42:5; Job 41:11; Dan. 4:35; John 1:1-3; Acts 17:24-25; Rom. 11:36; 13:1; 1 Cor. 8:6; 10:26; Col. 1:16-17; Heb. 1:3-4; 2:10; Rev. 4:11). Therefore, God Himself must be recognized as responsible for creating evil in the first place and thus foreordaining and enabling sin to occur. This was his original intent for us humans in this created world. And He implemented it and sustains it. How can anyone deny this, dare to challenge Him, question his sovereignty, criticize his ways, or be offended thereby?

So where did evil come from in the first place?

Nevertheless, while God is initially responsible for creating evil and creatures susceptible to temptation and sin, which He could have prevented, God in his sovereignty holds the fallen angels and us human beings responsible for our behavior in our committing sin and evil. But how then can God hold us responsible? Simply, it's because He's God and we are not. And He sets the rules.

So why did God do all this? Dr. Graham attempts to answer by lamenting that "theologians and Bible scholars have discussed this for centuries without coming up with a final answer" and "we'll never fully understand some things about him until we get to heaven. . . . Someday we will understand . . . but not yet."[7]

---

[6] Alcorn, *If God Is Good*, 226, 295. His solution is for God someday to create a New Earth and get it right this time—i.e., an evil-less, sin-less, suffering-less New Earth. But as we have seen, the last chapter of the Bible refutes this notion. Hence, I've labeled this futuristic belief: "fantasy Christianity." (See again Chapter 1, p. 47.)

[7] Billy Graham, "My Answer," *The Indianapolis Star* (Indianapolis, IN), 8 January 2013, E-4.

The Decisive Proof

With all due respect for Dr. Graham, once again, I assert that we can attain a much greater understanding of all this right now and much more than most of us have been led to believe. How so? It's because it has been adequately revealed in Scripture. And there is only one viable reason why evil has been and is present with us today. Here's the decisive proof that it was God's plan all along, before the beginning of the world, to create our world with evil, sin, and suffering in it. Scripture decisively documents God's premeditated intention in this matter. And based on this evidence, any responsible jury would so decide. Hence, the proper biblical answer to one simple question will prove beyond a shadow of a doubt that "this is my Father's world"[8]—i.e., He planned it this way and through Jesus Christ created it this way. This answer should settle this matter. That question is: When was Jesus slain? Was it in A.D. 30 or A.D 33 at the Cross, or long before then?

Scripture clearly states that Jesus "the Lamb that was slain from the creation/foundation of the world" (Rev. 13:8b). That means on or before day one of creation week (see Gen. 1:1-2; 2:5; Psa. 102:25). In other words, Jesus Christ lowering Himself and coming into our world to be born and slain was foreordained, pre-determined, settled, fixed, locked in place, and secured way back then. Accordingly, from that pre-creation time on, the redemptive and beneficial effects of his death and resurrection were not limited by time, could not be undone or thwarted, and were the same as if his sacrifice had already been made. Why so?

It's because God has also revealed that He will do all that He pleases (Isa.46:10-11; 14:24, 27; 55:11; Psa. 33:11; 115:3; 135:6; Dan. 4:35; Job 23:13; 42:2 – also see: Isa. 41:22-29; 42:8-9; 44:6-8; 45:18-24; 48:3-6). And He "works out everything in conformity with the purpose of his will" (Eph. 1:11, 5; Phil. 2:13; Heb. 6:17). Furthermore, his thoughts are not our thoughts; and his ways not our ways. His thoughts and ways are higher than ours (see Isa. 55:8-9). Rightly, Pink expounds upon this matter that "there is no ambiguity in these passages. They affirm in the most unequivocal and unqualified terms that it is impossible to bring to naught the purpose of Jehovah. . . . From all eternity God had

---

[8] See again the hymn in the Introduction, p. 8.

predestined every detail of that event of all events. Nothing was left to chance or the caprice of man."[9]

In a similar manner, "He [Jesus] was chosen before the creation of the world" (1 Pet. 1:20a). This is also why it is said that "his [God's] work has been finished since the creation of the world" (Heb. 4:3b; also see Heb. 9:26); why "I will utter things hidden since the creation of the world" (Matt. 13:35b; from Psa. 78:2); and why Jesus prayed, "Father, I want those you have given me to be with me where I am, and to see my glory, the glory you have given me because you loved me before the creation of the world" (John 17:24).

Scripture clearly states that Jesus "the Lamb that was slain from the creation/foundation of the world" (Rev. 13:8b). That means on or before day one of creation week.

Markedly, Billy Graham agrees that "Jesus' death was not a tragic mistake or unexpected accident; it was part of the eternal plan of God for our good."[10] Then Who killed Jesus back then? It was the same One Who created evil and ordained all these events in the first place? *God killed Jesus.* Certainly, He sentenced Him to death. Who can deny it? Moreover and also, "he chose us in him before the creation of the world to be holy and blameless in his sight. In love he predestined us to be adopted as his sons through Jesus Christ, in accordance with his pleasure and will – to the praise of his glorious grace . . ." (Eph. 1:4-6a; also see 2 Tim. 1:9). Hallelujah and Praise the Lord!

Consequently, Alcorn professes that "the Cross is God's answer to the question 'Why don't you do something about evil? . . . The drama of evil and suffering in Christ's sacrifice addresses the very heart of the problem of evil and suffering.'"[11]

Critical Objections: But Dr. Graham does not agree. He writes: "Adam and Eve's rebellion against God: It shattered his perfect plan for

---

[9] Pink, *The Sovereignty of God*, 35, 97.
[10] Billy Graham, "My Answer," *The Indianapolis Star* (Indianapolis, IN), 18 April 2014, E-4.
[11] Alcorn, *If God Is Good*, 206, 208.

the human race . . . . there is much about God's dealings with Adam and Eve that we will never fully understand this side of eternity."[12] "This present world isn't the way God intended it to be; God meant it to be a place of peace and joy."[13] Marguerite Shuster adds, "we don't know why God permitted the Fall."[14]

My Response: Oh, yes we do. Once again, and to the contrary, neither Satan's, Adam's nor Eve's rebellion frustrated or shattered God's perfect plan. Nor was it an "oops," an accident, or an unforeseen travesty necessitating a need for God to come up with a "Plan B." No, it was original intent, Plan A, from God's perspective. As Pink bluntly points out, "to declare that the Creator's original plan has been frustrated by sin, is to dethrone God. To suggest that God was taken by surprise in Eden and that He is now attempting to remedy an unforeseen calamity, is to degrade the Most High to the level of a finite, erring mortal."[15]

God had deliberately determined, planned, and foreordained the entire course of events. And the entrance of evil and sin into our world was completely under his ruling control and providence. It was the result of a settled design that the Godhead had formed in eternity in the secret counsels of heaven, and not by chance or accident. Rather, it was "by God's set purpose and foreknowledge" (Acts 2:23). Pink concurs that "before the foundation of the world God made a choice, a selection, an election. . . . It was not after Adam had fallen . . . [but] even before the world itself was founded . . . ."[16]

Eight Conclusions So Far

Certainly, Spykman's admonition, cited at the start of this chapter and taken from his textbook on systematic theology, is most apropos. "If

[12] Billy Graham, "My Answer," *The Indianapolis Star* (Indianapolis, IN), 22 December 2000,?.
[13] Billy Graham, "My Answer," *The Indianapolis Star* (Indianapolis, IN), 13 June 2009, C-11.
[14] Marguerite Shuster, "The Mystery of Original Sin," Christianity Today, April 2003, 39.
[15] Pink, *The Sovereignty of God*, 16.
[16] Pink, *The Sovereignty of God*, 40, 42.

we get the 'first things' wrong, 'last things' will also turn out wrong."[17] How true.[18] Then what does the foundational revelation of God's creation of evil mean for us today? I believe we can draw eight rather reformational conclusions, so far.

First, God's plan of redemption, for humankind to fall into sin and be redeemed, can be traced back to before God brought creation into existence. Otherwise, there would have been no reason or occasion for redemption (see again the Introduction, p. 2). It certainly was not an afterthought or a surprised response to an "oops." Clearly, God foreknew, foresaw, fore-planned, and foreordained evil, sin, the Fall, and suffering to be in our world. Morris agrees, for instance, that "the gospel is no afterthought. God had always planned to save people by the way of grace. It is the making of this known that is recent."[19]

Secondly, a major assumption and traditional emphasis of Christian eschatology has now been proven biblically invalid—i.e., that God, at the "restoration of all things" (Acts 3:21 NAS), must finally deal with evil and make an end to it in order to restore this world back to its original, pristine, pre-Fall, and evil-free condition—a.k.a. "paradise restored." This popular belief remains valid regardless of the time of consummation—past or future. Sadly, this futuristic hope of an evil-less, sinless, non-suffering world is a misguided myth. That is why I've termed it "fantasy Christianity." The biblically documented fact is, God created our world with evil in it from the very beginning. Thus, his sovereignty over all things created includes evil.

Thirdly, an omniscient God certainly knew about evil prior to its created material existence in the form of a tree in the garden. Following Adam and Eve's eating of the forbidden fruit, one verse proves this foreknowledge. *Elohiym* (plural for God) stated, "And the Lord God said, 'The man has now become like one of us, knowing good and evil . . . .'" (Gen. 3:22a). I would further contend that this is part of humans being made in the image and likeness of God (Gen. 1:26).

Fourthly, those who argue that evil originated with Satan when he rebelled against God, as discussed in Isaiah 14:12 (also see John 8:44), therefore claim that evil existed prior to the creation of the world. But

---

[17] Spykman, *Reformational Theology*, 152.

[18] Most of my other published books address "last things." See pp. 279-288.

[19] Morris, *The Epistle to the Romans*, 174.

there is no biblical account of the origin or creation of the angels. And in Isaiah 14:12, which most interpreters take as a typological description of Satan's fall, he was "cast down to the earth" upon his fall. Hence, the Earth had to have been created prior to Satan's fall. A similar account is contained in Ezekiel 28:11-19—in which God says typologically about Satan, "you were filled with violence, and you sinned. . . . So I threw you to the earth." On the other hand, Satan's rebellion was certainly the starting point of sin.

We also know from the beginning of the Book of Job that Satan still had access back into heaven (see his reappearance in Job 1:6-7f). Likewise, in the Book of Revelation we are told that after the birth of Christ, Satan and his demonic cohorts were again kicked out of heaven (Rev. 12:3-17). It stands to reason then that God must have created Satan and his gang of fallen angels with the capability and susceptibility to sin and rebel against Him, as well as to be and do evil (see again John 8:44; 1 John 3:8). But in none of these rebellions can Satan be accredited for being the first-cause Creator of evil. Only God through Christ created all things, including Satan and all the angels. That's one-hundred percent scriptural.

Fifthly, the proper identification of the ordained origin of evil breaks the impasse of the classic problem of evil's "awkward trilemma" or "inconsistent triad" that's used by traditionalists and atheists alike—i.e., God is good, God is all-powerful, evil exists. Throughout Church history most theodicies have functioned to obscure the fact that God is the origin, First Cause, and Creator of evil. In their misguided attempts to defend God's honor and absolved Him of any responsibility, they have depreciated his goodness and/or power attributes, while trying to sooth those who are suffering.

Sixthly, no doubt many Christians will continue to hold fast to verses like these to support their presumption that God could not have created anything evil and that evil was totally outside of God's original program until sin entered the world:

- "God is light and in him there is no darkness at all" (1 John 1:5).
- "For God cannot be tempted by evil, nor does he tempt anyone" (Jas. 1:13b).
- "Your eyes are too pure to look on evil; you cannot tolerate wrongdoing" (Hab. 1:13).

- "You are not a God who takes pleasure in evil" (Psa. 5:4a). "The LORD is righteous in all his ways and loving toward all he has made" (Psa. 145:17).

But there is no scriptural reason why God could not have created something that is incompatible with his own character and nature. After all, He is separate from his creation. And clearly, the Scriptures reveal that He created evil, at least in the form of a tree to start with and as we've seen so far. Thus, who can deny that both good and evil were structurally present in the original, pre-Fall garden?

Seventhly, failure to recognize this truth of creation has not only undermined the authority of the Bible and the integrity of the creation accounts; it has also created many unnecessary speculations and problems of understanding. We simply must square our discussions of evil with the fact that the origin of evil is God! Like it or not, He intended it. He created it. He sustains it. Is it any wonder, then, why we have so much confusion and conflict regarding the so-called problem of evil? In actuality, it is not a problem at all. It's a fact of creation. Nor does his creation of evil impugn upon God's existence, his power, or his goodness. Again, it was part of his sovereignty and original creative plan.

John Piper firmly grasps these truths, warns, and advises that:

> People who waver with uncertainty over the problem of God's sovereignty in the matter of evil usually do not have a God-entranced world view. For them, now God is sovereign, and now he is not. Now he is in control, and now he is not. Now he is good and reliable when things are going well, and when they go bad, well maybe he's not. . . . But when a person settles it Biblically, intellectually and emotionally, that God has ultimate control of all things, including evil . . . then a marvelous stability and depth come into that person's life . . . . embrace it for the day of your own calamity.[20]

Eighthly, when God is divested of any responsibility for evil, attempts to find a purpose or purposes for evil are rarely pursued or found. But the proper identification of the origin of evil (First Cause) is

---

[20] John Piper, "Is God Less Glorious Because He Ordained that Evil Be?" www.desiringgod.org/conference-messages/is-god-less-glorious-because-he-ordained-that-evil-be, 19 July 2014.

crucial if we sincerely desire to re-explore and find the godly purposes of evil and adjust our responses accordingly—the subjects of our last two chapters.

Critical Objection: "I could not worship a God who is responsible for evil."

My Response: People positing this denunciation are not contributing to our knowledge of God and our world. They are simply telling us something about themselves. Jennifer L. Bayne and Sarah E. Hinlicky capture the essence of this human theodic tendency, thusly:

> But even more heinous to some is the thought that God wants evil in the world for his ultimate purposes and that we are just pawns in the game. People want to protect God. It is easier to accept a world spun out of control, with evil abounding, than a world ordered by God where evil has a chosen place. [21]

In essence, they are closing their eyes to revealed truth about God and re-creating Him in their own image.

Critical Objection: "The Bible says God is not the Author of evil." [22] "It could not have come from God because He is absolutely good. . . . God did not create any evil thing. . . . Evil cannot come directly from the hand of the Creator." [23]

My Response: Scripture never says or teaches this. The closest scripture verse you can find reads that "God is not the author of confusion/disorder, but of peace . . . ." (1 Cor. 14:33 KJV/NIV). Big difference! God's decreeing, enabling, and allowing sin into our world does not make Him the "Author of sin" either. Yes, God wills all things. But He is not responsible for sinful occurrences. Why is he not? It's because God is not like us. Therefore, we must stop thinking this way lest He "rebuke you and accuse you to your face" because "you thought I was altogether like you" (Psa. 50:21). Certainly, there are similarities—

---

[21] Jennifer L. Bayne and Sarah E. Hinlicky, "Free To Be Creatures," *Christianity Today* magazine, 23 October 2000, 41.

[22] In quotation of Billy Graham's remarks spoken at the memorial service held at the National Cathedral in Washington, D.C. on Sept. 14, 2001 following the terror attacks on America -- "Graham on 9/11: Hope in the Midst of Great Evil," *Whistleblower*, December 2013, 23.

[23] Geisler, *If God, Why Evil?*, 27, 29.

image and likeness, for instance (Gen. 1:26). But there are huge differences. At the top of the list is God's sovereignty. He is the sovereign God and made the absolute sovereign rules. Accordingly, the Scriptures always assign the guilt for sin to us creatures and never to God. And as we've seen, Satan was the first to sin followed by many other angels in heaven. Thus, I concur with Piper who quotes and discusses Jonathan Edwards and Pink's excerpted comments (below) on this matter:

> "If by 'the author of sin,' he meant the sinner, the agent, or the actor of sin, or the *doer* of a wicked thing . . . . it would be a reproach and blasphemy, to suppose God to be the author of sin. In this sense, I utterly deny God to be the author of sin." But, he argues, willing that sin exist in the world is not the same as sinning. God does not commit sin in willing that there be sin. God has established a world in which sin will indeed necessarily come to pass by God's permission, but not by his "positive agency". . . . He uses the analogy of the way the sun brings about light and warmth by its essential nature, but brings about dark and cold by dropping below the horizon. . . ." Thus in one sense God wills that what he hates come to pass, as well as what he loves. [24]

> What is meant by "Author"? Plainly it was God's will that sin should enter this world, otherwise it would not have entered, for nothing happens save as God has eternally decreed. . . . for God only permits that which He has purposed. . . . No such distinction would have been invented had these theologians discerned that God could have decreed the existence and activities of sin without Himself being the Author of sin. [25]

Next, however, Pink admits that this realization "that God decreed the entrance of sin into His universe . . . at first may shock the reader." But he advises that "reflection should show that it is far more shocking to insist that sin has invaded His dominions against His will, and that its exercise is outside His jurisdiction . . . . No; to recognize that God has foreordained all the activities of evil, is to see that He is the Governor of sin. . . . Though nothing contrary to holiness and righteousness can ever emanate from God." Pink

---

[24] Piper, "Is God Less Glorious Because He Ordained that Evil Be?"
[25] Pink, *The Sovereignty of God*, 118, 195.

concludes by rightly recognizing that these are indeed "high mysteries . . . yet it is both our happy privilege and bounden duty to humbly receive whatsoever God has been pleased to reveal concerning them in His Word of Truth."[26]

Clark astutely expounds on this issue.

> Whether they be righteous acts or sinful acts . . . it is these agents [secondary causes] who are responsible. God is neither responsible nor sinful, even though he is the only ultimate cause of everything. He is not sinful because in the first place whatever God does is just and right. It is just and right simply in virtue of the fact that he does it. Justice or righteousness is not a standard external to God to which God is obligated to submit. Righteousness is what God does. Since God caused Judas to betray Christ, this causal act is righteous and not sinful. By definition God cannot sin. . . . There is no law, superior to God, which forbids him to decree sinful acts. Sin presupposes a law, for sin is lawlessness. . . . Man is responsible because God calls him to account. . . . God, on the contrary, cannot be responsible for the plain reason that there is no power superior to him; no greater being can hold him accountable. . . . there are no laws which he could disobey.[27]

Knoch argues likewise and adds:

> We have an innate repugnance, an instinctive abhorrence of any suggestion which seems to associate sin with God. So long as we think of evil as essentially sin, the door is barred to an understanding of its induction into the universe. . . . Sin did not *originate* in Adam. The serpent was in the garden before Adam sinned. . . . He was made an Adversary in the beginning, or it was dormant in him from his creation, or he was influenced from without after his creation. There must be an adequate cause for every effect. Many . . . are practicing the same deception when confronted with the origin of sin. . . . 'From the beginning is the Adversary sinning' (1 John 3:8). . . . It is the old, old attempt to relieve God of the responsibility of the creation as we know it, and to shift its shame to the shoulders of His creatures. . . . But if Adam, in his sin, fulfilled God's purpose, then the very sin of Adam proves the sinlessness of God.[28]

---

[26] Ibid., 202-203.
[27] Clark, *God and Evil*, 53-55.
[28] Knoch, *The Problem of Evil*, 16, 20, 32, 70. Romans 5:12 notwithstanding.

Knoch also reacts harshly to God being the so-called "Author of sin." He calls this expression "unscriptural" and characterizes it as: "an appeal to prejudice. It seems to smirch God with sin. It may or may not imply that God sins. Some do not think that it does. Others do."[29]

In essence, they are closing their eyes to revealed truth about God and re-creating Him in their own image.

Critical Objection: "God isn't the cause of evil . . . . he isn't to blame . . . ."[30] "Evil doesn't come from God. Evil comes from Satan."[31]

"But God's creation of a world in which the possibility of evil is necessary is *not* the same as God actually willing specific evil acts to occur."[32]

"No evil ever came from [God's] hands . . . Let this truth be fixed in our hearts . . . God made all things good, and avoiding hard thoughts of Him, say, An enemy has done this."[33]

My Response: The creation week was and is not the end of God's creation of evil. It was only the beginning. Not only is God the First Cause in the creation of evil, He also creates evil on an ongoing basis. As shocking as our first foundational revelation might have been, this second biblical revelation may be even more shocking. Let's see.

---

[29] Ibid., 189.
[30] Billy Graham, "My Answer," *The Indianapolis Star* (Indianapolis, IN), 24 July 2014, E-4.
[31] Billy Graham, "My Answer," *The Indianapolis Star* (Indianapolis, IN), 10 July 2012, E-4.
[32] Jill Graper Hernandez, "Leibniz and the Best of All Possible Worlds" in Meister and Dew, Jr., eds., *God and Evil*, 98.
[33] Boyd, *Satan and the Problem of Evil*, 293 – in quotation of G.H. Pember, "Earth's Earliest Ages."

God Creates More Evil

A biblically consistent and coherent theodicy must not seek to divert the responsibility for the creation of evil away from God by simply using the modest claims that God only allows, permits, or uses evil for redemptive purposes rather than He created evil in the first place. But shall we limit God to only this? That God sometimes creates more evil and sends it into our world and lives is often taught in the Scriptures.

"Many," as Knock notes, "may be tempted to cry, 'Blasphemy!' Many may insist that God could not do these things, no matter how clearly the Scriptures seem to certify to them."[34] So how can we know? Once again, the Bible tells us so. So what do you think are the implications of this astonishing statement?

> *I form the light, and create darkness; I make peace, and create evil:*
> *I the Lord do all these things.* (Isa. 45:7 KJV)

The Hebrew word *ra* (Strong's #7451) is translated as "evil" in the KJV. In more modern translations it's translated as "disaster" in the NIV, and as "calamity" in the NAS. It means "bad, evil, adversity, affliction, calamity, distress, disaster." It's derived from the Hebrew verb *raa* (Strong's #7489), which means "to spoil." The noun *ra* is used in some five hundred verses throughout the Old Testament and in a consistently applied manner.

Critical Objection: In answer to a reader's question – "A friend of mine . . . claims the Bible says God created evil. He even showed me a verse somewhere that seemed to say this" – Dr. Graham wrote: "Your friend is wrong; the Bible clearly teaches that God is good and evil doesn't come from God but from Satan. (Your friend may have used an older Bible translation which occasionally used the English word "evil" to translate the original Hebrew word for "disaster" or "judgment." . . . Your friend has tried to make the Bible say something it doesn't really say."[35]

---

[34] Knock, *The Problem of Evil*, 167.
[35] Billy Graham, "My Answer," *The Indianapolis Star* (Indianapolis, IN), 9 November 2010, E-4.

In a similar dismissive vein, Deem chimes in that the "use of this translation [KJV] is problematic these days, since it uses an archaic version of modern English, which doesn't necessarily mean the same things today as when it was translated over 400 years ago." Of course, the context of any verse in which the Hebrew word *ra* is used determines the proper translation. And since Isaiah 45:7 contrasts opposites, Deem insists that while "darkness is the opposite of light . . . . evil is not the opposite of peace"—God "is not the author of evil. However . . . God does bring judgment and calamity (either directly or through human authorities) on those who rebel."[36]

Another critic similarly disclaims that "the word translated evil in scriptures does not 'necessarily' mean evil in the same sense that we typically understand the word in our day." He suggests that it only means "something that is 'not good.'" Therefore, he submits that "it does not mean evil in the sense that we might think of the word today as wickedness."[37]

Popular author John MacArthur also puts down the King James Version's translation of *ra* as evil, preferring instead the NAS's translation as "calamity." He maintains that "God devises calamity as a judgment for the wicked. But in no sense is He the author of evil." He further assures his readers that "all evil in the universe emanates from the sins of fallen creatures. . . . He [God] simply permits evil agents to work, then overrules evil for His own wise and holy ends. Ultimately He is able to make all things—including all the fruits of all the evil of all time—work together for a greater good (Romans 8:28)."[38]

Alcorn also skirts the issue to protect God from any responsibility here in this way: "For good reason, most translators normally render *ra* as 'evil' when used of people disobeying God, but 'disaster' or

[36] Deem, "Did God Create Evil – Does the Bible Say So?"
[37] Tony Warren, "God Says He Creates Evil, Does That Mean God Creates Sin?" www.mountainretreatorg.net/faq/create_evil.html, 5/12/14. He cites Jer. 24:2, Prov. 15:10, Psa. 41:1b, Jas. 1:13-14, Lev. 26:25, Amos 3:6-7, Job 2:10 as examples. A similar argument is raised here: that *ra* sometimes means something milder, such as "hurtful (Job 35:12; 1 Sam. 30:22), merely an unpleasant experience (Gen.47:9; Prov. 15:10), or describing fierce beasts (Lev. 26:6) and even spoiled or inferior fruit (Jer. 24:3)" – from "Doesn't Isaiah say God made Evil?" www.cornereason.org/phil_qstn/phi025.asp., 19 July 2014.
[38] MacArthur, "Is God Responsible for Evil?"

'calamity' when used of God bringing judgment on sinful people. . . . (There can be righteous *ra* but not righteous *evil*.)"[39] He then compares it to "the surgeon [who] inflicts suffering on the patient and the parent [who] disciplines the child, but they do good, not evil. Likewise, God can permit and even bring suffering upon his children without being morally evil."[40] Later, at least, Alcorn does concede that "God can use any evil to accomplish good and sovereign purposes."[41]

My Response: Many translations and interpreters have modified this one scripture by citing a range of possible meanings for the Hebrew word *ra*. But its range is not wide. Essentially, all its meanings mean the same thing—bad stuff that spoils peace. Perhaps the more modern translations simply sought to find a more acceptable word in order to get around the stigma of the English word evil. Notably, however, *ra* is also the Hebrew word used in the expression "the tree of the knowledge of good and evil" in Genesis 2:9, 17.[42] In these two verses those two nouns of good and evil are certainly used as opposites. Accordingly, this tree did not become known as the tree of the knowledge of good and bad, good and disaster, or good and calamity. Furthermore, those who embrace God and follow in his ways are not immune from this evil, calamities, or disasters (check out what happened to Job, Joseph, David, and even Jesus, for instance). They are common to all humankind.

... the Hebrew word *ra*. But its range is not wide. Essentially, all its meanings mean the same thing— bad stuff that spoils peace.

Next, in my response to these above critics, let's take a comparative look at a few other consistent usages of *ra* in Isaiah, Deuteronomy, Micah, and Zechariah (KJV – *italics mine*): "Therefore shall *evil* come upon thee" (Isa. 47:11); "and keepeth his hand from doing any *evil* (Isa. 56:2); "righteousness is taken away from the *evil*" (Isa. 57:1); "Their feet run to *evil*" (Isa. 59:7); "he that departeth from *evil*" (Isa. 59:15), and "ye

---

[39] Alcorn, *If God Is Good*, 28.
[40] Ibid., 29.
[41] Ibid., 34.
[42] Also see: Gen. 3:5, 22; 6:5; 8:21.

did not hear, but did *evil* before mine eyes, and did choose that wherein I delighted not." (Isa. 65:12; also 66:4).

The passages in Deuteronomy are: "You will do *evil* in the sight of the Lord and provoke him to anger by what your hands have made" (Deut. 31:29). "You must purge the *evil* from among you" (Deut. 22:21b; 24b). "You must purge the *evil* from Israel" (Deut. 22:22b). Other relevant passages are: "Woe to those who plan iniquity, to those who plot *evil* on their beds" (Mic. 2:1a). "Turn ye now from your *evil* ways, and from your *evil* doings: but they did not hear, nor hearken unto me, saith the LORD" (Zech. 1:4b). "And oppress not the widow, nor the fatherless, the stranger nor the poor; and let none of you imagine *evil* against his brother in your heart" (Zech. 7:10; also 8:17).

Again, the noun *ra* is used some five hundred times throughout the Old Testament and in a manner comparatively consistent with its use in Isaiah 45:7.[43]

Critical Objection: Allowing, permitting, using, decreeing, and/or sending evil is not the same as creating it or doing it. God is holy and He would not create or do anything that is contrary to his nature. As Spykman supportively notes: "Classic Christian theology flatly refuses even to entertain the notion that the Creator himself is in some sense the Author, Source, or Cause of sin and evil. This option is repudiated in the strongest possible terms in the confessions of the Reformation era. . . . Evil has no divine origin, not even 'in a certain sense.' . . . Scripture sheds no light on the many attempts to ferret out a more ultimate 'explanation.' The *origin* of evil remains an inexplicable mystery." And yet he admits without skipping a sentence, "but its *beginning* is a matter of biblical record."[44]

My Response: The same Hebrew word *bara* used in Isaiah 45:7 and translated as "create" is used throughout Genesis, starting with "In the beginning God created . . . ." (Gen. 1:1; also – 1:21, 27; 2:3, 4; 5:1, 2; 6:7; and in many more Old Testament verses). Let's also note that this verb "create" in Isaiah 45:7 is in the present tense. That means that God is continually creating evil, disaster, calamity, even now. This biblical fact and ongoing reality is documented and demonstrated throughout the

---

[43] KJV translates *ra* as calamities once (Psa. 141:5) and does not translate it as disaster.

[44] Spykman, *Reformational Theology*, 305, 307, 311-312.

Bible. Oftentimes God has initiated suffering, punishment, and judgment by creating and sending evil. And yet, the critics contend that in his creating and sending, "God does not do evil," himself.[45] Or does He? "God is not the cause of evil."[46] Or is He? "Both piety and reason require the believer to dissociate God from the cause of evil."[47] How can we?

In critical retort, Sproul, Jr., unabashedly declares that Isaiah 45:7 "is no bare permission. God announces that he is the one who sends calamity."[48]

Critical Objection: Grudem offers this defensive but equivocating explanation in his textbook on *Systematic Theology*: "Isaiah 45:7, which speaks of God 'creating evil,' does not say that God himself *does* evil but should be understood to mean that God ordained that evil would come about through the willing choices of his creatures. . . . 'secondary causes' (human beings, and angels and demons) are *real* and . . . human beings do cause evil and are responsible for it. Though God ordained that it would come about, both in general terms and in specific details, yet *God is removed from actually doing evil,* and his bringing it about through 'secondary causes' does not impugn his holiness or render him blameworthy . . . . On the other hand, if we maintain that God does not use evil to fulfill his purposes, then we would have to admit that there is evil in the universe that God did not intend, is not under his control, and might not fulfill his purposes."[49]

Copan likewise argues, "but surely *permission* is not *causation.*"[50]

John Frame, however, counters: "What God permits or allows to happen will happen. God could have easily prevented Satan's attack of Job if he had intended to. That he did not prevent that attack implies that he intended it to happen. Permission, then, is a form of ordination, a form of causation."[51]

---

[45] Geivett, "Augustine and the Problem of Evil" in Meister and Dew, Jr., eds., *God and Evil*, 66.

[46] Ibid., 67.

[47] Ibid., 69.

[48] Sproul, Jr., *Almighty Over All*, 146.

[49] Grudem, *Systematic Theology*, 328.

[50] Copan, "Evil and Primeval Sin" in Meister and Dew, Jr., eds., *God and Evil*, 113.

[51] Grudem, *Systematic Theology*, 328, quoted from John M. Frame, *The Doctrine of God* (Phillipsburg, NJ: P & R, 2002), 178.

Sproul, Jr. adds: "Note that Satan did not ask for permission to torment Job but asked that God do it himself. God, not the devil, is the one with the power to destroy Job and his wealth. God, however, delegated this task to the devil [see Job 1:11-12]. . . . It is important to note that not only did the devil have to get permission to torment Job, he didn't even have the power to do so unless God granted him that power. . . . [Similarly] It was the Spirit who directed Jesus to go into the wilderness . . . . with the purpose that this temptation would take place. It was planned from the beginning. . . . . [And yet] God is not guilty of any wrongdoing in the story of Job."[52]

My Response: Yes, there are major disagreements over the sovereignty of God in creation, in the great sweep of history, in the plan of redemption, and in tiniest details of natural disasters, etc. But let's put the validity of this ultimate responsibility charge to a judicial test. Please consider the following argument:

> The analogy of a husband who hires a contract-killer to murder his wife. After the crime is committed, and both parties are arrested, do you suppose that in court, the husband will be declared "Not Guilty" by reason that he was merely the Conspirator? Will he be exonerated on the grounds that someone else, namely a *secondary* cause, was the one who actually pulled the trigger? In reality, however, the Prosecutor will, most often, offer to Plea Bargain with the secondary agent in order to levy the greatest charge against the primary agent. Therefore, not only does the "secondary causes defense" fail to *exonerate* the Conspirator, it further backfires as the Conspirator is the one held in *greatest* contempt.[53]

If you are up for it, check out this five-minute, YouTube video titled, "How Many Has God Killed?
(https://www.youtube.com/watch?v=6IrtdLukslY). It documents the specific instances in the Bible where God either directly killed or ordered people killed and only counts where the numbers killed are actually recorded in Scripture. Not included, therefore, were those who died in the flood in Genesis, the deaths of the first-borns in Egypt, or other

---

[52] Sproul, Jr., *Almighty Over All*, 117-118, 143.
[53] "Charge: Calvinism Makes God the Author of Sin," www.examiningcalvanism.com/Complaints/ac_sin.html, 19 July 2014.

massacres and slaughters in which no numbers are mentioned. But its tally does include Jesus. It's billed as "A light-hearted (yet sickening) look at the number of deaths God ordained in the Bible."[54]

So did you watch that video? Are you shocked? Joe Kovacs, in his book titled *Shocked by the Bible*, picks up on this carnage by asking "who is the biggest killer in the Bible?" He answers, "the fact is that it's God Himself." Kovacs further acknowledges that today, "Christians and non-Christians alike are so inundated with messages about God's love and forgiveness that they have simply never learned about the vast number of people God has slain . . . . It's part of God's nature that leaves some confused or even upset." Then he makes a startling claim. "One thing is certain: if we refuse to change our lives and live according to God's instructions, we shall also be killed by the Creator. Jesus said so Himself, twice. 'Except ye repent, ye shall all likewise perish' (Luke 13:3, 5)."[55]

Phillip Cary puts a different take on God's numerous commands for Israel to wipe out entire peoples. He argues that "the vast majority of Christians after the earliest decades of the church have been Gentiles." Hence "our origin lies not with the people who hear the command to kill, but with those who are to be killed. . . . To read the Canaanite genocide this way is to have our hearts formed the way the New Testament intends for Gentiles. We have to acknowledge that the holiness of God does indeed mean death for us. At precisely this point, it should be clear that we have entered familiar territory for Christian theology. We know the wages of our sin is death (Rom. 6:23) . . . which ought to drive us to faith in Christ."[56]

Interestingly, while writing this chapter, I posted the above YouTube video on my blog titled, "Does God Still Kill People Today?" and on several Facebook groups. Yes, it's not a popular thought or question. Needless to say, I received numerous responses. The two best and most accurate responses were these: (1) "Everyone who has ever lived. God proclaimed the death sentence at the Fall." (2) "The tragedy of the

---

[54] The home page of EvilBible.com tallies God directly killing 371,186 people and ordering another 1,862,265 murdered (8/26/14).

[55] Kovacs, *Shocked by the Bible*, 123, 130.

[56] Phillip Cary, "We Are All Rahab Now," *Christianity Today*, August 2013, 27-29.

destruction of Jerusalem . . . was from the fist or gavel of God. So, apparently, providential justice does continue. It's amazing how many people deny Yahweh's providence and it's even more amazing how many refuse to accept the fact that the potter discards some pottery when He desires to do so."[57]

Dr. Billy Graham doesn't have any problem believing that God still kills people. He's anticipating a mass-worldwide-killing event coming from and by God someday, possibly soon. In answer to a reader's question of "How will the world end?," he responds, "it will only pass away when God intervenes to bring it to an end. . . . it will be sudden and unexpected. Just as in the days of Noah's flood, a catastrophe will suddenly overtake the Earth – then it will be too late to turn to God. 'The heavens will disappear with a roar; the elements will be destroyed by fire, and the earth and everything . . . in it will be laid bare' (2 Peter 3:10)."[58] Of course, I totally disagree with Dr. Graham's eschatological assessment and perspective here and have extensively written in rebuttal.[59]

In this same regard, however, I now ask you this follow-up question as another responder to my blog so asked me:

> If an angel does the will of God, that's the same thing as saying God himself did it. Correct? Because if God commands someone to perform his will, then it is really God who does that act, even though another carries out his will. Likewise, assuming Satan is a literal being, if Satan does the will of God, that's the same thing as saying God himself did it. Correct? Satan cannot do what is against God's will, because God is sovereign. What God permits, God approves. And if Satan does God's will and acts as an adversary, then it is really God who acts as an adversary, or a "satan."Therefore . . . . whether it's God himself or an angel carrying out his will with his permission, it is really God who does it.[60]

---

[57] From my blog and FB postings, 8/27/14.

[58] Billy Graham, "My Answer," *The Indianapolis Star* (Indianapolis, IN), 12 September 2014, E-4.

[59] See Noē, *The Perfect Ending for the World*, entire book, especially, 21-106ff, 279-319. Noē, *Unraveling the End*, 141-169, 285-330.

[60] Miguel Figueiredo, "The Word 'Satan' in the Scripture," posted on the Facebook group Teologia & Apologetica, 1/15/14.

Examples of God Creating and Sending Bad '*Ra*'-Type Stuff

Scripture abounds with examples of God creating and sending evil (bad stuff) into people's lives and upon nations. Admittedly, as Morris remarks, "some commentators find the concept of the divine wrath distasteful and unworthy; so they write it out of Scripture."[61] We, however, shall not commit that error and or allow this omission, since wrath is a big part of Who our God is.

Consequently, below is a fairly extensive, but far from exhaustive, survey through the Old Testament to document the reality and firmly illustrate the severity of this greatly ignored and denied aspect of God's character and nature. To expedite your perusal, I have emphasized in bold the key words. As we shall see, divine wrath is how God has dealt with some of his creation throughout history.

From the Old Testament: (**bold emphasis mine**)

Genesis 6:5, 7: "The LORD saw how great man's wickedness on the earth had become, and that every inclination of the thoughts of his heart was only evil all the time. . . . So the LORD said, '**I will wipe mankind**, whom I have created, **from the face of the earth** – men and animals, and creatures that move along the ground, and birds of the air – for I am grieved that I have made them."

Genesis 19:24, 29b: "Then the LORD **rained down burning sulfur** on Sodom and Gomorrah – from the LORD out of the heavens. . . . and he brought Lot out of the catastrophe that overthrew the cities where Lot had lived."

Exodus 4:11: "The LORD said to him, 'Who gave man his mouth? Who makes him **deaf or dumb**? Who gives him sight or makes him **blind**? Is it not I, the LORD?"

Exodus 9:15-16: "For by now I could have stretched out my hand and **struck you** and your people with a **plague** that would have **wiped you off the earth**. But I have raised you up for this very purpose, that I

---

[61] Morris, *The Epistle to the Romans*, 180.

might show you my power and that my name might be proclaimed in all the earth.".

Exodus 14:17: "I will **harden the hearts** of the Egyptians so that they will go in after them [into the Red Sea]. And I will gain glory through Pharaoh and all his army, through his chariots and his horsemen."

Exodus 22:22-24: "Do not take advantage of a widow or an orphan. If you do and they cry out to me, I will certainly hear their cry. My anger will be aroused, and **I will kill you with the sword**; your wives will become widows and your children fatherless."

Exodus 32:35: "And the LORD **struck the people** with a **plague** because of what they did with the calf Aaron had made."

Leviticus 10:1-2: "Aaron's sons Nadab and Abihu took their incense; and they offered unauthorized fire before the LORD, contrary to his command. So **fire came out from the presence of the LORD** and **consumed** them, and they **died** before the LORD."

Leviticus 26:14-22: "But if you will not listen to me and carry out all these commands, and if you reject my decrees and abhor my laws and fail to carry out all my commands and so violate my covenant, then **I will do this to you**: I will bring upon you sudden **terror, wasting disease and fever** that will **destroy your sight and drain away your life.** You will **plant seed in vain**, because your enemies will eat it. I will **set my face against you** so that you will be **defeated by your enemies;** those who hate you will **rule over you**, and you will **flee** even when no one is pursuing you.

"If after all this you will not listen to me, I will **punish** you for your sins **seven times over.** I will **break down** your stubborn pride and make the **sky above you like iron** and the **ground beneath you like bronze.** Your **strength will be spent in vain**, because your soil will **not yield its crops**, nor will the trees of the land **yield their fruit.**

"If you remain hostile toward me and refuse to listen to me, I will **multiply your afflictions seven times over**, as your sins deserve. I will **send wild animals** against you, and they will **rob you of your children, destroy your cattle** and make you **so few in number** that your roads will be **deserted**."

Numbers 16:30f: "But if the LORD brings about something totally new, and the **earth opens its mouth** and **swallows them**, with everything that belongs to them, and they **go down alive into the grave**, then you will know that these men have treated the LORD with contempt."

Numbers 26:9a-10: ". . . and were among Korah's followers when they rebelled against the LORD. The **earth opened its mouth and swallowed them** along with Korah, whose followers **died** when the **fire devoured the 250 men**. And they served as a **warning sign**."

Deuteronomy 6:22: "Before our eyes the **LORD sent** miraculous **signs and wonders—great and terrible**—upon Egypt and Pharaoh and his whole household."

Deuteronomy 7:15: "The LORD will keep you free from every **disease**. He will not inflict on you the horrible **diseases** you knew in Egypt, but he **will inflict them on all who hate you**."

Deuteronomy 8:20: "Like the nations the LORD **destroyed** before you, so **you will be destroyed** for not obeying the LORD your God." .

Deuteronomy 20:17-18: "**Completely destroy them** – the Hittites, Amorites, Canaanites, Perizzites, Hivites and Jebusites – as the LORD your **God has commanded you**. Otherwise, they will teach you to follow all the detestable things they do in worshipping their gods, and you will sin against the LORD your God" (also see Deut. 7:1-2). This meant the extermination of men, women, and children and burning their cities.

Deuteronomy 28:20: "The LORD will send on you **curses, confusion, and rebuke** in everything you put your hand to, until you are **destroyed** and come to **sudden ruin** because of the **evil** you have done in forsaking him/me . . . ." (also see Deut. 28:21-29).

Deuteronomy 28:59-61: "The LORD will **send fearful plagues** on you and your descendants, **harsh and prolonged disasters, and severe and lingering illnesses.** He will bring upon you all the **diseases** of Egypt that you dreaded, and they will cling to you. The LORD will also bring on you every kind of **sickness and disaster** not recorded in this Book of the Law until you are **destroyed**."

Deuteronomy 32:23: "I will heap **calamities** [*ra*] upon them and spend my **arrows** against them." .

Deuteronomy 32:24, 35: "I will send **wasting famine** against them, **consuming pestilence and deadly plague**; I will send against them the **fangs of wild beasts**, the **venom of vipers** that glide in the dust. . . . their day of **disaster** is near."

Deuteronomy 32:39b: "There is no god besides me. **I put to death** and I bring to life, **I have wounded** and I will heal, and no one can deliver from my hand."

Joshua 6:20-21: "When the trumpets sounded, the people shouted, and at the sound of the trumpet, when the people gave a loud shout, the **wall collapsed**; so every man charged straight in, and they took the city [Jericho]. They devoted the city to the LORD and **destroyed with the sword every living thing in it – men, women, young and old, cattle, sheep and donkeys.**"

Joshua 11:20: "For it was the LORD himself who **hardened their hearts** to wage war against Israel, so that he might **destroy them totally, exterminating them without mercy,** as the LORD commanded Moses."

Joshua 23:15: "But just as every good promise of the LORD your God has come true, so the LORD will bring on you **all the evil** [*ra*] he has threatened, until he has **destroyed** you from this good land he has given you."

Judges 9:23a: "God **sent an evil** [*ra*] **spirit** between Abimelech and the citizens of Shechem . . ."

1 Samuel 2:25b: ". . . it was the LORD's will **to put them to death**."

1 Samuel 16:14: "Now the Spirit of the LORD had departed from Saul, and an **evil** [*ra*] **spirit from the LORD tormented** him" (also see 1 Sam. 19:9).

2 Samuel 12:11a, 15b, 18a KJV: "Thus saith the LORD, Behold, **I will raise up evil** [*ra*] against thee out of thine own house, and I will **take thy wives** before thine eyes, and give **them** unto thy neighbor, and he shall lie with thy wives in the sight of this sun. . . . And **the LORD struck the child** that Uriah's wife bare unto David, and it was **very sick**. . . . And it came to pass on the seventh day, that the child **died**."

2 Samuel 17:14b KJV: ". . . that the LORD might **bring evil** [*ra*] upon Absalom."

2 Samuel 24:1: "Again the anger of the LORD burned against Israel, and he **incited** David against them, saying, 'Go and count Israel and Judah'" (also see 1 Chron. 21:1, where it's said that **Satan incited** David to take this census).

2 Samuel 24:15-16a: "So the LORD sent a **plague** on Israel from that morning until the end of the time designated, and **seventy thousand** of the people from Dan to Beersheba **died**. When the angel **stretched out**

his hand to destroy Jerusalem, the LORD was grieved because of the calamity and said to the angel who was afflicting the people, 'Enough! Withdraw your hand'" (also see 1 Chron. 21:15).

1 Kings 9:9 KJV: ". . . the LORD brought upon them **all this evil**" [*ra*].

1 Kings 21:21a KJV: "Behold, **I will bring evil** [*ra*] upon thee, and will **take away thy posterity** . . . ."

1 Kings 22:21-23: ". . . **a spirit came forward**, stood before the LORD and said, 'I will lure him . . . . I will go out and be **a lying spirit** in the mouths of all his prophets' . . . 'Go and do it.' So now the LORD has put a **lying spirit** in the mouths of all these prophets of yours. The LORD has **decreed disaster** for you."

2 Kings 17:25b: ". . . the LORD; so he **sent lions** among them and they **killed** some of the people."

2 Kings 22:16a KJV: "Thus saith the LORD, Behold, **I will bring evil** [*ra*] upon this place, and upon the inhabitants thereof . . . ."

2 Chronicles 18:22 KJV: "Now therefore, behold, the LORD hath put a **lying spirit** in the mouth of these thy prophets, and the LORD hath spoken **evil** [*ra*] against thee."

2 Chronicles 34:24 KJV: "Thus saith the LORD, Behold, **I will bring evil** [*ra*] upon this place, and upon the inhabitants thereof, even all the **curses** that are written in the book which they have read before the king of Judah."

Proverbs 16:4 KJV: "The LORD hath made all things for himself; yea, even **the wicked** for the **day of evil**" [*ra*].

Isaiah 31:1b-2 KJV: ". . . but they look not unto the Holy One of Israel, neither seek the LORD! Yet he also is wise, and will **bring evil** [*ra*], and will not call back his words: but will **arise against** the house of the evildoers, and against the help of them that work iniquity."

Jeremiah 32:42 KJV: "For thus saith the LORD; like as I have brought all this **great evil** [*ra*] upon this people, so will I bring upon them all the good I have promised them."

Lamentations 3:38 KJV: "Out of the mouth of the most High proceedeth **not evil** [*ra*] **and good**?"

Ezekiel 5:13: "Then my anger will cease and my wrath against them will subside, and I will be avenged. And when I have **spent my wrath upon them**, they will know that I the LORD have spoken in my zeal" (also see 16:42; 24:13).

Ezekiel 5:15b-17 KJV: ". . . I the LORD have spoken it. **When I shall send upon them the evil [*ra*] arrows of famine,** which shall be for their **destruction**, and which I will send to **destroy you;** and I will **increase the famine** upon you, and will **break your staff of bread.** So will I send upon you **famine and evil [*ra*] beasts,** and they shall bereave thee; and **pestilence and blood** shall pass through thee; and **I will bring the sword upon thee.** I the LORD have spoken *it.*"

Amos 3:6 KJV: "Shall a trumpet be blown in the city, and the people not be afraid? Shall there be **evil [*ra*]** in a city, and the LORD hath not done it?"

Amos 4:10: "I sent **plagues** among you as I did to Egypt. **I killed your young men with the sword,** along with your captured horses. I filled your nostrils with the **stench** of your camps, yet you have not returned to me,' declares the LORD."

Micah 1:12 KJV: "For the inhabitant of Maroth waited carefully for good: but **evil [*ra*] came down from the LORD** unto the gate of Jerusalem."

Micah 2:3 KJV: "Therefore thus saith the LORD; Behold, against this family do **I devise an evil [*ra*]**, from which ye shall not remove your necks; neither shall ye go haughtily; for **this time is evil.**"

Zechariah 8:14: "'Just as I had determined to **bring disaster upon you** and showed no pity when your fathers angered me,' says the LORD Almighty."

Zechariah 9:4: "But the LORD will **take away** her possessions and **destroy** her power on the sea, and she will be **consumed by fire.**"

Zechariah 10:3a: "My anger burns against the shepherds, and **I will punish** the leaders."

Zechariah 14:18-19: "If the Egyptian people do not go and take part, they will have **no rain.** The LORD will bring on them the **plague he inflicts** on the nations that do not go up to celebrate the Feast of Tabernacles. This will be the **punishment of Egypt and the punishment of all the nations** that do not go up to celebrate the Feast of Tabernacles."

Also, quite notably, after Job suffered the loss of his oxen, donkeys, and the killing of his servants, sheep, and ten children at Satan's instigation, he would not give Satan the blame, causality, or responsibility. Rather he proclaimed, "The LORD gave and the LORD has taken away; may the name of the LORD be praised" (Job 1:21b). The next verse reveals that Job was not mistaken about Who was responsible. And yet, "In all this, Job did not sin by charging God with wrongdoing" (Job 1:22; also see Job 2:7). But God just didn't "allow" these horrendous evils to happen to Job and his family. He approved them and assigned and released Satan to cause them. Thus, God both allowed and enable it to happen, didn't He?

Let's also note that none of these evil "*ra*-type" acts, and many more in other scriptures, were contrary to the will of God. Rather, they were in accordance with his will and summed up by Piper as being "in sweeping inclusiveness about God's control covering them all" from this one passage in Isaiah: "I form the light, and create darkness; I make peace, and create evil: I the Lord do all these things" (Isa. 45:7 KJV). Piper further elaborates, it's "not that Satan is not involved; he is probably always involved one way or the other with destructive purpose (Acts 10:38). But his power is not decisive. He cannot act without God's permission. . . . This is a right view of God's sovereignty over Satan. . . . Therefore, I conclude with Jonathan Edwards, 'God decrees all things, even all sins.' Or, as Paul says in Ephesians 1:11, 'He works all things after the counsel of His will.'"[62]

Likewise, as Boyd specifically points out, "God ordains evil actions for greater good." For instance, "God intentionally orchestrated evil intentions of the brothers in order to get Joseph into Egypt."[63]

To top it all off, we are told by God Himself that "I the LORD do not change" (Mal. 3:6a). Or does He in the New Testament economy?

I Will CAUSE . . .

Lest there be any doubt Who caused this evil, here is an additional list of causational verses (caps and bolds mine):

"For yet seven days, and **I will CAUSE** it to rain upon the earth forty days and forty nights; and every living substance that I have made will I destroy from off the face of the earth" (Gen. 7:4 KJV).

". . . **I will CAUSE** thee to serve thine enemies . . ." (Jer. 17:4 KJV).

---

[62] Piper, "Is God Less Glorious Because He Ordained that Evil Be?"
[63] Boyd, *Satan and the Problem of Evil*, 396.

"Thus saith the LORD of hosts, the God of Israel, unto all that are carried away captives, whom **I have CAUSED** to be carried away from Jerusalem unto Babylon" (Jer. 29:4 KJV).

". . . **I have CAUSED** you to be carried away captives" (Jer. 29:7 KJV).

". . . **I have CAUSED** you to be carried away captives" (Jer. 29:14 KJV).

". . . **thou hast CAUSED** all this evil to come upon them" (Jer. 32:23 KJV).

"Out of the **mouth of the most High** proceedeth not **evil and good**?" (Lam. 3:38 KJV).

". . . **I will CAUSE** my fury to rest upon them . . ." (Ezek. 5:13 KJV).

"**I will CAUSE** them to perish out of the countries; I will destroy them" (Ezek. 25:7 KJV).

"For **I have CAUSED** my terror in the land of the living . . ." (Ezek. 32:32 KJV).

"**I will CAUSE** men to walk upon you, even my people Israel." (Ezek. 36:12).

"**I will CAUSE** to cease the kingdom of the house of Israel." (Hos. 1:4 KJV).

". . . **I CAUSED** it to rain upon one city, and **CAUSED** it not to rain upon another city." (Amos 4:7 KJV).

". . . for whose **CAUSE** this **evil** is upon us . . ." (Jonah 1:8 KJV).[64]

So once again we see that God does "cause" evil to come upon humankind, even his own people. Hence, we must now ask, is it possible that God is still creating evil and sending it upon us today, even upon his own people here in America, in Israel, in all countries, on and under the oceans, and in the sky?

Critical Objection: It's different now. We are under the New Covenant and under God's grace. No longer is God a vengeful and angry God. He's merciful and non-violent. This accusation of Him still being a murderer and killing people because He does not change is at odds with how God is expressed in Jesus.

---

[64] This list of scriptures is taken from my friend John Bray's newsletter, "Biblical Perspectives," January 15, 2010, 1.

My Response: The holy people chosen by the Lord for Himself in Old Testament times (Deut. 7:6) were under God's grace as well when they were obedient to his law.[65] But in the New Testament we find another "chosen people" (1 Pet. 2:9-10) and yet the same dynamic still being set forth of God creating and sending *ra* (evil, disaster, calamities), with one major difference. During his earthly ministry, Jesus announced that God "the Father judges no one, but has entrusted all judgment to the Son" (John 5:22).

... is it possible that God is still creating evil and sending it upon us today, even upon his own people here in America, in Israel, in all countries, on and under the oceans, and in the sky?

Therefore, in his longest and most dramatic prophecy concerning the soon-coming destruction and total desolation of Jerusalem and the Temple, Jesus prophesied that "upon you will come all the righteous blood that has been shed on the earth . . . ." (Matt. 23:35a) and "at that time the sign of the Son of Man will appear in the sky, and all the nations of the earth will mourn. They will see the Son of Man coming on the clouds of the sky, with power and great glory" (Matt. 24:30). He also foretold when this judgment would befall them. "I tell you the truth, this generation will certainly not pass away until all these things have happened" (Matt. 24:34; also see 1 Pet. 4:7, 17; 1 John 2:18). The fact is, Jesus used an evil nation—the Roman Empire, like the God the Father had used Babylon and other evil nations in the Old Testament—as his instrument of judgment and punishment against his own people Israel.[66]

Forty-some years later it was over. Josephus records that 1.1 million Jews were killed in the fall and destruction of Jerusalem and the Temple circa A.D. 70. Many others were killed or taken into captivity during the entire Roman-Jewish War of A.D. 66-70 and through the fall of Masada in A.D. 73. These tragic yet redemptive events were also the fulfillment

---

[65] Check out the some thirty-eight applications of the word "grace" in the Old Testament in a concordance.

[66] For more, see Noē, *The Perfect Ending for the World*, 91-93, 171-202. Noē, *Unraveling the End*, 312-315.

of several Old Testament prophecies (Deut. 32; Isa. 5:1-7; Dan. 12; Hab. 2:3; Hag. 2:6; Zech. 13 and 14). And there is more.

Other New Testament verses and passages talk about similar *'ra'*-type stuff being sent by God.

From the New Testament

Evidence of God's ability and willingness to continue using evil for his purposes (bold emphasis mine):

- First and foremost, was the **crucifixion** of Jesus (Acts 3:18; Matt. 26:39, 53-54; Luke 22:22; John 18:11; 19:10-11). Knoch terms "this sin, in God's hands . . . the corrective of all sin. . . . actually and absolutely they were carrying out the purpose of God?"[67]
- Others being **condemned and cast into** *Gehenna* (Matt. 5:21-22, 29-30; 10:28; 18:8-9; Mark 9:42-49; Luke 12:4-5; 23:33)[68]
- "**Weeping and gnashing** of teeth" (Matt. 8:12; 13:42, 50; 22:13; 24:51; Luke 13:28).[69]
- "The servant who knows his master's will and does not get ready or does not do what his master wants will be **beaten with many blows**. But the one who does not know and does things deserving punishment will be **beaten with few blows**. From everyone who has been given much, much will be demanded; and from the one who has been entrusted with much, much more will be asked" (Luke 12:47-48).
- "Simon, Simon, **Satan has asked to sift you as wheat**. But I have prayed for you, Simon, that your faith may not fail" (Luke 22:31-32a). Yes, Jesus granted Satan access to Peter in order to test him.
- God's Spirit **killing** Ananias and Sapphria **for lying** to the Holy Spirit (Acts 5:1-11).
- Jesus **blinding** Saul on the road to Damascus (Acts 9:1-12).

---

[67] Knoch, *The Problem of Evil*, 51-52.
[68] For more on what this entails, see Noē, *Hell Yes / Hell No*, 55-74.
[69] Ibid., 87-88.

- "The **wrath** of God is being revealed from heaven against all the godlessness and wickedness of men who suppress the truth by their wickedness. . . . Therefore, God **gave them over** in the sinful desires of their hearts . . . ." (Romans 1:18, 24a). God giving wicked human beings over means He takes away his protection and abandons them to the depraved and evil consequences of their "shameful lusts" (Rom. 1:26-32).

- Paul's command to "**hand this man over to Satan**, so that the sinful nature may be destroyed and his spirit saved on the day of the Lord" (1 Cor. 5:5).

- Many believers in the Church coming under the judgment of the Lord and being made **weak, sick, and fallen asleep** (a euphemism for death) for partaking of the Lord's Supper in an unworthy manner (1 Cor. 11:27-32). Hence, many church people die before they reach old age.

- See the mentions of Paul's many **great sufferings** which he had to endure during this faithful ministry up to that time (Rom. 8:35; 1 Cor. 4:9-13; 2 Cor. 4:8-9; 6:4-5; 11:23-30; 12:10).

- The revelation that God wants to make known and show his wrath, therefore, has made some people as vessels/objects of **"dishonor" and "of wrath"** for that purpose (see Rom. 9:16-24 KJV).

- All of Jesus' original twelve Disciples, and also Paul, **were killed** except for two—John who was **imprisoned** in exile on the isle of Patmos and Judas who killed himself.

- The Apostle Paul was given "**a thorn in the side**, a messenger of Satan, to **torment** me" and to keep him "from becoming conceited." Three times Paul pleaded with God to remove it. But God refused in order that his power would be made perfect in Paul's weakness (2 Cor. 12:7-10).

- ". . . for because of such things God's **wrath comes on** those who are **disobedient**" (Eph. 5:6b).

- "For this reason God sends them **a powerful delusion** so that they will believe the lie and so that all will be **condemned** who have not believed the truth but have delighted in wickedness" (2 Thess. 2:10-11).

- **Seven seals of judgment** being unsealed and released upon the earth (Rev. 6:1-2ff).
- **Seven trumpets of judgment** being sounded (Rev. 8:6ff).
- **Seven bowls of God's wrath** (plagues) being pour out on the earth (Rev. 15:1ff; 16:1).
- **Punishment** of the great prostitute, who sits on many waters on the earth (Rev. 17-18).[70]
- People being thrown into the **lake of fire** (Rev. 20:14-15; also 20:10).[71]
- Satan being "released out of his prison **to deceive** the nations . . . to gather them **for battle**" with all the war and slaughter that that did and/or will entail (Rev. 20:7). Seems Satan is still as much under God's control and a necessary part of his plans as is the angel Gabriel.
- The final warning of Scripture. "**I warn everyone** who hears the words of the prophecy of this book: If anyone adds anything to them, **God will add to him the plagues** described in this book. And if anyone takes away from this book of prophecy, **God will take away** from him his share in the tree of life and in the holy city, which are described in this book" (Rev. 22:18-19).

Critical Objection: I cannot believe that our God kills people today! "In no way is God responsible for evil; He is only responsible for using evil to bring forth good."[72]

My Response: Yes, many Christians may find this above list of New Testament verses troubling and refuse to believe it. But what, pray tell, was and is the purpose of Paul's lengthy and emphatic warning and admonitions in 1 Corinthians 10:1-13? This passage refers to the judgments that fell upon Old Testament Israel during their Exodus wandering in the wilderness. As Paul wrote, this was where "God was not pleased with most of them; their **bodies [dead]** were scattered over the desert. **Now all these things occurred as examples**, to keep us from setting our hearts on **evil things** as they did. . . . We should not test the

---

[70] For the identification of this great prostitute today and more, see Noë, *The Greater Jesus*, 251-289.

[71] For the proper identification of this reality, see Noë, *Hell Yes / Hell No*, 90-92.

[72] D'Souza, *What's So Great About Christianity*, 278.

Lord, as some of them did – and were **killed** by snakes. And do not grumble, as some of them did – and were **killed** by the destroying angel. These things happened to them **as examples** and were written down **as warnings for us**, on whom the fulfillment of the ages has come" (1 Cor. 10:5-11; also see Num. 21:6 – bold emphasis mine). These judgments befell them by the hand of God.

So does God through Christ still create and send this kind of bad 'ra'-type stuff today? Apparently so, Romans 5:9 notwithstanding. Of course, many Christians don't like to think of Him in these terms. But if Christ does not, then why would Paul, by inspiration, make this above comparative warning and give these admonitions to New Testament saints? Likewise, why would the writer of Hebrews warn New Testament believers: "See to it that you do not refuse him who speaks. If they [Old Testament Jews] did not escape when they refused him who warned them on earth, how much less will we, if we turn away from him who warns us from heaven?" (Heb. 12:25).

Perhaps, we should carefully consider Pink's explanation that these examples of God's sovereignty are "designed as a motive for godly fear." He further elaborates that they are "made known to us for the promotion of righteous living . . . revealed in order to bring into subjection our rebellious hearts . . . . humbles as nothing else does or can humble, and brings the heart into lowly submission before God, causing us to relinquish our own self-will and making us delight in the perception and performance of this Divine will."[73]

Most appropriately, Pink then asks, if this doctrine of God's sovereignty can be "'horrible' and 'dangerous' which affords the saints a sense of security in danger, that supplies them comfort in sorrow, that begets patience within them in adversity, that evokes from them praise at all times?" He answers, "No; a thousand times, no. Instead . . . this doctrine of the Sovereignty of God is glorious and edifying, and a due appreciation of it will but serve to make us exclaim with Moses, 'Who is like unto thee, O Lord, among the gods? who is like Thee, glorious in holiness, fearful in praises, doing wonders?' (Exod. 15:11)."[74]

As we've seen above, this ra–sending reality of God is repeatedly presented and taught throughout both the Old and New Testaments.

---

[73] Pink, *The Sovereignty of God*, 143.
[74] Pink, *The Sovereignty of God*, 181-182.

However, this realization does not make God the so-called "Author of evil" or "Author of sin." Bringing that charge against God is not our privilege or prerogative, anymore than it was Job's, Jesus' or Paul's. The sovereign fact is, God has both the right and the power to do as He pleases, regardless of what we think or believe—with this one caveat— as long as it doesn't contradict his Word. Would you now agree?

... this *ra*–sending reality of God is repeatedly presented and taught throughout both the Old and New Testaments.

Would you also agree that all the verses we've cited above and more make it abundantly clear that at least some evil, pain, and suffering are sometimes sent directly from the hand of God? Who are we to say otherwise? And sometimes He acts and intervenes in the midst of evil. Either way, He is sovereign over all causes and realities. All things are under his oversight and control. Not recognizing this high level of sovereignty means that one will never truly know God. To his credit, Dr. Graham has seriously and accurately recognized this consequence and reality as he writes: "if we have a false view of God, we may end up believing a lie about him—and that would be tragic. Is God basically kind and loving, or is he basically strict and judgmental? Both!"[75]

Of course, Satan, the fallen angels, human beings, natural disasters, and even animals are secondary causes of evil. But God in his sovereignty and providence remains the First Cause of everything that happens. Would you now agree?

My Working Definitions of Evil and Sin

As promised in our last chapter, below are my working definitions for evil and sin. I welcome your input.

---

[75] Billy Graham, "My Answer," *The Indianapolis Star* (Indianapolis, IN), 4 September 2014, E-4.

My definition of evil is based on the meaning of the Hebrew noun *ra* and verb *raa* covered above.

Evil = is an ethical and moral reality produced by a spoilage or loss of a substance deemed good by the victim/recipient and/or by God. For instance, most would characterize the loss of a job, health, relationships, marriage, money, possessions, position, opportunity, and life itself as being evil. Yet sometimes these situations turn out for the good. Of course, the "last enemy . . . is death," according to the Bible (1 Cor. 15:26). And Who sent death into our world? Wasn't it God (see Gen. 2:17)?[76]

AmericanVision broadly defines evil "not merely as a bunch of bad action 'out there' but rather as 'anything and everything which is opposite of God'"[77]

Barclay says that "Evil (*adikia*). *Adikia* is the precise opposite of *diaiosunē*, which means *justice;* and the Greeks defined *justice* as *giving to God and to men their due.* The *evil* man is the man who robs both man and God of their rights. He has so erected an altar to himself in the centre of things that he worships himself to the exclusion of God and man."[78]

Knoch astutely suggests that "we must have our eyes opened to the difference between evil and sin. Evil need not be wrong, while sin always is a mistake."[79]

Therefore, my definition of sin is:

Sin = is an angelic or human condition, thought, or act of disobedience to God's will or violation of his law. It can be either an omission or a commission. Based on Romans 3:23, it could also be defined as simply falling short of the glory of God, of his standards, his law, or his righteousness. Some term sin as merely missing the mark.

Paul Tillich defined sin as "an estrangement or separation from God, from self, and from neighbor."[80]

---

[76] It is debated by some whether animal and vegetation death was present in the pre-Fall garden.

[77] AmericanVision, "Epicurus and the problem of evil, www.americanvision.org/7989/epicurus-problem-of-evil/, 5/23/13.

[78] Barclay, *The Letter to the Romans*, 34.

[79] Knoch, *The Problem of Evil*, 193.

[80] Paul Tillich, *The Courage to Be* (New Haven, CN: Yale University Press, 1952, 2000), *xxi*.

Clark directly quotes Scripture for his definition, "'sin is lawlessness.' Sin is any want of conformity unto or transgression of the law of God"[81] (1 John 3:4).

"The essence of sin" for Barclay " to put self in the place of God. . . . the root of all sin is disobedience."[82]

But God in his sovereignty and providence remains the First Cause of everything that happens. Would you now agree?

The Bible teaches that after Adam and Eve's fall, all human beings are born with a sinful nature. That means that as fallen creatures, we have sinful desires that produce sinful thoughts that flow into sinful acts. In other words, we sin because we are sinners. So sin is a condition that produces thoughts, and acts of evil. Of course, Adam and Eve were not born with a sinful nature. But they were created by God with the susceptibility to be tempted and to fall into sin, as were the fallen angels.

Thus, sin entered the world as a result of creature rebellion—Satan's and man's (Rom. 5:12). That's why sin is man's fault, not God's. Thus, Bernard W. Anderson concludes that like Adam and Eve in the original garden, "sin . . . is an act of the will in revolt against God. It is occasioned by Man's ambition to overstep his status as a creature, to become 'like God' or perhaps 'like the gods' . . . . the determination to do as one pleases, as though God's commands were not to be taken seriously."[83]

Supportive Scholarly Insights

Please be assured, once again, that on this side of heaven we shall never be able to account for all the evil, pain, suffering, and sin in our world with a single model—including the one I'm presenting.

---

[81] Clark, *God and Evil*, 53.

[82] Barclay, *The Letter to the Romans,* 28, 53.

[83] Bernhard W. Anderson, *Understanding the Old Testament* (Englewood Cliffs, NJ: Prentice-Hall, Inc., Third Ed., 1975, 1966, 1957), 212.

Nonetheless, I'd like to suggest that we adopt a fresh worldview. Let's begin by accepting the world as God chose to create it and have us face. No, we shall never be able to answer all the questions and remove all the doubts. That would be to remove all need for faith. Instead, let's take on the attitude of Job, "Though he slay me, yet will I trust him" (Job 13:15). Job remained faithful in the face of adversity, as did Jesus, Paul, and so many others in the Bible and in Church history. We'll have much more to say on this aspect of evil in our last two chapters.

Let's also stop hoping for and teaching a future, evil-less earthly existence coming at some unscriptural "end of time," or at any time. That's "fantasy Christianity." The testimony of Scripture is: God, knowingly and intentionally, created a world in which evil exists, and that world is without end (Eph. 3:21 KJV; also see Eccl. 1:4; Psa. 78:69; 89:36-37; 93:1; 96:10; 104:5; 119:90; 148:4, 6).[84] And He is responsible for and is sovereign over all of it.

Critical Objection: "John, I have read your views on the creation of evil in your book *Off Target.* I respectfully counter that God is not the Creator of evil. . . . to suggest God created evil is morally indefensible and unlikely from a biblical exegetical viewpoint."[85]

My Response: As we've seen, this objection is exactly what most Christians have been told, taught, and believe—that God did not and does not create evil or have any responsibility in its perpetuation, expect for allowing, permitting, and somehow using it. Another problem is, some people think they know everything God does and does not do. But obviously God is infinite and cannot be pigeonholed by a finite being. After interacting with many of these types of people over the years, and while working on and developing this book, I'm convinced that the bottom line for accepting or rejecting God as the First-Cause Creator of evil is not based on what Scripture clearly states, but rests more on one's position on this core issue—the sovereignty of God versus the "sovereignty" of human free will. And while there are many who will disagree with what has been presented so far in this book, several scholars have offered supportive insights that confirm different aspects.

---

[84] See Noë, *The Perfect Ending for the World,* 21-106ff. Noë, *Unraveling the End,* 146-155ff.

[85] Mike Edwards posting two comments on my blog titled, "The Creation of Evil" on PRI's website, 8/26/14 and 5/12/14.

Arthur W. Pink offers this sage advice: "It is not for us to pick and choose from the truths revealed in God's Word."[86]

Greg Foster's opinion is: "We have a tendency to idolize individual choice. . . . We want to think we have a sovereign 'self.'. . . We want to be as free as possible. . . . [it's] a seductive idea."[87] Hence, we tend to believe what we want to believe. This tendency is especially true in these two significant areas of human thought and belief . . .

Basil Mitchell elaborates: "In politics, as in religion, men become committed to positions which they will not readily give up and which involve their entire personalities. On neither of these subjects are differences easily resolved by argument."[88] This tendency is especially true for those professionally tied to their view.

R.C. Sproul emphasizes: "Not even an event such as 9/11 can happen apart from His providence." He notes, however, that "there is much confusion about this. . . . we reject the idea that God could have been involved in any way in the tragedy itself. We allow for God's providence as long as it is a blessing, but we have no room for God's providence if that providence represents some kind of judgment. . . . Within His providence come both blessings and calamity. . . . If God did not ordain all things, He would not be sovereign over all things." But he concedes that "theologians argue endlessly over *how* God ordains all things" and "I do not know why God ordained 9/11." Finally, he characterizes this aspect of God as, "one of the most difficult concepts even for devout Christians to deal with. Yet the concept is found on almost every page of sacred Scripture. It is at the very heart of the Christian faith. . . . It is that concept that is on a collision course with every philosopher in human history that would deny the sovereignty of God over human life. Does that mean God is sovereign over tragedy? Yes."[89]

Sproul further adds that "in present-day America, our view of God's character is an idol. It is an idol of a God who has been stripped of His true attributes. He's a God who is defined in terms of love and mercy and

---

[86] Pink, *The Sovereignty of God*, 83.

[87] Greg Forster, *Joy for the World* (Wheaton, IL: Crossway, 2014), 72-74.

[88] Basil Mitchell, *The Justification of Religious Belief* (New York, NY: A Crossroad Book, 1973), 1.

[89] Sproul, *When Worlds Collide*, 23, 29, 30, 32, 33, 36.

grace, but we have thrown out any idea of His being just and holy and wrathful. If we are going to be faithful to the biblical understanding of God, we have to understand that He is, among other things, a God of wrath. . . . the idea of mercy is an empty concept if He has no capacity for wrath."[90]

Timothy Keller points out: "God who controls the affairs of the world . . . that is far more comforting than the belief that our lives are in the hands of fickle fate or random chance."[91]

Gordon H. Clark insists: "Let it be unequivocally said that this view certainly makes God the cause of sin. God is the sole ultimate cause of everything. There is absolutely nothing independent of him. He alone is the eternal being. He alone is omnipotent. He alone is sovereign. Not only is Satan his creature, but every detail of history was eternally in his plan before the world began; and he willed that it should all come to pass. . . . God determined that Christ should die; he determined as well that Judas should betray him. There was never the remotest possibility that something different could have happened."[92]

R.C. Sproul, Jr. rightly differentiates: "God is the Creator; we are not. . . . He does not merely see ahead of time that it will happen. He makes sure it happens. He planned for it to happen, and he set things up to ensure that it would happen. . . . But even if God works through secondary causes—hires someone else to do his work for him—he cannot cease to be the primary cause. In a human trial, we recognize that hiring a hit man does not shift the blame from the hirer to the hiree. . . . The same could apply to Adam and Eve and the fall. . . . All these events in Eden were so that the Son might glorify the Father and the Spirit, that the Spirit might glorify the Son and the Father, that the Father might glorify the Spirit and the Son. It all hinges on the fall, on the changing of Eve's (and Adam's) inclination from good to bad, an event which was, on the one hand, a terrible tragedy, but on the other, the means by which God might be glorified. . . . All the rest of history . . . is the unfolding of this plan, of his plan. . . . God is so almighty that . . . . All of creation is under his absolute control."[93]

---

[90] Ibid., 68.
[91] Keller, *Walking with God through Pain and Suffering*, 58.
[92] Clark, *God and Evil*, 51.
[93] Sproul, Jr., *Almighty Over All*, 112, 56-57, 59, 135.

John Hick summarizes quite well: "We have . . . found it to be an inescapable conclusion that the *ultimate* responsibility for the existence of sinful creatures and of the evils which they both cause and suffer, rests upon God Himself. . . . there is no one else to share that final responsibility. The entire situation within which sin and suffering occur exists because God willed and continues to will its existence; and we must believe that from the first He has known the course that His creation would take. To say this is not to deny man's blameworthiness for his own sins . . . . We are undoubtedly here at one of the major watersheds of theodicy. On the one hand, we must treat sin as *wrong* and evil as *bad*. . . . But on the other hand, we must not so magnify this contrary power as to create a final dualism. *Ultimately* God alone is sovereign, and evil can exist only by His permission. . . . And this brings us back . . . to some kind of instrumental view of evil. . . . This then is the starting-point from which we propose to try to relate the realities of sin and suffering to the perfect love of an omnipotent Creator. . . . God is Himself ultimately responsible for the existence of evil and yet that evil is truly evil and truly subject to His condemnation and rejection."[94]

Randy Alcorn fairly concludes: "The problem of evil is man's problem with God, not God's problem. . . . We want to reconcile what seems irreconcilable—human choice and divine sovereignty. We want to remove God from any hint of blame for injustice or suffering. But biblically, it just doesn't work. We shouldn't take on the mantle of God's public relations team. We do not need to put a spin on Scripture, air-brushing the Almighty so he can win the popular vote. He doesn't ask us to get him off the hook of public opinion, but to believe what he has told us about both our meaningful choice and his complete sovereignty."[95]

"Remarkably, God takes full credit for giving these disabilities [see Exod. 4:11]. God does not say the Fall makes people deaf or Satan makes them blind, but that *he* does. God doesn't attempt to give a full list. But doesn't he intend us to understand that he also gives people Down syndrome, deformities, cancer, and insulin-dependent diabetes? The fact that we don't like the idea that deformities, diseases, and

---

[94] Hick, *Evil and the Love of God*, 228, 233, 261, 353 .
[95] Alcorn, *If God Is Good*, 106, 267.

suffering come from God's own hand does not alter Scripture. Our discomfort will not change God's mind."[96]

William Barclay contends: "Bluntly, it is that God can do what he likes and that man has no right whatever to question his decisions, however inscrutable they may be. The clay cannot talk back to the potter .... That, said Paul, is what God has a right to do with men."[97]

"Everything is of God; behind everything is his action; even the things which seem arbitrary and haphazard go back to him. Nothing in this world moves with aimless feet."[98]

"It is one thing to say that God *used* an evil situation to bring good out of it; it is quite another thing to say that he *created* it to produce good in the end. Paul is saying that God deliberately darkened the minds and blinded the eyes and hardened the hearts of the mass of the Jewish people in order that the way might open for the Gentiles to come in. . . . In the end the only answer Paul can find is that God did it."[99]

Westminster Confession of Faith states: "Although, in relation to the foreknowledge and decree of God, the first Cause, all things come to pass immutably, and infallibly; yet, by the same providence, he ordereth them to fall out, according to the nature of second causes, either necessarily, freely, or contingently."[100]

A.E. Knoch offers up an astute transition into our last two chapters: "The evil in the world is in accord with the Scriptures, and an essential ingredient in God's plan, and also the only way to the highest blessings for ourselves and for the human race . . . . May we prayerfully grasp the necessity of evil as a background for the display of God's grandest glories and our perpetual praise of Him. Only then will we be prepared to endure with thankful hearts all the trials and tragedies in the present which He sends to us. . . . Let us not fall back upon traditional scholarship. It . . . dares not acknowledge its own deficiencies."[101]

---

[96] Ibid., 231.
[97] Barclay, *The Letter to the Romans*, 120.
[98] Ibid., 129.
[99] Ibid., 132-133.
[100] Westminster Confession of Faith, chapter 5, section 2.
[101] Knoch, *The Problem of Evil*, 5, 137 .

Another astute but non-scholarly option wraps us up, most succinctly: "He made it all . . . The Good . . . The Bad . . . The Ugly . . . But hey . . . what can ya do . . . he's the only God we got!"[102]

In Sum

The proper identification of the First-Cause origin of evil solves and resolves the so-called problem of evil. The fact is that God chose to create both good and evil as part of his original creation. He intended both, He foreordained both, He created both, and He called it all "very good." Moreover, He sustains it all for his own purposes. Yet in no way does this biblical truth and documented reality compromise or limit his goodness or power, since He is separate from his creation. We simply cannot apply our standards to God.

Thus, the "awkward trilemma" and "inconsistent triad" — composed of God's goodness, omnipotence, and the existence of evil—is over. That means God is not obliged to eliminate evil or remove it in some past (A.D. 70) or future consummatory terminus at the "restoration of all things" (Acts 3:21 NAS), or in a so-called "paradise-restored" earth. As unsettling as this realization may be, the promise of a heavenly evil-less existence, and not an earthly evil-less one, must suffice.

With this realization that God is primarily and ultimately responsible for evil, sin, and suffering in our world, the long trail of failures to find an adequate theodicy is possibly now resolvable. Our challenge next becomes to make better sense of our God-created world.

Unfortunately, we are up against scriptural revelations that have been taken captive by philosophical presuppositions and avoidance tactics. Therefore, I agree with Robert Jeffress who suggests "another alternative" to the various compromising theodicies of the past. Here's how he lays it out in a nutshell:

---

[102] Response to my Facebook post "The Creation of Evil," from Rich Cassidy, 8/30/14.

- "God exists.
- He is loving and all-powerful.
- *and* He assumes full responsibility for everything that happens in His creation."

Jeffress appropriately recognizes that "such an idea is not only grounded in Scripture, but it is also the only answer that provides genuine and lasting comfort to those who find themselves caught in the maelstrom of inexplicable heartache and unanswered questions." He bemoans that "unfortunately, many people believe in a God of their imaginations rather than the God revealed in Scripture." He then compares this inconsistency with "the idolatry that was so roundly condemned in the Old Testament," which "was reducing God and His majesty to a deity of our own making." He concludes by asking this basic question: "What does the Bible reveal about the true God and His relationship to suffering and evil?" He answers, "God is ultimately responsible for all suffering. . . . He must also assume responsibility for the evil that is in the world. Amazingly, He does just that."

Finally, however, he warns that "some theologians, in their attempts to let God off the hook for tragedies in the world, make the distinction between God's *causing* and God's *allowing* suffering." He retorts by asking another poignant and indicting question. "But if God is not the direct cause of suffering and yet He has the power to prevent it, isn't He at the very least guilty of negligence?" He answers his own question by exclaiming that "to allow suffering when you are capable of preventing suffering is to be responsible for suffering." Then after listing several verses talking about God's love, he ends with this most pertinent question: "How do we reconcile God's love with the horrendous evil we see in the world?"[103]

Critical Objection: "All evil proceeds from wills other than God. . . . from agents having say-so in how things transpire over and against God. . . . Though God of course anticipated this possibility, the age-long battle between God and Satan with all the suffering it has caused is not something the beneficent Creator would ever will. . . . He [Christ] never

---

[103] Robert Jeffress, *Hell Yes! . . . and other outrageous truths you can still believe* (Colorado Springs, CO: WaterBrook Press, 2004), 56-57, 59-61.

encouraged accepting evil as coming from God. "[104] "The creator has not given up on creation and is working to salvage and restore the world (human and nonhuman) to the fullness of shalom and flourishing intended from the beginning. . . . the grip of terrible evil . . . has blocked God's purposes from coming to fruition . . . God has been at work throughout history—through a series of redemptive agents and ultimately through Jesus—to overcome all that impedes his purposes from being fulfilled. . . . eschatological redemption consists in nothing other than the renewal of human cultural life on earth. . . . Heaven was never part of God purposes for humanity . . . and has no intrinsic role as the final destiny of human salvation. . . . the term 'heaven' simply does not describe the Christian eschatological hope. . . . Ultimately, this leads to the New Testament's vision of a new heaven and new earth as the eternal home of the redeemed (2 Pet. 3:13; Rev. 21:1)."[105]

My Response: These traditional beliefs remain entrenched and a serious objection to my central argument. But let's now call out these defensive and deflecting objections for what they really are. Pink discerns this well as he summarizes that "almost all doctrinal error is really, Truth perverted."[106] God's creation of evil and ongoing creating of evil is part of why we need to fear Him, obey Him, and serve Him. And how we perceive and understand the ordained origin of evil will shape how humbly and effectively we see life's '*ra*'-type events and respond to them.

Critical Objection: "I cannot believe God created evil then sentenced man to thousands of years of sickness, disease, death, and punishment because of it. . . . I couldn't live that way."[107]

My Response: What a great objection to segue into our next chapter. So why didn't God create a perfect, evil-less world in the first place, instead of this "very good" evil one? Since most of the world does not believe or even know that the origin of evil was God, they also have largely failed to understand his purposes for creating evil in the first place and allowing, permitting, using, and even creating evil ever since. Not surprisingly, the question once again, becomes, "Why?"

---

[104] Boyd, *Satan and the Problem of Evil*, 216, 290, 320, 406.
[105] Middleton, *A New Heaven and a New Earth*, 27, 71-73, 87.
[106] Pink, *The Sovereignty of God*, 183.
[107] Facebook post, 8/19/14.

In our next chapter we are going to make the case that God planned and created this world exactly as it is, with evil, sin, and suffering in it, not for our convenience and pleasure but for our advantage and benefit.

The proper identification
of the First-Cause origin of evil solves and resolves
the so-called problem of evil.

<u>Part III – The Outworking</u>

Chapter 4

The Dualistic Dynamic of Evil

I f God's works "are perfect and all his ways are just. A faithful God who does no wrong, upright and just is he" (Deut. 32:4) . . .
If "as for God, his way is perfect; the word of the LORD is flawless" (Psa. 18:30a) . . .

If "the LORD is righteous in all his ways" (Psa. 145:17) . . . and "who works out everything in conformity with the purpose of his will" (Eph. 1:11b) . . .

And if God is all-powerful, all-good, and all-knowing, as most Christians believe, then why didn't He create a world without any evil, pain, suffering, risk, or danger? He could have, couldn't He? But He didn't create that type of world.

From a human standpoint, this perceived conundrum forces us to more thoughtfully and seriously consider the possibility that there may be divine reasons and valid purposes for the existence of evil. Perhaps God created—*both* pre-fall and post-fall—the best of all possible worlds and placed us in this environment not for our comfort and convenience, but for our advantage and benefit.

Does this possibility seem bizarre? If so, perhaps our perplexity is because, as William Lane Craig and Michael Tooley intimate: "we tend to think that if God exists, then his goal for human life is happiness in this life" and that "God's role is to provide a comfortable environment for his human pets." But what if "man's end is not happiness as such but rather a personal relationship with God, which in the end will bring true and everlasting human fulfillment. . . . It's not at all improbable that only in a world suffused with natural and moral evil would the optimal number of people freely come to know God personally and so find eternal life."[1]

Certainly, the presence of evil is a part of the "mystery of iniquity" (2 Thess. 2:7 KJV) and "the secret things" that "belong to the LORD our God" (Deut. 29:29a). But "to deny the sovereignty of God" in this matter, as Pink warns, "is to enter upon a path which, if followed to its logical terminus, is to arrive at blank atheism."[2]

Therefore, we must trust that God in his sovereignty knew and knows that evil in this world really is "good" and "very good" (Gen. 1:12, 1:31). And that this dualistic dynamic of evil and good is necessary. I use the word dualistic to mean the philosophical and theological doctrine "that all phenomena of the universe can be explained by two separate and distinct substances or principles . . . in conflict, one good and one evil."[3] I do *not* use the theological term of dualism, which means "the existence of two equally ultimate powers, one good and the other evil," nor to imply that "sin surprised God or challenged or overcame his omnipotence or providential control over the universe."[4] Again, please remember that we are undertaking this re-exploratory effort in this book in order to better prepare and equip ourselves for how to respond when evil adversities cross our path in life.

Perhaps God created—both pre-fall and post-fall— the best of all possible worlds and placed us in this environment not for our comfort and convenience, but for our advantage and benefit.

---

[1] William Lane Craig and Michael Tooley, "The Craig-Tooley Debate" in Meister and Dew, Jr., eds., *God and Evil*, 308.

[2] Pink, *The Sovereignty of God*, 16.

[3] *The World Book Dictionary* (Thorndike-Barnhart, 1982 Edition).

[4] Grudem, *Systematic Theology*, 492.

The Dynamic of Polarity

This is a broken world,"[5] claims Dembski and many others (who also believe that "all evil in the world ultimately traces back to human sin."[6]) Circumspectly, he adds that "we can all think of changes that we would make if we were God."[7]

Spykman refutes this human opinion in recognizing that "others have argued that evil is a *necessary condition* for the good to come to its own. It is a negative agent to stimulate the good. Just as there can be no light without darkness, so the argument goes, so there can be no good without evil. Evil is the shadow side of the good."[8]

Undeniably, we humans live in a three-dimensional, physical, material, and observable world. In addition, many of us believe that it's surrounded and interpenetrated by a spirit dimension (see Heb. 12:1, 22-24).[9] It's also a world comprised and defined by many polar opposites. Some term this multi-faceted environment and dualistic dynamic of polarity the human predicament. And they are correct. Yet this is the type of world into which God has chosen to place us. We are here to live in it, discern between its polar opposites, make choices, and die.

Below is a partial list of many polar opposites with which we must contend every day. Some contain continuums of degrees in between the two poles. Others may not. Hick, however, maintains "that all that is exists in this contrast and antithesis."[10] Perhaps you can think of more.

North/South, East/West, up/down, high/low, left/right, in/out, hot/cold, soft/hard, light/heavy, wet/dry, clean/dirty, mountain/valley, fast/slow, large/small, opened/closed, empty/full, positive/negative, plus/minus, protons/electrons, light/dark, day/night, winter/summer, past/future, (the present only lasts for the blink of an eye), loud/silent, sweet/sour (bitter), beautiful/ugly, beginning/end, yes/no, true/false, fact/fiction, right/wrong, love/hate, sacred/profane, joy/sadness-sorrow, laughter/tears, justice/injustice, well/sick, hope/despair, pleasure/pain,

---

[5] Dembski, *The End of Christianity*, xiv.
[6] Ibid., 8.
[7] Ibid., *xiv*.
[8] Spykman, *Reformational Theology*, 316.
[9] Some scientists speculate there may be more dimensions.
[10] Hick, *Evil and the Love of God*, 129.

feast/famine, blessings/curses, riches/poverty, success/failure, victory/defeat, peace/war, contentment/anger, forgiveness/bitterness, reward/punishment, gain/loss, less/more, growth/decay, young/old, birth/death, and, of course, thesis/antithesis (A/not A), and good/evil.

Thus, a dualistic dynamic permeates and penetrates almost, if not everything, around us, as "nature always has a double aspect."[11] So why would God structure his creation this way? As we shall increasingly discover, God, in his omniscience, knew it would be necessary in order to accomplish his purposes for us humans—physically, morally, emotionally, spiritually, and eternally.

The Apostle Paul bears witness to this necessity of polarity in creation when he rhetorically questions and argues: "But if our unrighteousness brings out God's righteousness more clearly, what shall we say? That God is unjust in bringing his wrath upon us? (I am using a human argument.) Certainly not! If that were so, how could God judge the world?" (Rom. 3:5-6).

Some term this multi-faceted environment and dualistic dynamic the human predicament. And they are correct. Yet this is the type of world into which God has chosen to place us.

Of course, "there are numerous alternative worlds that God could have created" writes physicist Paul Davies:

There are endless ways in which the universe might have been totally chaotic. It might have had no laws at all, or merely an incoherent jumble of laws. . . . One could imagine a universe in which conditions changed from moment to moment in a complicated or random way, or even in which everything abruptly ceased to exist. There seems to be no logical obstacle to the idea of such unruly universes.[12]

---

[11] Boyd, *Satan and the Problem of Evil*, 244.
[12] Paul Davies, *The Mind of God* (New York, NY: Touchstone Books, 1992), 195.

But the fact is, God didn't place us into a random and inconsistent mishmash of a world. Let's illustrate the necessity of this dualistic dynamic of polarity in creation by looking at some familiar comparatives:

For Physical Development:

The major physical force on planet Earth is gravity. It's essential. Without it we couldn't walk, ride around, drink water, or perform a host of other daily activities. And God put just the right amount of gravity in our world for our benefit:

- "If the Earth was 25% larger, we would . . . weigh 25% more if the density stayed constant." If it was much larger than that, our muscles would not be strong enough to lift us or get us around. Some hefty people might manage. But life would be difficult if not impossible.
- If the earth was smaller, gravity would be less and the air would be lighter and rarer. The earth's nitrogen-oxygen atmosphere would also be affected. If it was not just the right width and composition (oxygen 21%, nitrogen 77%, and traces of argon, carbon dioxide, and water), the earth's daily heat gain and loss would be out of balance and our present-day climates would be drastically altered.[13]

Hence, in a weightless world, babies would not grow up very well. And in a world with more gravity, it would be tough to get around, perhaps overwhelming. D'Souza speculates that "God could have created a world where gravity sometimes works but sometimes doesn't. . . ."[14] But He didn't. Gravity is a consistent downward force against which we inhabitants of planet Earth must constantly contend.

In a similar manner, physical strengthening and development require exercise and training. This is why, as Keller points out, "a good coach puts you through exercises . . . . They are ways to cause stress or put pressure on various parts of your body. Bicep curls with weights put

---

[13] Excerpt from Noē, *The Perfect Ending for the World*, 5.
[14] D'Souza, *Godforsaken*, 93.

pressure on the biceps. Forearm curls . . . . Running does many things, including taxing the respiratory and circulatory systems."

Moreover, "a good coach will not put too much pressure on your body. To lift too much or run too much would cause your body to break down. But if, on the other hand, you exercise too little . . . your body will also break down and age faster. What you need is exactly the right amount of pressure and just the right amount of discomfort and pain. The biblical author is right when he says that suffering is painful 'at the time' but later yields a harvest. That is exactly how exercise works."[15]

Dr. Graham concurs and extrapolates thusly from muscle development into our next comparative area:

> . . . just as muscles need to be exercised to become strong, so our spiritual 'muscles' need exercise if we're to become spiritually strong.[16]

> Think of it this way: Suppose you never got any physical exercise; all you did was sit in your chair or lie in bed all day. What would happen to your muscles? They'd grow weaker and weaker. Our muscles only become strong if we exercise them and challenge them to do more. The more resistance they face, the stronger they'll get. The same is true spiritually. If our faith is never challenged . . . if we never have to put it to work . . . then our spiritual 'muscles' will grow weaker and weaker. But when hardships and trials come into our lives, we'll be forced to exercise those muscles – and when we do, our faith will grow stronger.[17]

For Moral and Spiritual Growth:

Let's face it. Most of our physical, moral, and spiritual growth comes through facing, pushing through, and overcoming resistance and adversity. How else could virtues like truthfulness, patience, courage, loyalty, mercy, compassion, faithfulness, forgiveness, and repentance

---

[15] Keller, *Walking with God through Pain and Suffering*, 194.

[16] Billy Graham, "My Answer," *The Indianapolis Star* (Indianapolis, IN), 17 October 2013, E-4.

[17] Billy Graham, "My Answer," *The Indianapolis Star* (Indianapolis, IN), 7 February 2013, E-4.

develop and flourish if there is no opposite from which to discern, differentiate, and choose?

Usually, these virtues are not innate. They are developed through circumstances that test us. Hence, Keller is spot on when he recognizes that "at the simplest level, we know that only if there is danger can there be courage."[18] Likewise, Evans supports this polar necessity in noting that "the experience of evil is inextricably connected to the development of these character traits and, as such, provides a morally sufficient reason for God's permitting the evil that pervades our world."[19]

Hence, just as pushing on and overcoming resistance is necessary for growing muscles, a world of polar opposites is a necessary condition for producing authentic moral and spiritual growth and maturity. Thus, Sittser, who has personally experienced horrendous evil, insists that "we need adversity, at least some of the time. It exposes our smallness, weakness, and selfishness; it reveals our need for God and enlarges our inward capacity for true happiness." He further explains how this works. "Adversity does this work in the same way exercise grows muscle by first breaking it down. Only people whose circumstances would appear to cause unhappiness can actually become truly happy. They stop requiring it from the world and learn to find it in God, the source of all that is good. Without adversity we would remain spoiled children who expect the world to conform to our every whim and wish."[20]

Sittser calls adversity and prosperity "tools in his [God's] hand, like the hammer and chisel Michelangelo used to sculpt his figures, setting them free from their marble prison."[21] Caroline Leaf adds that this is how "God pulls us along in exciting suspense in this enjoyable discovery of his creation. . . . [as] God is taking us through the material world into the spiritual world to get to know him more deeply. Why . . . did he put our soul and spirit in a physical body and place us in a physical world? "[22]

---

[18] Keller, *Walking with God through Pain and Suffering*, 117.

[19] Evans, *The Problem of Evil*, 14.

[20] Jerry Sittser, *A Grace Revealed: How God Redeems the Story of Your Life* (Grand Rapids, MI: Zondervan, 2012), 80.

[21] Ibid., 87.

[22] Caroline Leaf, *Switch on Your Brain*, (Grand Rapids, MI: Baker Books, 2013), 119.

Yes, a polarity of opposites is the dualistic dynamic it takes and what it means to live in a morally structured universe. We learn about one opposite from the other. Hence, evil serves a critical role of distinguishing and revealing what is good, righteous, and just. It's the only way we can know and answer the question of what is good and what is evil? According to Evans, "answering this question takes us to the very foundation of ethics."[23] Spykman terms evil "the dialectical counterpole of the good"[24]

Let's face it. Most of our physical, moral, and spiritual growth comes through facing, pushing through, and overcoming resistance and adversity.

Apparently but arguably, God knew that this type of environment would be the best and most authentic way for us to develop a personal, meaningful, and loving relationship with Him. Thus, He said and challenged us long ago: "I set before you today life and prosperity, death and destruction. . . . life and death, blessings and curses. Now choose life . . . ." (Deut. 30:15, 19). Aren't these choices meaningless unless they are comprised of clear, distinct, and polar opposites that produce different causes and effects? After all, how could we call for justice, compassion, and love if there were nothing to compare them with and against? Hence, the meaning of good depends on the meaning and knowledge of the contrary of evil, and vice versa. And, of course, before Adam and Eve sinned, they had no knowledge of either good or evil.

Knoch explains that this is "how God uses evil as a background to make good appear good."[25] The fact is, good cannot be known or appreciated apart from the knowledge and experience of evil, just like light cannot be known or appreciated apart from the experience of darkness. We know by contrast. Also, how is God going to demonstrate grace and mercy and show love if there are no evil and sin and people who hate Him? As impossible as it is to imagine a world without light, it is equally hard to imagine a world without darkness. Likewise, how can

---

[23] Evans, *The Problem of Evil*, 138.
[24] Spykman, *Reformational Theology*, 326.
[25] Knoch, *The Problem of Evil*, 193.

we do good if there is no wrong to right? The bottom line is, evil enables God to put these good aspects of his nature on display.

Leaf, in her amazing book, *Switch on Your Brain*, captures the essence of this "process of thinking and choosing." She characterizes it as "the most powerful thing in the universe after God, and it is a phenomenal gift from God to be treasured and used properly." And it plays "a central role in who God has made us to be."[26]

Of course, God could have created us as race of automatons or robots who always did the right thing. But Kyle Blanchette and Jerry L. Walls argue that a race of automatons or robots "would have had none of the rich moral and personal significance that can only come with genuine moral freedom." Rather, they add, "a big part of what justifies many of the evils that God permits are the intrinsic goods tied up with moral freedom, and to override that freedom in the end would be to undercut our overall theodicy, as well as to subvert God's purpose for humankind."[27] Others, however, take a more condescending tack, believing we must "simply accept" evil "as a part of the mystery of our existence."[28]

Notably, in Romans 1 and by inspiration, Paul reveals that God's power and nature are made known through the created order around us, so that men are without excuse (Rom. 1:20). That created order contains many polar opposites. He also emphasizes that God has written his moral law upon all men's and women's hearts. Thus we are all morally responsible before Him (Rom. 2:15). And to become people of virtuous character we must be able to distinguish between right and wrong, good and evil, and choose appropriately.

This is why, according to Dembski, "God has precisely ordered the physical world to enlighten our minds about him. Creation elucidates the Creator. . . . Impurity presupposes purity, unrighteousness presupposes righteousness, transgression presupposes a boundary that has been

---

[26] Leaf, *Switch on Your Brain*, 103-104.

[27] Blanchette and Walls, "God and Hell Reconciled" in Meister and Dew, Jr., eds., *God and Evil*, 253.

[28] Giberson and Collins, "Evil, Creation and Evolution" in Meister and Dew, Jr., eds., *God and Evil*, 281.

'stepped across,' deviation presupposes a way . . . from which we've departed, sin . . . presupposes a target that we missed, etc."[29]

And yet some people in our world don't believe there is a right and a wrong. The Bible, however, casts "woe" onto those who confuse them. It both admonishes and advises: "Woe to those who call evil good and good evil, who put darkness for light and light for darkness, who put bitter for sweet and sweet for bitter" (Isa. 5:20). "Hate what is evil; cling to what is good" (Rom. 12:9; also see Rom. 16:19; Amos 5:15; Heb. 1:9; 1 Pet. 3:11; 3 John 11). "But solid food is for the mature, who by constant use have trained themselves to distinguish good from evil" (Heb. 5:14). Yes, we are challenged by God to know, understand, and choose between these polar opposites.

As a matter of agreed upon fact, God could have created other worlds for us. But as Dembski variously suggests, "God may have chosen to create this world because the good to be achieved through Christ's death on the Cross surpasses the good achievable in other worlds. . . . Or perhaps God's purposes are inscrutable, and we shall never understand why he chose to create this world rather than another."[30] Or are his purposes truly inscrutable? We shall visit this topic in Chapter 6.

For the Drama of Life:

Think for a moment about the types of dramas we are drawn to see and fondly remember. Also, don't we want to see our sports teams fight through and overcome their opposition? Don't our favorite stories, books, plays, and movies usually utilize "a dose of darkness." As N.D. Wilson describes: "Stories . . . use hardship to burn away the dross in characters. Stories that honor the honorable and damn the damnable. . . . To reveal triumph, we must build enemies. To tell the truth about what it means to be heroic, we must spin a fiction full of danger."[31] Yes, we want to see drama from our heroes facing something to triumph over and defeating some nasty antagonist. Why is this so? It's because we have

---

[29] Dembski, *The End of Christianity*, 143, 145.
[30] Ibid., 169.
[31] N.D. Wilson, "Why Kid's Stories Need a Dose of Darkness, *Christianity Today*, January / February 2014, 30.

been created in the image and likeness of God (Gen. 1:26). And God desires to see the same fight, overcoming drama, and victorious result from us, as well. Oh, yes, He does, as we shall continue to see in this chapter and the rest of this book. Not only is this commonality factor a central tenet of Christian thought, Evans terms it our "ontologically grounded . . . image."[32]

> ## "God has precisely ordered the physical world to enlighten our minds about him. Creation elucidates the Creator. . . ."

Alcorn sums up this ubiquitous human desire thusly: "The greatest character virtues we know would never appear in a story without evil and suffering. . . .The same is true of *Les Misérables* and nearly every great story. It's also true of the Bible, the archetypal redemptive story."[33] The same is true for you and me in the story of our lives.

Most assuredly, the things we value the most are not the things that come easily, but the things we've had to work hardest for. The victories we treasure are those over the toughest of battles. And God has surrounded us with both blessings and battles, with provisions and difficulties. John Eldredge frames this reality appropriately in writing: "Life is not a problem to be solved, it is an adventure to be lived. That's the nature of it and has been since the beginning when God set the dangerous stage for this high-stakes drama and called the whole wild enterprise *good*. He rigged the world in such a way that it only works when we embrace *risk* as the theme of our lives, which is to say, only when we live by faith."[34]

"For our life *is* a quest, my brothers, arranged by our Father, for our initiation."[35]

---

[32] Evans, *The Problem of Evil*, 148.

[33] Alcorn, *If God Is Good*, 198, 204.

[34] John Eldredge, *Wild at Heart* (Nashville, TN: ThomasNelson, 2001), 200.

[35] John Eldredge, *The Way of the Wild Heart* (Nashville, TN: ThomasNelson, 2006), 298.

Special Insights from Scholars

John Hick simply believes that "the world's 'original perfection' is thus simply its suitability as an environment for the emergence of man's God-consciousness."[36]

He further explains and warns that "the entire situation – the polarity of sin and salvation – thus exists within the sovereign purpose of God. To deny God's omni-sovereignty, and therefore His omni-responsibility, would be to take the decisive first step towards Manichaean dualism."[37] Thus, "sin has been ordained . . . by God, not indeed sin in and of itself, but sin merely in relation to redemption; for otherwise redemption itself could not have been ordained."[38] He elaborates that: "these concepts have no clear application if men are built wholly good. . . . goodness would be emptied of content if there were no such experience as temptation and therefore no occasion to choose good as distinct from evil."[39]

He additionally conceives that in an evil-less world, "the daunting fact that emerges is that in such a world moral qualities would no longer have any point or value. . . . It would be a world without need for the virtues of self-sacrifice, care for others, devotion to the public good, courage, perseverance, skill, or honesty. . . . Perhaps most important of all, the capacity to love would never be developed, except in a very limited sense of the word, in a world in which there was no such thing as suffering. . . . It is . . . difficult to see how it could ever grow to any extent in a paradise that excluded all suffering. For such love presupposes a 'real life' in which there are obstacles to be overcome,

---

[36] Hick, *Evil and the God of Love*, 221, in interacting with Friedrich Schleiermacher.

[37] Ibid., 229, in interacting with Schleiermacher. Boyd defines "dualism" as follows: "the belief that there are two ultimate powers running the world, one good and one evil. Metaphysical dualism . . . holds that this sharing of power is built into the nature of things. . . . Scripture clearly rules out such a view, for it consistently depicts God as the single Creator of all this is. What Scripture does not rule out, however, is viewing God *for a period of time* as sharing power with others. This constitutes a *provisional* dualism . . . ." (Boyd, *Satan and the Problem of Evil*, 421.)

[38] Ibid., 231, in interacting with Schleiermacher.

[39] Ibid., 270, in interacting with Anthony Flew.

tasks to be performed, goals to be achieved, setbacks to be endured, problems to be solved, dangers to be met. . . . The same is true in relation to the virtues of compassion, unselfishness, courage, and determination. . . . For moral and spiritual growth comes through response to challenges; and in a paradise there would be no challenges."[40]

Thus, Hick concludes that "there can be no evil where there is not good. . . . Nothing evil exists in *itself,* but only as an evil aspect of some actual entity."[41] "How," for instance Hick asks, "if we had no knowledge of the contrary, could he [we] have had instruction in that which is good?"[42] "This is the general character of our world and the universe we inhabit. [It's] a work of art made by God. . . . In a painting, for example, contrasts arising from the presence of dark as well as light colours, and even of elements that are in themselves ugly and repellent, may contribute to the beauty of the whole; and this fact may suggest by analogy a positive function for the dark patches of evil within a universe which in its totality is morally harmonious, well-ordered, and beautiful."[43]

Likewise in music, the "clash and disharmony at one stage of the musical development [functions] in order to make possible a later triumphant resolution in which the dissonant notes are worked into a complex harmony that would not be possible without them."[44] Hence, Hick views our universe as "a complex picture or symphony or organism whose value resides in its totality, and whose perfection is compatible with much suffering and sin in some constituent units"[45]

A. E. Knoch expresses God's creative purposefulness this way: "Sin has an essential, though transient, part in God's purpose. God made due preparation for it before it came. The Lamb was slain from the disruption [sic] of the world. Creation may reveal some aspects of God's power and wisdom, but His love can be displayed only where sin has sown the seeds of hate. There can be no Saviour apart from sin. There can be no

---

[40] Ibid., 324-326, 374.
[41] Ibid., 48.
[42] Ibid., 214.
[43] Ibid., 97, 192.
[44] Ibid., 192-193.
[45] Ibid., 195.

reconciliation apart from enmity. God locks all up together in stubbornness that He should be merciful to all (Rom. 11:32)."[46]

"Evil alone lacks contrast. It must be seen in the light of good. Wrong must be viewed in the presence of right. . . . [Hence] The function of evil in this world is to impart an appreciation for the good. It's God's background on which He will paint the highlights of His grace. . . .the presence of sin in the universe is not a mistake on God's side, but a part of His plan for reaching the hearts of His creatures. . . . Sin is not His tyrant, but His slave. It crushes that He may cure. It kills that He may make alive. Its function is to show God's creatures their utter dependence on His power. It gives them a wholesome horror of existence without Him. . . . It will drive them into His bosom."[47]

Knoch further expounds on "the principle," which he claims is "the key to unlock the great problems that most perplex us. It is this: Our knowledge is relative; it is based on contrasts. The knowledge of good is dependent upon the knowledge of evil." Hence the tree of the knowledge of good and evil "in the garden was not, as we usually think of it, merely the means of knowing evil, it was the means, primarily, of the knowledge of *good*. Adam and Eve had good but did not realize it because they had had no experience of evil.[48]

He concludes by observing that "the great purpose of God during the eons is to provide a background for the display of His love. . . . The groundwork of the plan is very simple. The sinner experiences evil that he may know good. . . . [It's] His plan for reaching the hearts of His creatures."[49]

Randy Alcorn, likewise, notes that "grace and forgiveness, both expressions of God's eternal character, are moral goods, but without evil they wouldn't have become clearly evident."[50]

Norman L. Geisler agrees that "we can only know something is evil (not good) if we know what is good. We can't know something is *injust* [sic] unless we know what is just."[51]

---

[46] Knoch, *The Problem of Evil and the Judgments of God*, 21.
[47] Ibid., 57, 67, 69, 86.
[48] Ibid., 53.
[49] Ibid., 56, 69.
[50] Alcorn, *If God Is Good*, 26.
[51] Geisler, *If God, Why Evil?*, 13.

Bruce Little terms the dualistic dynamic of polarity as being God's "moral ordering of the universe" in which "God voluntarily commits to working with humans within this creation order so that, as a real person, they can have a person-to-person relationship with God—one mind to another mind, where the second mind is patterned after the first mind."[52]

Rousas John Rushdoony likewise concurs that "man is born into a world of total meaning" and "all life thus has direction in terms of God's creative purpose."[53] If however, as he illustrates, "all the world is black, no concept of black is possible, since no differentiation exists. Everything being black, there is no principle of definition and description left. When all the world is in blasphemy, no definition of blasphemy is possible: everything is the same."[54]

William A. Dembski thus surmises that "we live in a meaningful world whose meaning was placed there for our benefit."[55]

Rabbi David Aaron finds "it is strange that we cry in moments of pain but also in moments of intense joy." Therefore, he asks, "what do pain and joy have in common that they can both move us to tears?" He answers that "both pain and joy can bring us face-to-face with the bedrock of life and this encounter is overwhelming. . . . mysterious, miraculous, and incomprehensible."[56]

Dinesh D'Souza rhetorically inquires, "Could an omnipotent God create a world with free will but no evil?" He speculatively answers that "to create creatures capable of *moral good*, therefore, he must create creatures capable of moral evil, and he cannot leave these creatures *free* to perform evil and at the same time prevent them from doing so."[57]

Gregory A. Boyd dubs the world we live in as an "objective environment" and states that we humans "can only interact with each

---

[52] Little, "God and Gratuitous Evil" in Meister and Dew, Jr., eds., *God and Evil*, 45.

[53] Rousas John Rushdoony, *The Institutes of Biblical Law* (n.l.: The Presbyterian and Reformed Publishing Company, 1973), 224.

[54] Ibid., 118.

[55] Dembski, *The End of Christianity*, 144.

[56] Rabbi David Aaron, *Inviting God In* (n.l: Trumpeter, 2007), 54-55.

[57] D'Souza, *Godforsaken*, 91-92.

other" in such an environment.[58] He insists that we must have this type of environment "in order to render certain phenomena intelligible."[59]

R.C. Sproul factually points out that "the word 'tragedy' presupposes some kind of order or purpose in the world. If the world has purpose and order, then all that occurs in it is meaningful in some respect . . . [Yet] their ultimate purpose might elude us for the present."[60] Hence, "the only way to understand mercy is against the background of the reality of wrath."[61]

C.S. Lewis wrote, "In a word, unless we allow ultimate reality to be moral, we cannot morally condemn it."[62]

Timothy Keller ramps up the stakes by eschewing that if "morals are totally subjective . . . God is unnecessary. . . . and you can't condemn evil. How tenable is that?"[63]

Gordon H. Clark accurately notes that "it is his [God's] will that establishes the distinction between right and wrong, between justice and injustice; it is his will that sets the norms of righteous conduct."[64]

Philip Yancey understands, in his quoting Bishop Desmond Tutu of South Africa, that "this universe has been constructed in such a way that unless we live in accordance with its moral laws we will pay the price for it."[65]

William Barclay believes *that moral order is the wrath of God at work.* God made this world in such a way that we break his laws at our peril. Now if we were left solely at the mercy of that inexorable moral order, there could be nothing for us but death and destruction. . . . But into this dilemma of man there comes the love of God, and that love of God, by an act of unbelievable free grace, lifts man out of the consequences of sin and saves him from the wrath he should have incurred. . . . Break the laws of agriculture—your harvest fails. Break the laws of architecture—your building collapses. Break the laws of health— your body suffers. Paul was saying [Rom. 1:18-23] 'Look at the world!

---

[58] Boyd, *Satan and the Problem of Evil*, 425.
[59] Ibid., 429.
[60] Sproul, *When Worlds Collide*, 38.
[61] Ibid., 68.
[62] C.S. Lewis, *Christian Reflections* (Grand Rapids, MI: Eerdmans, 1967), 70.
[63] Keller, *Walking with God through Pain and Suffering*, 106.
[64] Clark, *God and Evil*, 45.
[65] Yancey, *The Question That Never Goes Away*, 122.

See how it is constructed! From a world like that you know what God is like.' The sinner is left without excuse."[66]

James Spiegel recognizes the universality of polar opposites and expresses his understanding in this rather unique manner: "Indeed, when one reflects on the various vocations, it is difficult to think of any field or career that isn't advanced by, if not entirely a consequence of, the need to respond to sin and suffering. From medicine and health, to science, law and criminal justice, to construction and road repair—all are cases in point. And the ingenuity we have developed in dealing with evil better equips us to make advances in fields that are not necessarily responsive or preventative regarding evil, such as transportation, communications and the fine arts, though even in these fields we find ways in which our struggles drive advancement."[67]

Jill Graper Hernandez summarily concludes that: "our actual world is the result of the convergence of God's perfection and freedom . . . . even though this created world is not perfect, it is the best possible, and so it would be impossible for God to create a better world . . . . A perfect God would create only the best out of any world that could be conceived; since this is the world God created, this is the best of all worlds that could be conceived—the best of all possible worlds. . . . [it] requires that humans may choose certain evil acts, and this is harmonious with God's perfection of intellect and will. . . . God cannot be blamed morally when he creates the opportunity for his people to flourish and to help others flourish, and they freely choose to do otherwise.[68]

Critical Objection: Alcorn disagrees and contends that "this is not the best possible world." But he also allows that "it may be the best possible means of achieving the best possible world." He explains that "a world that had never been touched by evil *would* be a good place. But would it be the best place possible? If we acknowledge that evil and suffering facilitate the development of significant human virtues, then we must answer no."[69]

---

[66] Barclay, *The Letter to the Romans*, 26-27.
[67] James Spiegel, "The Irenaean Soul-Making Theology" in Meister and Dew, Jr., eds., *God and Evil*, 84.
[68] Hernandez, "Leibniz and the Best of All Possible Worlds" in Meister and Dew, Jr., eds., *God and Evil*, 96, 101, 102.
[69] Alcorn, *If God Is Good*, 194.

Still, Alcorn struggles with this tough realization: "If I had to believe that what we now see represents God's best for this world, I would not be a Christian. If not for the redemptive work of Christ, I would not believe in God's goodness."[70]

Critical Objection: Metaphysical dualism must be rejected. Boyd defines metaphysical dualism thusly and elaborates: ". . . any view that understands the conflict between good and evil to be a matter of metaphysical necessity (i.e., it could not be otherwise). The Christian tradition has rightly always rejected this philosophy as undermining the omnipotence of the Creator. At least since Augustine, the classical philosophical tradition by logical implication tended towards metaphysical monism: the view that only the good is ultimately real and thus the conflict between good and evil is only apparent."[71]

My Response: Out of an infinite range of possibilities, our God has chosen to create and sustain our world with the dualistic dynamic of good and evil functioning in it. This world, as it is, has been determined by God in his sovereignty to be the best world possible for humankind and for purposes we shall further explore in Chapter 6.

But first, what are we to make of all the confusion surrounding natural evil and disasters?

"man is born into a world of total meaning" and "all life thus has direction in terms of God's creative purpose."

---

[70] Ibid., 212.
[71] Boyd, *Satan and the Problem of Evil*, 424.

Chapter 5

The Confounding Confusion of Natural Evil

M ost of our physical world is beautiful and beneficial. But it is also a violent and dangerous place. Why is that? It's because of what Boyd terms the "antithetical potentials in all natural objects and in the natural laws."[1]

Yes, we can fall and be killed, be hit by falling objects and crushed, drowned in water, be burned by fire, bitten or ravaged by an animal, blown away by a storm, swallowed up by the ground, or attacked by a disease. Most certainly, confounding confusion reigns supreme over the cause and nature of these so-called "natural" events, which have burdened and plagued the human race for eons. For instance . . .

(Used with permission)

---

[1] Boyd, *Satan and the Problem of Evil*, 279.

Let's face it. The same gravity that enables us to walk can cause us to fall. The same water that sustains us can drowned us. The same fire that heats our homes and cooks our food can burn. The same rain that moistens our crops can also flood. The same breeze that refreshes can also destroy. The same ground that stabilizes our buildings can also crumble. The same sun that nourishes our plants and trees can also parch and bring drought. The same electricity that lights and powers our world can also electrocute.

All natural forces manifest this same dualistic dynamic and potential as do we humans, the animals, and the angels—i.e., to bless or curse, do good or evil. It's popularly called natural evil. It's defined as being evil that's produced by nonhuman causes, such as: volcanoes, earthquakes, tsunamis, floods, hurricanes, typhoons, monsoons, tornadoes, infectious diseases, landslides, avalanches, wildfires, lightning strikes, hailstorms, droughts, animal attacks, many birth defects, and death and decay of vegetation, etc. Evil produced by human beings is termed moral evil. Evil produced by angels is a somewhat mixed bag between moral evil and supernatural evil.

On the other hand, unnatural disasters, such as airplane and automobile accidents, occur because we humans have invented objects that both utilize and defy natural laws. Hence, airplanes sometimes fall from the sky and automobiles sometimes run into one another or other objects, and with disastrous results.

The two big questions regarding natural evil and disasters are: (1) Who or what causes them? (2) Are they truly evil, good, or neither?[2] Boyd readily concedes that "this category of evil is difficult to explain."[3] Even worse, Keller believes that "natural evil offends those who believe in a God who exists for us, and confounds those who don't believe we are all sinners needing salvation by sheer grace."[4] In a nutshell, the confounding confusion that exists over the nature of so-called "natural evil" and who is responsible is huge. Hence, Win Corduan appropriately asks, "Is evil a part of the natural order without cause, or is it a disruption

---

[2] Greek philosophy and Gnosticism assert that the material universe is evil and only spiritual realities are good.

[3] Ibid., 424.

[4] Keller, *Walking with God through Pain and Suffering*, 59.

of how things should be?"[5] In a partial answer, DeWeese reports that "while many have offered defenses in reply to the problem of moral evil, only a few have addressed the problem of natural evil."[6]

Further compounding this confusion is the fact that biblical evidence exists for a number of different causes. Moreover, God has never given humankind a full explanation of the operation and purposes of these natural forces, preferring instead to deflect the issue by simply proclaiming through the prophet Isaiah: "For my thoughts are not your thoughts, and your ways are not my ways. . . . For as the heavens are higher than the earth, so are my ways higher than your ways and my thoughts than your thoughts" (Isa. 55:8-9). Or He intimidates with questions to Job like: "Where were you when I laid the earth's foundation. Tell me, if you understand" (Job 38:4).

Who's Responsible?

Given that the world was designed and created by God to be both three-dimensional and consist of polar opposites that can be beneficial as well as adversarial. And given, as Evans submits, that "it is generally agreed that the regularities in nature provide a great good to the overall well-being and daily functions of creatures in the world."[7] And with the understanding that "world" here refers to the physical structure of the earth—from its center to surface to atmosphere—and the balances that nature contains within itself . . . who, then, is the culprit or culprits responsible for evil natural disasters? Are they God-caused and controlled, human sin-caused, Satan and his demonic cohorts-caused and empowered, or simply mechanistic laws of nature, or a mixture, or what? Let's explore.

---

[5] Win Corduan, "Evil in Non-Christian Religions" in Meister and Dew, Jr., eds., *God and Evil*, 176.

[6] DeWeese, "Natural Evil: A 'Free Process' Defense" in Meister and Dew, Jr., eds., *God and Evil*, 54.

[7] Evans, *The Problem of Evil*, 114.

God-Caused and Controlled

As we saw in Chapter 3, the Bible frequently informs us that our God creates and causes many natural disasters, such as: the great flood, raining down burning sulfur on Sodom and Gomorrah, birth defects, plagues, wasting diseases, fever, illnesses, famine, and pestilences, making the ground become like bronze, sending wild animals against people, killing cattle, opening up the earth and swallowing people up, and unleashing fire from the sky to destroy people and places.

A few years ago, I was asked to be one of three "clergy and religious experts" to contribute to an article in the "Faith + Values Faith Forum" section of *The Indianapolis Star* on a topic titled: "We see God's role in disasters differently." Here was my contribution. See if you agree or not.

> Distancing God from any responsibility for natural disasters has become fashionable today. But is this detachment simply an expression of wishful thinking, scriptural ignorance, or painful avoidance?
>
> The Bible documents many instances of God causing natural disasters. Here are a few:
>
> Who produced the great flood in Noah's time that killed the vast majority of human beings (Gen. 7-8)?
>
> Whose anger "shut the heavens so that it will not rain and the ground will yield no produce" (Deut. 11:17)?
>
> Who opened up the earth and swallowed Korah's men along "with their households and all their possessions" (Num. 16:30-34)?
>
> Who answered Elijah's two prayers and caused no rain for 3-1/2 years before "the heavens gave rain, and the earth produced its crops" (Jas. 5:17-18).
>
> Who directs the "four angels standing at the four corners of the earth, holding back the four winds of the earth . . . who had been given power to harm the land and the sea" (Rev. 7:1-2)? Some believe these are the earth's four jet streams that control the weather.
>
> Lastly, God told Isaiah that "I bring prosperity and create evil/disaster/calamity" (Isa. 45:7). The Hebrew word variously translated as "evil, disaster, or calamity" is *ra*. It comes from the Hebrew verb *raa* meaning "to spoil."
>
> So when God never, sometimes, or always causes natural phenomena, is it good or bad? For me, never is not an option since God's Word proclaims that He does not change (Mal. 3:6). But

between the latter two possibilities, I simply don't know which is right. And I don't know anyone who truly does.

For me, this would seem to be the irony of ironies. Why do we often term natural disasters "acts of God" while taking for granted and rarely giving Him credit for years, decades, or even centuries of pleasant, peaceful, and beneficial weather? [as well as a physically stable and life-enabling earth and universe? – this later portion was edited out of the article].

There is one other fashionable idea as the reason for natural disasters nowadays. Let's blame climate change, which is human-caused, of course. But is it really?[8]

Needless to say, this article drew a wide variety of comments—from the ridiculous to sublime. However, I'm not going to encumber this chapter with them. If you are interested, email me and I'll send them to you.

Opinions from Scholars

Dembski claims that "another way to justify that natural evils are not morally significant is to grit one's teeth and boldly assert that God takes full responsibility for natural evil, that he directly created it, that he even takes pleasure in it, and that, however counterintuitive it may seem, natural evil is entirely compatible with the goodness of God in creation."[9]

Yes, the fact is, that the Holy Scriptures abound with testimonies and revelation that God controls the weather (see Psa. 78:26; 104:4; 105:16; 135:6-7; 147:18; 148:7-8; also see Zech. 9:14; 10:1; 14:18-19; Duet. 28). According to Piper, this means "that all calamities of wind and rain and flood and storm are owing to God's ultimate decrees. One word from him and the wind and the seas obey."[10] Ralph L. Smith agrees and adds that "nature has been created to proclaim His power."[11]

---

[8] John Noē, "We see God's role in disasters differently," *The Indianapolis Star* (Indianapolis, IN), 10 November, 2012, B-3.
[9] Dembski, *The End of Christianity*, 80.
[10] Piper, "Is God Less Glorious Because He Ordained that Evil Be?"
[11] Ralph L. Smith, *Old Testament Theology: Its History, Method, and Message* (Nashville, TN: Broadman & Holman Publishers, 1993), 98.

Hence, God has demonstrated his ability and willingness to control nature. Since He created it all in the first place, moving it around as He wills is no big deal for Him. And again, if God doesn't change, as He says He doesn't (see Mal. 3:6a), then the question becomes: Is God the cause behind *all* instances of natural evil or only *some*? And if only some, who might be the other culprits?

Critical Objection: God merely allows or permits natural evil. Geisler and Corduan take this position and explain that "it is necessary for God to permit physical evils (as the condition) by which he can produce the morally best world."[12]

Critical Objection: In answer to a reader's question about "How do you explain natural disasters like hurricanes and tornadoes?" Dr. Graham conceded: "To be honest, we often don't understand why God permits things like this to happen." Then he offered this caveat: "I know God is ultimately in control of the universe – but I also know many things happen that aren't his perfect will, because they end in suffering and death. But notice that I said God 'permits' some things to happen, not 'causes' them to happen."[13]

My Response: Drs. Geisler, Corduan, and Graham here are flying directly in the face of a lot of Scripture to the contrary. And isn't God either in control or not? Additionally, according to Scripture, God the Father did not merely create the universe through Christ (John 1:1-3; Col. 1:16), He also sustains it through Christ—i.e., keeps it in existence and functioning (see Heb. 1:3; Col. 1:17).

God has demonstrated his ability and willingness to control nature. Since He created it all in the first place, moving it around as He wills is no big deal for Him.

---

[12] Norman Geisler and Winfried Corduan, *Philosophy of Religion*, 2nd ed. (Grand Rapids, MI: Baker, 1988), 373.

[13] Billy Graham, "My Answer," *The Indianapolis Star* (Indianapolis, IN), 8 February 2001, E-5.

Human Sin-Caused

We live on a fallen planet in a world broken, and all because of human sin. Or so we are told by many theologians, pastors, and well-meaning Christians. Keller lays out this traditional belief this way:

> The world is now in a cursed condition that falls short of its design. Human beings were not created to experience death, pain, grief, disappointment, ruptured relationships, disease, and natural disasters. The world we were made to live in was not supposed to be like that. A frustrated world is a broken world, in which things do not function as they should, and that is why there is evil and suffering.[14]

The citing of this causational culprit goes back to the Augustinian tradition and its free will theodicy to explain the origin of both moral and natural evil. In this view, they are all "byproducts of the Fall." And granted, "this is an appealing argument in which all good things in nature . . . can be attributed to God, and all the bad things in nature . . . can be attributed to human sin."[15]

Not surprisingly, proponents, like Geisler, despise the notion "that much physical evil is not the result of free choices" but "can be blamed on God." Adamantly, he protests: "all physical evil can be related to free choice either directly or indirectly. According to one view, Adam's sin alone could account for all physical evils. Add to that the evils inflicted by Satan and evil spirits and one need look no further for the possible explanation of all physical evil. . . . The bottom line is this: The above explanation . . . can account for all physical evil in the universe."[16] Oh really? On the moon and on others planets as well—after all, they don't sin or make choices? And yet Geisler also believes that "God is in complete control over the whole universe" and "Nothing can thwart God's purposes."[17]

Similarly, a local pastor in a recent sermon emphasized that "natural disasters (tornados and hurricanes) trace their origins back to the

---

[14] Keller, *Walking with God through Pain and Suffering*, 131.

[15] Giberson and Collins, "Evil, Creation and Evolution" in Meister and Dew, Jr., eds., *God and Evil*, 275.

[16] Geisler, *If God, Why Evil?*, 80-81.

[17] Ibid., 100.

sinfulness of mankind that led to what Paul calls . . . 'We know that the whole creation has been groaning as in the pains of childbirth right up to the present time.' Romans 8:22."

On March 17-19, 2014 and in response to my original post on this topic of human sin causing natural evil, many Facebookers responded with both pro and con assertions. Their pros far outweighed their cons:

PRO – "Adam's sin affected creation itself and brought the curse on the created order." And one of these days, "the sons of God will deliver creation from its curse and death will no longer affect the created realm."

PRO – "For the creation was subjected to futility, not willingly, but because of Him who subjected it, in hope that the creation itself also will be set free from its slavery to corruption into the freedom of the glory of the children of God. (Rom. 8:20, 21)."

PRO – "I do think that the precipitation of lies had an effect on the physical constitution of the perishable world."

PRO – "Thinking that sin affected the created realm seems pretty clear to me."

PRO – "The idea that sin affected the world and the weather and the animals is not Biblically far-fetched in my opinion."

PRO – "I do not believe that hurricanes, tornados and devastating earthquakes are 'good.' Rather, I believe they are a result of a world in turmoil and spiritual derision."

PRO – "Does that mean there was once a time that weather was perfect and then man sinned and screwed the weather up?"

PRO – "I, like you, have trouble with the idea that God is responsible for evil. He is responsible for creating beings with free will, but that only makes evil possible. . . . bad stewardship of the authority (dominion) given to the first couple and handed over to the evil one certainly accounts for the evil in the world without in any way indicting God."

PRO – "This is a consequence of sin, of the actions of people."

PRO -- "I never said God is responsible for evil. God is responsible for his creation."

CON – "I don't think that sin changed the constitution of material physics."

CON – "I do not see anywhere where it [Scripture] makes any of those claims. I think those are more legend. There is a lot of extra-biblical mysticism surrounding the garden, Adam and Eve, etc. –

especially medieval legends and such that have attached themselves to the Bible stories and people think they are truth."

This same divergence of opinion exists among theologians. While a few argue the CON position that natural evil does "not occur as a direct consequence of human choice," the vast majority argue the PRO that "natural disasters do indeed occur as a consequence of humanity's free choice to sin, which brought ruin to the earth (see Genesis 3:17; Romans 9:19-22)."[18]

Alcorn further details this retroactive corruption and transference process like this. "The moral evil of Earth's stewards caused God to curse Earth with natural disasters." Also citing Romans 8:20-22, he expounds that "earthquakes, volcanoes, and tsunamis reflect the frustration, bondage, and decay of an earth groaning under sin's curse."[19]

But even if Alcorn and his PRO compadres are correct, doesn't this culprit of human sin still leave God ultimately responsible for the infliction of natural evil? After all, we humans are not capable of changing the physical dynamics and nature of tectonic plate movements or weather patterns with our sins. As Spiegel points out, natural evils cannot be "the product of any human volition."[20] There would have to have been some sort of metaphysical connective. And only God could make that connective and change to his physical creation, right?

Conversely, how can human free will, obedience, and volition explain the goodness of nature? It cannot. That's God's doing, exclusively, isn't it? Evans certainly recognizes this divergent problem as he retorts that "these evils . . . are not connected to the exercise of free will" and "the concept of natural evil is not as clearly delineated as that of the problem of moral evil. For instance, in what sense can we say that natural events are *evil*?"[21]

Furthermore, how has human sin here on Planet Earth possibly affected the entire cosmos? After all, "the universe appears fine-tuned for

---

[18] Alcorn, *If God Is Good*, 256.
[19] Ibid., 85.
[20] Spiegel, "The Irenaean Soul-Making Theodicy" in Meister and Dew, Jr., eds., *God and Evil*, 81.
[21] Evans, *The Problem of Evil*, 114.

life."[22] That precision does not seem to be evil or demonic in nature, does it?

Somehow this desire and concept of keeping God away from any involvement or responsibility in this metaphysical transaction leaves much to be desired. The fact is, we do not have strong scriptural grounds for determining how human sin, stemming from the consequences of Adam and Eve's fall, transfers into producing a corruption, perversion, disordering, or disintegration upon the nature of creation from "very good" to essentially evil. That assertion is certainly more than the Scriptures themselves reveal. Essentially, this line of speculation is based on one passage of Romans 8:19-22 and what we think "the creation [that] was subject to frustration," its "bondage," and liberation that was to be "brought into the glorious freedom of the children of God" was, or is.

Conversely, how can human free will, obedience, and volition explain the goodness of nature? It cannot. That's God's doing, exclusively, isn't it?

I maintain in another book that this creation, its frustration, bondage, and freedom can better be understood and explained as the change of covenants then underway and not the change of cosmos—i.e., the covenantal creation, and not the physical creation. For one thing, compare its "bondage" with the covenantal "bondage" Paul speaks about in Galatians 4:21-26 KJV.[23] For more insights, compare the frustration to which this Romans 8:19-22 creation was subjected to these verses about the imperfections of the old covenantal system (Heb. 10:1, 4; 7:18-19 versus 7:25; 9:9-10) and also to this covenantally determined "a new creation" (Gal. 6:15).

Hick hits this issue head on in noting that "to throw the discussion into metaphysical regions . . . to which the already sufficient difficulties of knowing whether we are talking sense or nonsense are compounded to a point that is, literally, beyond all reason."[24] The link between human

---

[22] Ibid., 124.

[23] For more, see: Noē, *The Perfect Ending for the World*, 279, 309-310, 319. Noē, *The Greater Jesus*. 366-368. Noē, *Unraveling the End*, 109-110.

[24] Hick, *Evil and the God of Love*, 13.

sin and natural evil is far from clear. On the other hand, Dembski speculates that all of nature has been this way all along, with the Garden of Eden being "a perfect creation" in a "segregated area."[25] He suggests that "only after they sin and are ejected from the Garden do they become conscious of the difference" and "the tragedy they now face by being cast into a world full of natural evil and devoid of a tree that could grant them immortality."[26]

If Dembski's scenario is correct, then "there never was a chronological moment when the world we inhabit was without natural evil." And, "it may seem pointless to speculate about what would have happened if there had been no Fall."[27] So Dembski concludes that while "speculations about worlds that never were are interesting . . . . they ought not to distract us from the world that we actually inhabit. Our world is dynamic and messy. There never was any other, so far as we are concerned." Hence, "in the mind of God, creation always presupposed the Cross. . . ."[28]

Finally, he warns that "in the metaphysics of evil, this temptation is the most fundamental of all temptations. Rather than find meaning and purpose in creation as put there by the Creator, the temptation here is to invent meaning and purpose on one's own without recourse to the Creator.[29] . . . . [We] must do more than merely connect the world's going haywire to human sin."[30]

Satan and His Demonic Cohorts-Caused and Empowered

Another popular culprit to blame natural evils upon is Satan and his demonic cohorts. Boyd is a major proponent of this view. He insists, in a mixed manner, that "ultimately there is no such thing as 'natural' evil (which is why I place quotation marks around the word). In my view, *all*

---

[25] Dembski, *The End of Christianity*, 152.

[26] Ibid., 153.

[27] Ibid., 171.

[28] Ibid., 172.

[29] Ibid., 133.

[30] Ibid., 151.

evil ultimately derives from the wills of free agents. What cannot be attributed to the volition of human agents should be attributed, directly or indirectly, to the volition of fallen angels. . . . [Hence] all evil . . . originates in the will of self-determined creatures. It cannot be traced back to the Creator."[31] He further believes that "it is obviously as gross an oversimplification to blame, for example, the Holocaust completely on Hitler as it is to blame all the evil of the world on Satan. Evil on a grand scale, like goodness on a grand scale, always involves cooperation on a grand scale."[32]

Wright, however, specifically tags this "enslavement of creation" to "the satan . . . it seems is opposed not only to humankind, to Israel and to Jesus but to creation itself" and "is constantly pressing to undo the project of God, the world which God said was very good (Gen. 1:31). . . . [and is] bent on attacking and destroying creation in general and humankind in particular."[33]

Dr. Graham joins this chorus. In answer to a reader's question, "How do you know the devil is real?" Dr. Graham here blames Satan for natural disasters. He wrote: "famines, injustices, natural disasters, accidents, wars, illnesses and so forth? The total sum of evil and human misery is staggering. . . . it happens because a powerful, evil spiritual being is behind it. Just as the creation bears witness to its creator, so evil bears witness to its creator: Satan."[34]

Yet in another newspaper column, when Dr. Graham was asked, "How do you explain something like the earthquake in Haiti?" he replied: "To be honest I do not have a full answer as to why tragedies like this occur. What I do know is that we live in a broken world, where evil and suffering often seem to gain the upper hand. The Bible traces this back to the rebellion of the human race – along with that of Satan and his fallen angles – against the authority of God. As a result the Bible

---

[31] Boyd, *Satan and the Problem of Evil*, 24, 46.
[32] Ibid., 174.
[33] Wright, *Evil and the Justice of God*, 109.
[34] Billy Graham, "My Answer," *The Indianapolis Star* (Indianapolis, IN), 25 February 2009, C-12.

says, 'The whole creation has been groaning as in the pains of childbirth right up to the present time (Rom. 8:22).'"[35]

However, only one place in Scripture that I know of documents a natural disaster brought by Satan to inflict suffering—i.e., the wind and a lightning storm. Job 1:19 records that "when suddenly a mighty wind swept in from the desert and struck the four corners of the house. It collapsed on them and they are dead . . . ." And in Job 1:16 "the fire of God fell from the sky and burned up the sheep and the servants . . . ." But this was only done by Satan with God's permission (Job 1:12).

Nowhere else in Scripture is there a hint of demonic causality or metaphysical dualism in the physical creation or in natural disasters. In fact, this causality notion is similar to the Gnostic dualism that was fought against by the early Church. Gnostics also viewed our physical world as ugly, fallen, and contaminated with sin.

Notably, however, the Psalmists didn't view our world in that way. Neither did Jesus, or Paul, or any New Testament writer. Rather, they taught that the creation is glorious and reveals God's glory. And if we look at how creation works (stars in the sky, birds of the field, lilies of the valley, how rock badgers gather their food, how the ant works – for examples see Proverbs, etc.) we see the glory and goodness and creativity of God, and not a "broken" and "fallen" physical creation and universe.

But if creation (the natural realm) was indeed metaphysically altered or its mechanisms reprogrammed, corrupted, and made unholy by Satan and his demonic cohorts, how did they manage to change the nature of tectonic plates, the ground, weather, and plants and animals and how all this operates? Was this also when the law of thermodynamics (entropy) was introduced? I must again reassert that these notions are more than the Scriptures themselves reveal. No scripture lends any support to the theory that the physical creation is other than good, except perhaps Romans 8:19-22 and how it is interpreted and understood.

Furthermore, the idea of Satan and fallen angels being in charge of the natural world or different aspects of nature, the earth's crust or tectonic plates, etc. (like the gods of ancient Greece) or that they could corrupt and pervert nature presents the same problem as with human sin

---

[35] Billy Graham, "My Answer," *The Indianapolis Star* (Indianapolis, IN), 17 February 2010, C-13.

doing this. They no more have this capability than do we humans. Only God can change the nature of his creation. Or He can allow, assign, and empower someone else, as a secondary agent, to do it on an ad hoc basis. But that still makes God ultimately responsible as the First Cause, does it not? And as we've seen, his angels are in charge of the four winds and brought down fire on Sodom and Gomorra.

... Satan and his demonic cohorts, how did they manage to change the nature of tectonic plates, the ground, weather, and plants and animals and how all this operates?

Rightly, Hick terms this notion "a speculation." But he also recognizes that it "has its attractions." Therefore, he warns that this speculation "would lead to a gnostic rejection of the natural order as evil." Rather, he finds: "for the most part mankind has found it to be otherwise and our minstrels, the poets of all ages, have celebrated the goodness of the earth, the bountifulness of nature, and the infinite delights and ever-changing beauties of earth's seasons. Both Jewish and Christian poets have been in the forefront of this celebration, directing it upwards in gratitude to God." Next, he circumspectly asks: "Are we, then, to split the seamless coat of nature and say that the lilies of the field, together with rich harvests and beautiful sunsets, are ruled by good spirits, whilst diseases, earthquakes and storms are produced by evil spirits? This would indeed be a desperate expedient. For all that the sciences teach us about the workings of nature tends to emphasize its unity as a single system of cause and effect exhibiting the same laws throughout."[36]

What is more, Scripture tells us that both good and bad weather comes from God (Jonah 1:12; Psa. 147:18; Job 37:13; Amos 4:6-7, 9; Matthew 5:45). Alcorn is also right on when he retorts that "those who argue that God has given the operation of the world over to Satan contradict these passages."[37]

---

[36] Hick, *Evil and the Love of God*, 332-333.
[37] Alcorn, *If God Is Good*, 86.

Therefore, Hick concludes that "all harsh features of the world, which we call natural evil, are integral to its being an environment in which a morally and spiritually immature creature can begin to grow towards his perfection"[38] (one of the topics in our next chapter).

Even Evans admits that "Scripture gives no indication that every atrocity that results from the natural order is caused by the misuse of free will by either human or demons." Yet he reverts to his human sin position "that some unknown quantity of suffering that is usually described as resulting from natural causes may have a non-natural explanation for its coming about, and these instances are more evidence of the moral problem, rather than a natural problem, of evil. . . . So even if there is no explanation for how free will is involved in a hurricane, sin is an explanation for every calamity that is an affront to human well-being."[39]

Alcorn both insists and relents that: while "Satan may bring about a natural disaster . . . the book of Job makes clear that God continues to reign, even while selectively allowing Satan to do evil things. Satan knew he didn't have the authority to incite humans to do evil, to bring down lightning to cause fires, or to send the wind to blow down a building and take lives *without God's explicit permission.* We should know this too."[40]

The bottom line for me is, I see nothing in Scripture that would suggest that anything in creation changed at such a fundamental level as tectonic plates, weather patterns, etc. immediately after the Fall other than perhaps "thorns and thistles," and man to labor and toil to get the ground to produce its yield—more on this later in the chapter.

Perhaps, however, the real reason our physical world has been perceived as "fallen" and "broken" is because that is the way God created it from the beginning. Perhaps, as Dembski speculated above, the Garden of Eden may have been a special and unique place within it. But the whole world wasn't this garden or a garden. The rest of the world into which Adam and Eve were cast was different and subject to thorns the thistles, life and death—just the way God created it. And there they would have to toil and "be fruitful, multiply, and replenish the earth,

---

[38] Hick, *Evil and the Love of God,* 369.
[39] Evans, *The Problem of Evil,* 115-116.
[40] Alcorn, *If God Is Good,* 88.

increase in number, and work to produce a "garden-like" nature as they gradually brought the world more and more under their control.

Also, the Bible doesn't say that pre-Fall animals were vegetarians or that plants and animals – even bugs and ants – were immortal or weather was perfect. Contentions such as these are difficult to prove from Scripture. Sad to say, we have added many such ideas and brought them into the church via the traditions of men that make the word of God of little or no effect (see Matt. 15:6; Mark 7:13).

Critical Objection: To "prove" the evil nature of God's post-Fall creation and Satan's primary responsibility, Boyd cites the poetic section of Isaiah 11:6-9 as a proof text, and takes literally the wolf living with the lamb, the leopard lying down with the kid, the lion eating with the ox, the child playing over the hole of the asp and handling adders (highly poisonous snakes). He then feebly deduces that "this passage suggests that when nature is brought [back] into perfect alignment with God's will—that is, when it is 'full of the knowledge of the LORD'—there will be no violence in it."[41]

Not surprisingly, Boyd then labels as "inadequate" all theodicies that "attempt to explain 'natural' evil by identifying a purpose that the Creator has for it. That is, it contributes to the beauty of the whole, it punishes sinners, it builds our character, or it participates in God's suffering, self-sacrificial love."[42] The bottom line for Boyd is, "it fails to explain how the Bible can offer us hope that someday the creation shall be set free of 'natural' evil."[43]

Consequently, Boyd asserts: "this . . . is the perspective that best explains the viciousness of nature and the perspective most consistent with the perspective of Jesus and the New Testament. . . . Jesus never attributed genetic mutations, deformities, blindness, deafness, leprosy, blood diseases, fevers, falling towers, barren trees, life-threatening storms or death itself to God's providence or to 'natural' features of his Father's creation. He consistently identifies them as evidence of the reign of the kingdom of darkness here on earth, a kingdom that his [Jesus'] whole ministry was intended to destroy."[44] Then he offers up this

---

[41] Boyd, *Satan and the Problem of Evil*, 266.
[42] Ibid., 269-270.
[43] Ibid., 280.
[44] Ibid., 292.

futuristic eschatological deferment statement about "Scripture's promise that nature will not manifest these features in the kingdom of God. . . . It is Scripture . . . that suggests that these features are not inherent features of God's creation."[45]

Finally, he adds that "throughout his ministry Jesus opposed all infirmities and diseases as things that God does not will. Never once did he ascribe these things to his Father's will. Never once did he encourage people to find comfort in the notion that these things were part of God's plan. Rather, infirmities and diseases were consistently rebuked as the result of Satan's activity, which is why Jesus and his disciples always delivered people from them."[46]

My Response: Oh really? But Boyd's contentions above are part and parcel of the appeal of "fantasy Christianity," which we discussed in Chapter 1 pp. 33-48. Here are two brief retorts. First, just because Jesus demonstrated his command over nature by calming the storm via rebuking the wind and waves doesn't mean that bad weather is evil or demonically controlled (Matt. 8:23-26; Mark 4:39), any more than Jesus cursing the fig tree meant that tree was evil (Matt. 21:18-21; Mark 11:12-13, 20-23). Secondly, regarding Boyd's "never once" assertion above, when Jesus' disciples questioned Him about a man born blind and the relationship between sin and suffering, Jesus responded, "Neither this man nor his parents sinned, said Jesus, but this happened so that the work of God might be displayed in his life" (John 9:3). Who, then, do you think created that man blind?

Simply Mechanistic Laws of Nature

In an article titled, "3 Reasons Bad Things Happen to Good People: 'Why doesn't God stop earthquakes and genocides?,'" Rabbi Daniel Lapin believes "the answer is that God avoids interfering in nature's laws, as He set them up" and cites "the laws of gravity" as his example.[47]

---

[45] Ibid., 306.
[46] Ibid., 397.
[47] Rabbi Daniel Lapin, "3 Reasons Bad Things Happen to Good People: 'Why doesn't God stop earthquakes and genocides?'" *Whistleblower* December 2013, 38.

Knoch simply observes: "nature and natural laws. They operate without fail or favor for either saint or sinner. The just and the unjust are often engulfed in the same doom."[48]

Likewise, Evans takes this neutral position that the disastrous events in nature "are not in themselves considered to be evil but take on the label of being evil when they cause human or animal suffering." Thus, "nature" is "an impersonal force [that] does not commit evil." Of course, human moral evil can also produce natural disasters and evil, so-to-speak, such as starting forest fires. On the other hand, "there are violent, natural states of affairs that never affect any human in any negative way . . . ."[49] So Evans defines "natural evil" as being "evil resulting solely or chiefly from the operation of the laws of nature. Alternatively, and perhaps more precisely, an evil will be deemed a natural evil only if no non-divine agent can be held morally responsible for its occurrence."[50]

Keller as well seems to support this concept and adds that "without natural laws, life is impossible, but suffering is then inevitable. The natural evils that hurt so much are the by-products of something that brings us even greater good."[51]

D'Souza further affirms that our Creator God created a world and universe filled with "discoverable and predictable laws." But he then challenges us to: "imagine . . . living in a world where events are truly random, unpredictable, and indescribable through laws. Obviously, science would become impossible and so would most of modern technology. Moreover, freedom would lose most of its moral significance. Certainly virtue and vice would become meaningless in a world where actions don't have foreseeable consequences. . . . Thus . . . God creates for man an independent, lawful universe. . . . Natural suffering is part of this universe. . . . as the unavoidable consequence of a lawful world inhabited by free, conscious creatures like us."[52]

Pink, however, characterizes this notion of "(impersonal and abstract) 'laws of nature'" as "the Creator [being] banished from His

---

[48] Knoch, *The Problem of Evil and the Judgments of God*, 229.
[49] Evans, *The Problem of Evil*, 4-5.
[50] Ibid., 116.
[51] Keller, *Walking with God through Pain and Suffering*, 94.
[52] D'Souza, *Godforsaken*, 111, 176.

own creation."[53] Keller rightly categorizes it as "the idea of Deism . . .
that God created the world for our benefit and now it operates on its own,
without his constant or direct involvement. This world works like a clock
and can be understood scientifically, without any need for divine
revelation."[54] This is also the mechanistic "view [that] has resurfaced
today in the writings of scientific materialists . . . ."[55]

Dembski cites this same mechanistic belief from another theologian
who also believes that "nature does result entirely from the capacities
that God has given it."[56] But, once again, doesn't this admission still
make God the One ultimately responsible? Dembski, however, disputes
this premise by charging that "invoking the freedom of nature does little
to answer the worries raised by such evils." He then rhetorically asks this
series of intriguing questions: "Was the Lisbon or Haiti earthquake really
nothing more than a consequence of the freedom of the earth's crust?
How does such an answer comfort the victims and survivors? Why . . .
didn't God simply place us on a less dangerous planet where earthquakes
don't ravage human life? Or was this not an option for the Creator, and if
not, why not? What are we to make of divine providence in a world with
the freedom to crush us? Why, in most classical liturgies of the Christian
churches, do we pray for favorable seasons and good crops if the
freedom of nature means that the land is going to do whatever it will
regardless of our wishes? Or does God constrain the freedom of nature?
But, if so, why doesn't God place tighter constraints on this freedom in
relation to evil?"[57]

So the issue remains. Is "evil inherent in the [post-Fall] structure of
creation . . . [as] nature's potential for blessing is balanced by an equal
capacity to curse," as Boyd suggests?[58] Or is it simply impersonal and
mechanistic? "To be sure," Boyd continues, "creation *does* display
remarkable purposiveness and design, enough to proclaim the wisdom of
a grand designer (Rom. 1:20). But it also displays the antithesis of

---

[53] Pink, *The Sovereignty of God*, 8.

[54] Keller, *Walking with God through Pain and Suffering*, 54.

[55] Ibid., 134.

[56] William Dembski, "Evil, Creation and Intelligent Design" in Meister and
Dew, Jr., eds., *God and Evil*, 266.

[57] Ibid., 267.

[58] Boyd, *Satan and the Problem of Evil*, 243.

unified purposiveness and design."[59] Consequently, he is forced to conclude in a traditional manner that "nature in its present state, I believe, is not as the Creator created it to be, any more than humanity in its present state is as the Creator created it to be."[60] Again, who's right?

Not surprisingly, Boyd struggles with the confounding confusion that "it is not clear what the word *good* means if it is used to describe the 'design' that orchestrates such things as killer diseases, mudslides that bury children alive or typhoons that drown thousands. If such things are in any sense good, what does evil look like? If such things are the work of a loving and all-good God, what would the work of a hateful devil look like?"[61]

In Boyd's view, "God created the world such that when morally responsible agents fall, everything they are morally responsible for will become adversely affected. . . . Thus, there is no contradiction in saying that God cursed the earth because of Adam's sin and that Satan and his legions also plague the earth because of Adam's sin. . . . they twisted the laws of nature governing the cosmos in a destructive direction. . . . Nature became hostile, creatures became vicious, and the whole planet became subject to God's enemy and was no longer fit for the purposes for which it was originally created. . . . In short, Satan and his legions are directly or indirectly behind all forms of 'natural' evil."[62]

Critical Objection: This objection to the above is quoted by Boyd himself from a critic of his trinitarian warfare theodicy. It "is overly speculative . . . . Scripture does not pay that much attention to these invisible agents and does not explicitly give them the authority the trinitarian warfare theodicy gives them."[63]

Boyd's Response: "I agree that the trinitarian warfare theodicy is speculative, but I deny that it is *overly* speculative. It is no more speculative than any other theodicy one might suggest. . . . all theodices inevitably go beyond Scripture insofar as they attempt to resolve certain intellectual problems that Scripture does not resolve. . . . I argue that . . . it not only is consistent with Scripture; it reconciles the scriptural portrait

---

[59] Ibid., 245.
[60] Ibid., 247.
[61] Ibid., 249-250
[62] Ibid., 313-314, 318.
[63] Ibid., 372.

of our loving Father with our experience of horrific evil. . . . Scripture tells us that God accepted the full consequences of our rebellion."[64]

My Response: I agree with Alcorn on this issue. "The Bible never speaks of nature as an impersonal mechanism. Nature does not govern the universe; God does."[65] And Jeffress puts this issue in a proper biblical perspective by affirming that: "natural forces do not hold our supernatural God hostage. One can only imagine how many laws of physics and biology were violated by the parting of the Red Sea, the virgin birth of Christ, the feeding of the five thousand, and the resurrection of Christ from the dead."[66]

Furthermore, I believe the theodicy we are presenting in this book—that God in his sovereignty foreordained, planned, created, implemented, and sustains everything in our world, including evil—is more true to Scripture than Boyd's or many other theodicies I've come across. If correct, then God created the whole universe and this world to function just the way it has and still does today.

Notwithstanding, of course, the fact that God did curse the ground at the Fall (Gen. 3:17-19). But how much of our planet was affected by that curse? In other words, how deep down into the ground did that curse go—to the tectonic plates and molten core levels? The answer is, no. The extent of this passage's curse on the ground only speaks of "thorns and thistles," "painful toil" in order to eat, and "to dust you will return." That's only speaking of surface level. Yet God Himself declares: "the whole earth is mine" (Exod. 19:5b) and "the earth is the LORD's and everything in it" (Psa. 24:1a). That would certainly include tectonic plates and molten core levels, would it not? Also, weather patterns are not mentioned in this curse at all. Truly, truly how much of the physical creation was "lost" in the Fall?

In actuality, our planet functions with incredible durability and adaptability. For instance, the oil that was dumped in the Gulf of Mexico a few years ago. Gone. Remember, Bikini in the Marshall Islands? It has recovered rather nicely after twenty-three nuclear explosions in the 1940s and 1950s. Even Jupiter seems to be surviving rather well after massive, multi-comet crashes in 1994. Our earth (what some call

---

[64] Ibid., 372-373, 391.

[65] Alcorn, *If God Is Good*, 86.

[66] Jeffress, *Hell Yes*, 53.

"nature") has a way of cleaning up itself. I believe it was created from the beginning with this "very good" capability (Gen. 1:31).

Similarly but shockingly for some, in an article titled, "The good side of disasters," Dennis McCafferty acknowledges that while "Mother Nature can be devastating . . . natural disasters serve valid purposes, scientists say. Without them, our Earth wouldn't resemble its current state, and we'd lose some of our most precious resources." He lists "a wide range of productive, even needed contributions made possible by wildfires, earthquakes, hurricanes and other disasters." Here's a highlighted recap:

<u>Wildfires:</u> "The truth is without wildfires, our forests would have a difficult time existing. . . . Periodic fires keep the dead material from accumulating and remove the ladder fuels. . . . also pump nutrients into the forest soil. . . . and they're crucial for plant growth."

<u>Volcanoes:</u> ". . . are responsible for the existence of places like the Hawaiian Islands, the Galápagos and Iceland. More volcanic activity occurs underwater than on the Earth's surface, and eruptions can provide the foundation for eventual landmasses. And much of what these volcanoes transport is 'good stuff' that helps civilizations to survive, with heat and gases from magma beneath volcanoes forming deposits of lead, zinc, silver and gold. As decades pass, volcanic ash falling on the surrounding ground creates fertile soil for crops."

<u>Landslides:</u> "Like earthquakes, landslides serve an aesthetic purpose. Without them, gorgeous outcroppings such as those along the South's Blue Ridge Parkway wouldn't exist. Landslides also create habitats in streams, which allow fish to thrive."

<u>Hurricanes:</u> "Wetlands can be destroyed by hurricanes, but they also can benefit from them because the storms import good dirt. Flooding from the sea brings sediment that can nourish the marsh vegetation, while adding a protective element by building the land higher."

<u>Earthquakes:</u> "A great deal of our fuel resources are made possible by the same forces that cause quakes. Miles underground, hydrocarbons are making oil and gas trapped underground. Picture these underground areas as a large carpet. Without quakes, this carpet is relatively flat, its valuable oils and gasses spread far and wide. When tectonic plates collide, however, causing the earth to rumble, the carpet bends into folds, trapping those fuels in the tops of the folds and making the drilling process possible. . . . And earthquakes create much of the

natural beauty we value. Over time, they move the earth and pave the way for mountains and other landscapes."

McCafferty concludes that "extreme events are the price we pay for living on a dynamic planet. . . . over time they've split continents, formed great ocean basis and built mountains. . . . So earthquakes are still a potential hazard . . . but its mountains are the reward."[67]

Rushdoony offers this additional benefit for the presence of weeds, or what the Bible terms as "thorns and thistles" (Gen. 3:18). "Weeds have their place in God's plan, in that they penetrate deep into the subsoil and bring necessary minerals to the top soil. To treat weeds simply as an enemy rather than as a God-given ally is to despise creation. Weeds have rightly been called 'guardians of the soil' for their restorative work."[68] Hence, he advises that "*First*, the world is not an enemy, nor a hostile element, but is God's handiwork and man's destined area of dominion under God. Man therefore must work in harmony with creation, not attack it as an alien and hostile force. *Second*, although the world is by nature essentially good, it is all the same a fallen world. To ascribe perfection to it, and to assume that the 'natural' way is the perfect way is not Christian but humanistic. Because the world is fallen, and the ground itself under a curse . . . what is natural is not therefore of necessity good. Man has a restorational and healing work to do. . . . He must respect the basic pattern of creation and work within its framework."[69]

Likewise, Yancey observes that "the tectonic forces that proved so destructive in 2011, however, are the same ones that formed the islands of Japan in the first place. The hurricanes and cyclones that wreak such havoc are essential to the weather systems that spread moisture across the globe." And yet he still sees our world in a traditional manner as "'in process' – flawed, incomplete, imperfect."[70]

As a quick aside, irresponsible building in earthquake- or hurricane-prone areas exaggerates the potential for disaster. *USA TODAY*, in an

---

[67] Dennis McCafferty, "The good side of disasters," *USA Weekend*, 20-22 February 2009, 6-7.
[68] Rushdooney, *The Institutes of Biblical Law*, 261 – in quotation of Joseph A. Cocannouer, *Weeds, Guardians of the Soil* (New York, NY: Devin-Adair, 1964). n.p.
[69] Ibid., 262.
[70] Yancey, *The Question That Never Goes Away*, 45-46.

article titled, "IT WON'T SURVIVE," states that: "Experts say a major hurricane could devastate Miami, which because of a lack of investment is a sitting duck," for "a massive surge of water like those produced by Hurricane Katrina or Superstorm Sandy." It further cites Miami and New York City as "the most vulnerable in the USA the next time a hurricane packing a high storm surge roars through."[71]

"extreme events are the price we pay for living on a dynamic planet. . . . over time they've split continents, formed great ocean basis and built mountains. . . . So earthquakes are still a potential hazard . . . but its mountains are the reward."

On the other hand, Giberson and Collins explain the so-called "freedom" of natural laws this way. "God created the world with an inbuilt capacity to explore novelty and try new things, but within a framework of overall regularity. This is the way the world is."[72] Hence, "God is off the hook. Unless God micromanages nature so as to destroy its autonomy, such things are going to occur." They then make this comparison. "Likewise, unless God coercively micromanages human decision making, we will often abuse our freedom."[73] Hence, "physical evil is the necessary accompaniment of [a] structured world."[74]

"Perhaps," they further contend, "this is actually the very best way to create a world that is interesting and meaningful like this one. Bland worlds without the possibility of disasters were, in Leibniz's view, inferior to this world. . . . the same forces that produce a life-sustaining planet, including the laws of physics, chemistry, weather and tectonics, can also produce natural disasters. As with the free will of humans, God cannot constantly intervene in these areas without disrupting the inherent

---

[71] Alan Gomez, "It Won't Survive," *USA Today*, in *The Indianapolis Star*, 10.18.14, B-1-2.
[72] Giberson and Collins, "Evil, Creation and Evolution" in Meister and Dew, Jr., eds., *God and Evil*, 279.
[73] Ibid., 280.
[74] Ibid., 281 – in quotation of Frederick Robert Tennant.

freedom of the creation and disrupting his consistent sustaining of all the matter and energy in the universe. Without this consistency, science would be impossible, moral choices would be subverted and the world would not be as rich with meaning and opportunity."[75]

Critical Objections: Sproul opposes this mechanistic view arguing that "in our age, we have a tendency to view nature as functioning independently from any governance or rule by God."[76] But Sproul insists that "God in His providence is a sovereign God, who not only governs nature and the laws of nature but who raises nations up and brings nations low."[77]

Pink agrees with Sproul and objects to these so-called "laws of nature" in that they "deny that God is governing matter, deny that He is 'upholding all things by the word of His power' (Heb. 1:3), and all sense of security is gone!"[78] Rather Pink maintains that "God governs inanimate matter, that inanimate matter performs His bidding and fulfils His decrees" and that this governance "is clearly shown on the frontispiece of Divine revelation . . . . in Genesis one."[79] That "God governs" the animal kingdom, as well as "the angels . . . . and men."[80]

He also notes that "a very superficial observation of 'the laws of Nature' reveals the fact that they are not uniform in their working. The proof of this is seen in the fact that no two seasons are alike."[81]

Hence, Pink submits that "while . . . the material world appears to be governed by laws that are stable and more or less uniform in their operations, yet Scriptures, history, and observation compel us to recognize the fact that God suspends these laws and acts apart from them whenever it pleaseth Him to do so. In sending His blessings or judgments upon His creatures He may cause the sun itself to stand still, and the stars in their courses to fight for His people (Judges 5:20). He may send or withhold 'the early and the latter rains' according to the dictates of His own infinite wisdom; He may smite with plague or bless with health; in

---

[75] Ibid., 282.
[76] Sproul, *When World Collide*, 22.
[77] Ibid., 30.
[78] Pink, *The Sovereignty of God*, 27.
[79] Ibid., 28.
[80] Ibid., 31-34.
[81] Ibid., 26.

short, being God, being absolute Sovereign, He is bound and tied by no laws of Nature, but governs the material world as seemeth Him best."[82]

Sproul, Jr. simply puts it like a friend of his told him: "the universe cannot contain both a sovereign God and 'one maverick molecule,' one small speck outside of God's control" and "nature itself communicates God's sovereign control over all things (Rom. 1:20)."[83]

The bottom line for Swinburne is, the "God who is so much more the source of our being than are our parents" has chosen "the laws of nature under which we live."[84]

Other Causes

DeWeese cites "chaos systems . . . to help us understand why the world is such that natural evils occur . . . [and] make natural evil possible." Hence, "wildly erratic systems in the natural world cause natural evil." Consequently, he believes "that even God cannot make such a world where natural evil never occurs."[85] He elaborates that "our world is made up of a vast number of interacting chaos systems" and that "the past five decades have seen tremendous progress in discovering, analyzing and understanding chaos systems. Weather patterns, of course, are chaos systems, but so are many other phenomena in the world"[86] Also "plate tectonics causes earthquakes, and tsunamis, and unleashes volcanic fury, destroying forests and cities. And on and on. Our world of interacting chaos systems is a much wilder, more disorderly place than was long thought."

As physical proof that we live in this type of "a dynamic world" and that it "is better than a static world,"[87] DeWeese offers up this evidence: "trees and ferns, snowflakes and clouds, shorelines and faces would all be predictable, with perhaps only a small number of variations within

---

[82] Ibid., 90.
[83] Sproul, Jr., *Almighty Over All*, 91.
[84] Swinburne, *Providence and the Problem of Evil*, 230.
[85] DeWeese, "Natural Evil: A 'Free Process' Defense" in Meister and Dew, Jr., eds., *God and Evil*, 55.
[86] Ibid., 57.
[87] Ibid., 58.

well-defined limits. . . . Surely our world is much more interesting and beautiful as a result."[88]

". . . we have a tendency to view nature as functioning independently from any governance or rule by God."

For theological support, DeWeese relies on "Genesis 1 God bringing order out of the chaos of verse 2, and then in Genesis 1:28 and 2:15, assigning to humanity the duty to exercise responsible stewardship of the earth." He claims that "those commands imply that humans can indeed affect the natural world, so the world must be a dynamical one that will respond to human activity."[89]

He concludes that "even God cannot make a dynamic world in which natural evil could not occur."[90] But he points out that "both human and demonic agents can cause natural free processes to become chaotic in behavior. To the degree that this is so, the resultant 'natural' evil would be moral evil after all."[91] Thus, we "must allow for some sort of interaction between the material realm and the immaterial."[92]

Does Anybody Really Know?

Rabbi Lapin reports but laments that "the most common answer is that it is hopeless for us to try to understand God's mysterious ways."[93]

Graham concurs. To a reader's question, "Are natural disasters sometimes an instrument of God's judgment?" he responds: "God certainly can use natural disasters to speak to us, just as he can use other

---

[88] Ibid., 59.
[89] Ibid., 59-60.
[90] Ibid., 61.
[91] Ibid., 62.
[92] Ibid., 63.
[93] Rabbi Lapin, "3 Reasons Bad Things Happen to Good People," 38.

difficulties and tragedies to turn our hearts toward him. . . .[But] we don't know why God allows natural disasters to occur."[94]

Critical Objection: William Hendriksen disagrees. As part of his discussion of the first four trumpets judgments of Revelation 8:7-13 that result in "a storm of hail and fire" and which burns up "the third part of the earth, the third part of the trees and all the green grass," he claims "that these calamities, of whatever nature they be, are controlled in heaven, and in a certain organic sense are sent by our governing Lord is clearly indicated by the clause 'they were cast upon the earth.'" Regarding the second trumpet, he states that God "also employs the *sea* as a tool . . . . [of] maritime calamities."[95]

Likewise, David Chilton believes that "we need a theological interpretation of disaster, one that recognizes that God acts in such events as captivities, defeats, and crucifixions." Hence, he asserts that "the Bible can be interpreted as a string of God's triumphs disguised as disasters."[96] Concerning natural events, Chilton emphatically states:

> . . . the association of angels with 'nature' is not 'mere' imagery. God through His angels really does control weather patterns, and He uses weather as an agency of blessing and judgment. . . . God did not create a self-sustaining universe which is now left to operate in terms of autonomous laws of nature. The universe is not a giant mechanism, like a clock, which God wound up at the beginning of time. Ours is not a mechanistic world, nor is it an autonomous biological entity, growing according to some genetic code of the cosmos. Ours is a world which is actively sustained by God on a full-time basis (Job 38-41). All creation is inescapably *personal* and *theocentric*. . . . (Rom. 1:20). If the universe is inescapably personal, then there can be no phenomenon or event in the creation which is independent from God. . . . Nothing in the universe is *autonomous*. . . . Nothing in the creation generates its own conditions of existence, including the law structure under which

---

[94] Billy Graham, "My Answer," *The Indianapolis Star* (Indianapolis, IN), 19 January 2010, C-5.

[95] William Hendriksen, *More Than Conquerors* (Grand Rapids, MI: Baker Book House, 1982, 1940), 118.

[96] David Chilton, *The Days of Vengeance* (Ft. Worth, TX: Dominion Press, 1987), 284 – in quotation of Herbert Schlossberg, *Idols for Destruction: Christian Faith and Its Confrontation with American Society* (Nashville., TN: Thomas Nelson Publishers, 1983), 304.

something operates or is operated upon. Every fact in the universe, from beginning to end, is exhaustively interpreted by God in terms of His being, plan, and power."[97]

Likewise, Jill Graper Hernandez is forced to agree that "because only God could prevent natural disasters and the suffering that results from them. . . . physical evil seems to come directly from God."[98]

Boyd takes a lesser position in writing that God could have "designed an exhaustively predetermined world, devoid of chance and challenges. Instead, the sovereign God wisely, courageously and lovingly chose the risky cosmos we find ourselves in. . . . things do not always go as God would desire. . . . Hence God chose to create this world rather than the safer but uninteresting world of predestined puppets."[99]

But Grudem clings with the "fantasy Christianity" tradition. Regarding Romans 8:19-23, he writes: "In this renewed creation, there will be no more thorns or thistles, no more floods or droughts, no more deserts or uninhabitable jungles, no more earthquakes or tornadoes, no more poisonous snakes or bees that sting or mushrooms that kill. There will be a productive earth, an earth that will blossom and produce food abundantly for our enjoyment."[100]

Perhaps, however, what Grudem and so many others are looking for someday has already been provided in Christ as the prophet Isaiah proclaimed long ago: "The LORD will surely comfort Zion and will look with compassion on all her ruins; he will make her deserts **like Eden**, her wastelands like **the garden of the LORD**. Joy and gladness will be found in her, thanksgiving and the sound of singing" (Isa. 51:3 – bold emphasis mine). For a statement by Jesus contextualizing and encompassing this prophecy's past fulfillment, see Luke 21:20-22.

---

[97] Ibid., 204 – in quotation of *The Dominion Covenant: Genesis* (Tyler, TX: Institute for Christian Economics, 1982), 1-2, 425-54.
[98] Hernandez, "Leibniz and the Best of All Possible Worlds" in Meister and Dew, Jr., eds., *God and Evil*, 104.
[99] Boyd, *Satan and the Problem of Evil*, 392.
[100] Grudem, *Systematic Theology*, 836.

Wise Advice

The testimony of Scripture is that God was the First Cause Who created both good and evil and placed them in our world. And while He also creates evil, as He has told us, He also allows others to manifest it. Therefore, we must stay open to these revelations from his Word and realize that God can use any means He wants (and has) to send and manifest evil: directly from Him and/or through angels, people, animals, or nature.

In an article in *Christianity Today* appropriately titled "The Fear That Draws Us: What Happens When We Really Grasp That God Is Almighty," Mark Galli draws these insightful perspectives about spectacular mountains regions of our world: "When we go to places like Glacier Point, we find ourselves attracted to the very thing that makes us afraid. And rather than running from it, we want to get closer, at least as close as we can without getting killed."[101]

My Response: Seriously, the massive power that it took to shove the mountains high into the sky, sweep away the massive granite slabs and blocks from the valleys, and split others in half in locations all around the world and under the seas—was that evil-caused, human sin-caused, chaos-caused, or God-caused? Then why claim otherwise today when relatively minor events of this nature still occur?

Also insightfully, John Hick cites this particular purpose for natural evil being in our world: "The very mystery of natural evil, the very fact that disasters afflict human beings in contingent, undirected and haphazard ways, is itself a necessary feature of a world that calls forth mutual aid and builds up mutual caring and love."[102]

Dr. Graham offers this bit of advice. "We must be very cautious about saying that God judged a nation's sin by causing a specific disaster to take place – because we simply don't know."[103]

---

[101] Mark Galli, "The Fear That Draws Us," *Christianity Today*, November 2013, 46-49.

[102] John Hick, "An Irenaean Theodicy," *Encountering Evil*, ed. Stephen T. David (Louisville, KY: Westminster John Knox, 2001), 50.

[103] Billy Graham, "My Answer," *The Indianapolis Star* (Indianapolis, IN), 16 November 2010, E-4.

For me, however, the bottom line is this. Since we cannot rule out the possibility that any particular natural disaster was or was not an act of judgment from God, and because Scripture informs us that "God does bring calamities from time to time upon nations as acts of judgment;"[104] we should not jump to conclusions. As Sproul wisely advises, we must not forget that, "the error of the disciples and the error of Job's friends was assuming that in *every* situation there is a direct correlation between sin and judgment. This is refuted by Jesus' teaching in John 9 and by the entire book of Job." Also, "what was Paul's sin that caused him to have a 'thorn in the flesh' (2 Cor. 12:7)? That thorn was given to him for his own sanctification, to manifest the goodness of God, so that Paul would rely constantly on divine grace (v. 9)." Therefore, Sproul concludes that "there are many reasons why God visits His people with what we call tragedy without its being a direct judgment on sin, though at times it is judgment." And yet humbly he concedes that "if asked why 9/11 happened, the only honest answer I can give is, 'I don't know.'"[105]

"because only God could prevent natural disasters and the suffering that results from them. . . . physical evil seems to come directly from God."

Lastly, philosopher Michael Peterson offers this poignant piece of advice. "God has designed a natural order to serve as an arena in which free human beings can respond to real dangers and challenges. 'Pointless' evils, though tragic, are a necessary part of that system. Hence, an evil could itself be pointless, which the natural order that permits it is not. . . . God may permit such evils to exist not *for* a greater good, but because of one."[106]

---

[104] Sproul, *When Worlds Collide*, 48.

[105] Ibid., 53-54.

[106] Alcorn, *If God Is Good*, 371 – in summary of philosopher Michael Peterson's position.

Has the Genesis 3 Curse Been Lifted—More Confusion?

Of course not, most Christians would answer. Then why do we Christians sing this third stanza from "Joy to the World" every Christmas season?

> No more let sins and sorrows grow
> Nor thorns infest the ground
> He comes to make
> His blessings flow
> Far as the curse is found
> Far as the curse is found
> Far as, far as the curse is found[107]

God's curse on the ground was an integral part of the Genesis 3:14-19 curse. And there are other curses (Gal. 3:10 – the curse of the law, also see Deut 27 and 28 and the curse of not tithing – Mal. 3:9).

Critical Objection: Doesn't the ground still bring forth thorns and thistles? Don't we still have to toil to grow plants and crops? Don't snakes still crawl on the ground, and isn't childbirth still painful? Moreover, look at the many deserts and soils around the world today that are still no good for anything. Even with our modern scientific advances with chemicals, fertilizers, insecticides, and preventatives, we still have a lot of hard work to do to make things grow. Hence, the battle against this curse still continues (also see Deut. 28:15-63). It will only be lifted when Jesus Christ returns, does final battle with sin, and the earth is restored to a garden paradise as Christ begins his 1,000-year reign (Rom. 8:19-22; Rev. 20:1-10).

My Response: Admittedly, this is the belief of many Christians. But is it scriptural? The nature of fulfillment of Christ's four "Did He fail" propositions (covered in Chapter 1, p. 37) should, at the least, give us a cause for pause before continuing to futurize this lifting.

But while many Christians, such as Alcorn, insist that today "natural disasters ordinarily are general results of the Curse,"[108] others are

---

[107] Peter Korbel, Issac N. Watts, "Joy to the World," third stanza.
[108] Alcorn, *If God Is Good*, 87.

claiming that the curse in totality has been lifted or, at the least, the antidote provided. Various scriptures are cited. So let's take look at them in chronological order and you decide.

Some say the curse expired with the death of Adam and birth of Noah. "He named him Noah and said, 'He will comfort us in the labor and painful toil of our hands caused by the ground the LORD has cursed'" (Gen. 5:29). Anderson believes that this "story implies, the curse on the ground was removed (see 5:29; also 3:17-19) and Noah himself was successful as a farmer."[109] But this verse does not say that God removed or will remove the Genesis 3 curse.

Others claim the flood was the curse of the ground. After the flood, God's promise that "Never again will I curse the ground because of man . . . . As long as the earth endures, [there would be] seedtime and harvest, cold and heat, summer and winter, day and night will never cease" (Gen. 8:21-22). That promise removed the curse. John Gill takes this position and writes in his Bible commentary (bold emphasis mine):

> I will not again curse the ground for man's sake, or drown it for the sin of man, as he [God] had cursed it for the sin of Adam, and which continued till this time; **but now was taken off**, and it became more fruitful, and very probably by means of the waters which had been so long upon it, and had left a fructifying virtue in it, as the waters of the Nile do in Egypt. Some interpret the phrase, "for man's sake," for the man Christ's sake, for the sake of his sacrifice, of which Noah's was a type, and the sense be, **that God would no more curse the earth;** for by his sacrifice the curse of the law is removed, with respect to his people; they are redeemed from it, and shall inherit that new earth, of which this earth, renewed after the flood, was a type, in which there will be **no more curse,** (Revelation 21:1) (22:3) . . . .[110]

Once again, however, these verses do not say that God removed the Genesis 3 curse. Another verse used to support the proposition that God's curse on the ground was apparently lifted after the flood is when "Lot looked up and saw that the whole plain of Jordan was well watered,

[109] Anderson, *Understanding the Old Testament*, 215.
[110] *John Gill's Exposition of the Entire Bible,*
http://www.biblestudytools.com/commentaries/gills-exposition-of-the-bible/genesis-8-21.html.

like the garden of the LORD, like the land of Egypt, toward Zoar" (Gen. 13:10).

Others cite the Hebrew meaning of the name of the mountain range on which Noah's ark came to rest—"the mountains of Ararat" (Gen. 8:4). "Ararat = the curse reversed; precipitation of curse."[111] Not surprisingly, this meaning is contested.[112]

But most adherents say this curse is only removed spiritually for those "in Christ" because of what Christ accomplished on our behalf on the cross, and in his resurrection, and ascension. Even futurist Grudem agrees that "the redemption of Christ is aimed at *removing* the results of sin and of the fall in every way."[113] Hence, our only disagreement here is the time factor for when "there shall be no more curse" (Rev. 22:3) at "the times of restitution of all things" or "time comes for God to restore everything" (Acts 3:21 – KJV / NIV), "the time of the new order" (Heb. 9:8-13; 8:13), and as a part of our "faith that was once for all delivered to the saints" (Jude 3). For me, I believe these verses speak of realities fulfilled circa A.D. 70. But most Christians have been told and believe that this fulfillment still awaits some yet-future millennial reign or the end of time. In the meantime, the Genesis 3 curse remains in effect.

Notwithstanding these differences, let's address how the complete, triple-faceted, Genesis curse possibly might have been lifted, removed, or the antidote provided "in Christ," circa A.D. 30 – 70. Of course, you may or may not agree with this type (the physical) and antitype (the spiritual) explanation. But please keep in mind that this explanation is in keeping with the nature of how Jesus fulfilled the four "Did He fail?" propositions of abolishing death, putting away sin, destroying the works of the devil, and removing the distinctions of "neither Jew nor Greek, slave nor free, male nor female, for you are all one in Christ Jesus" that we presented in Chapter 1, pp. 37-38. Also, this explanation would be considered part of our "faith that was once for all delivered to the saints"

---

[111] www.biblestudytools.com/lexicons/hebrew/nas/arart.html., 11/30/14. And, classic.netbible.org/dictionary.php?word=ARARAT, 11/30/14.

[112] "The word *ararat* is probably from a foreign language and it doesn't really mean anything in Hebrew" (www.abarim-publications.com/Meaning/Ararat.hlml#.BHt3nzHR_lA, 11/30/14.

[113] Grudem, *Systematic Theology*, 465.

(Jude 3), and past tense. See what you think as we dissect it, curse by verse:

The curse against the Serpent (crawl on your belly, eat dust, enmity between you and the woman, crush your head, you strike his heal – vss. 14-15). First, let's note that this portion of the Genesis curse was upon Satan and not upon all snakes—after all, snakes don't sin. Yes, all snakes literally crawl on their bellies, but no snake in the world literally eats dust. Rather, they suck eggs, and eat small animals and other snakes. (Side note: worms, however, both literally crawl on their bellies and eat dust.) Spiritually, however, Satan's crawling on his belly could signify his low-life status and his eating dust could mean that he seeks "someone to devour"—i.e., human beings and we humans are called "dust" in Scripture. Sound far out? Try comparing 1 Peter 5:8 with Genesis 3:19b.

Furthermore, the enmity was obviously between Satan and Jesus. Satan's strike was getting Jesus sent to the cross. In my view, the crushing of Satan involved not only Jesus' death, resurrection, and ascension, but also his cloud-coming in destruction and desolation of the Old Covenant system circa A.D. 70, the opening up of heaven, the resurrection of the dead ones, and the casting of the devil, death, and Hades into the lake of fire (Rev. 20:10, 14). However, being cast into the lake of fire does not necessarily render Satan inactive or ineffective.[114]

The curse against the woman (increased pains in childbirth, desire for your husband, he ruling over you – vs. 16): There is no childbirth pain in the spiritual second birth of being born again. Of course there may be pain for some in getting to the second birth, but not in the birth itself. And when this occurs, for both males and females, Jesus becomes your husband. He, then, is the One Who rules over you.

The curse against the ground and Adam/humankind (thorns and thistles, painful toil to eat of it, returning to dust [i.e., dying] – vss. 17-19): None of this curse spiritual applies whenever one inherits and enters the Holy City, the New Jerusalem, that's located in the new heaven and new earth, which came down to earth from heaven, back then and there (see Gal. 4:26; Rev. 21:1-10).[115] But this spiritual reality is only available

---

[114] See: Noē, *Hell Yes / Hell No*, 90-93. Also: Noē, *Unraveling the End* and Noē, *The Perfect Ending for the World.*

[115] For more, see: Noē, *The Greater Jesus*, 339-389; Noē, *The Perfect Ending for the World*, 279-319.

to enter for those believers here on earth who are overcomers (see Rev. 21:7 and 12:10-11). I further believe that this how we enter God's rest, here and now (Heb. 4:1-11). Hence, we are now "God's field" or last and ultimate garden (1 Cor. 3:9). And there is "no more curse" (Rev. 22:3 KJV). Thus, no more thorns and thistles in God's field or garden.

Lynn Hiles recognizes this New Covenant reality in writing, "God has removed from you the curse that brings forth thorns and thistles in your earth. Those things that have choked out the good seed of the Kingdom are removed by the redemptive work of Jesus Christ, who wore a crown of thorns as a symbol of earth's curse. He wore it there on His head because the place where we need His redemptive power is in our mind and thinking. . . . It is . . . coming into a revelation of the finished work of Jesus Christ . . . ."[116] Amen!

Additionally, those nations whose God is the Lord are promised land-produced blessings and more if they are obedient, or "a curse" if they aren't (see Mal. 3:8-12; 4:6b; Matt. 6:31-33). Rushdoony explains this spiritual/physical reality this way: "The ground is cursed because of man's sin (Gen. 3:17). The earth flourishes and is blessed as man is holy and obedient to the Lord; it is cursed and profane when man is disobedient (Deut. 28 . . . also in Isaiah 24. . . . when man forsakes his required dominion over the earth, the earth then gains a dominion of judgment over man. The earth is pictured as pursuing man vengefully as God's agent of destruction (Isa. 24:18). The cause of this is the Lord, who uses the earth as a means of judgment against man. . . . Scripture gives us one Lord, one covenant, one plan of salvation, and one law. . . . It is an everlasting covenant. It governs man, and it governs the earth."[117]

Therefore, "the Bible very plainly declares that there is a relationship between man's faithfulness and the earth's fertility. If men are lawless, the earth will by God's providence exact a judgment from man. . . . All things having been created by God therefore serve His purposes alone. . . . but, when they continue in sin and defile the earth (Isa. 24:5), then the heavens become as brass, and the earth as iron to those who despise the

[116] Lynn Hiles, *The Revelation of Jesus Christ* (Shippensburg, PA: Destiny Image Publishers, 2007), 107-108.
[117] Rousas John Rushdoony, *Law and Society* (Vallecito, CA: Ross House Books, 1986, 1982), 315, 317.

Lord and His law (Deut. 28:23-24). . . . Those who deny God's law will have the earth itself against them."[118]

No doubt, this is why the Psalmist proclaims that "the earth is the LORD's and the fulness thereof: the world and they that dwell therein." (Psa. 24:1; also see Exod. 19:5; Lev. 25:23).

Regarding the curse on work, Rushdoony recognizes work as being part of the original pre-Fall mandate "to subdue or work the earth, and to exercise dominion over it (Gen. 1:28)." But he adds these insights. Following "the fall came a curse on man's work, but work is not a curse. With redemption, the effects of sin are steadily overcome, as man works to restore the earth and to establish his dominion under God. . . . under the sixth commandment, man has a mandate to restore the earth by work and to inhibit and limit the injuring and killing effect of sin. . . . Work thus has a position of importance in Biblical thought. Proverbs repeatedly stresses its necessity, dignity, and importance: 'he that gathereth by labour shall increase' (Prov. 13:11; also 12:24; 13:4; 22:29). . . . Work thus has as its goal the restored kingdom of God; work therefore is a religious and moral necessity."[119]

Lastly, Rushdoony summarizes that "the purpose of curses is also restitution: the curse prevents the ungodly from overthrowing God's order."[120]

So what do you think? Do these spiritual explanations make sense to you? Do they possibly demonstrate how every single component of God's Genesis 3:14-19 curse was redeemed "in Christ," if we have eyes to see and ears to hear (see Matt. 11:15; 13:9, 13-16, 43; Rev. 2:7,17, 29; 3:6,13, 18, 22)? Do you?

From the Lips of Children (Matt. 21:16)

One day last year I was having a theological conversation with two of my thirteen grandchildren (which I do occasionally). They are quite bright and biblically astute for their age. First, I asked what they thought was the purpose for evil being in our world. Without hesitation,

---

[118] Ibid., 318, 320-321.
[119] Rushdoony, *The Institutes of Biblical Law*, 308-309.
[120] Ibid., 13.

Christian, age 9, blurted out, "It just makes people work harder." Then Elisabeth, age 10, responded, "It brings God more glory to know we have two choices."

One year later (as I'm completing the writing of this book), and during another theological discussion time with Elisabeth and her other brother, Eli, age 7, I asked them, what is sin? Elisabeth immediately replied that "sin is what you do after evil temps you . . . . Sin is the evil you commit." I followed up with this question. What is the difference between good and evil? Eli, not wanting to be out done by his sister, pounced on my question with this bit of wisdom: "Good is what God wants; evil is what Satan wants."

In our next chapter, we'll see just how close to being theologically spot on, their above answers truly are.

"the Bible very plainly declares that there is a relationship between man's faithfulness and the earth's fertility. If men are lawless, the earth will by God's providence exact a judgment from man. . . ."

Chapter 6

The Planned Purposes of Evil

"Every quest for some deeper insight or more ultimate answer leads inescapably into dead-end speculations."[1]

N o subject throughout the history of all religious thought has been so difficult to deal with as the idea that there is a divine purpose or purposes for evil in our world. Sensitive Christians, especially, have reacted with horror at the mere suggestion that a loving Creator God even allows humans and animals to suffer some horrendous things—not to mention the biblically revealed facts that He both created evil in the first place and continues to create and send some of it even today.

Not surprisingly, the vast majority of scholars and theologians have described the intended purpose or purposes of evil as being "unknowable," "not soluble," "illogical," "inexplicable," "no answer," "a mystery," "doesn't make sense," "a by-product of freedom," "hidden," "not explained," "no general explanation," "beyond our capacity to understand," etc. Moreover, they warn that Scripture itself admonishes us not to try and comprehend the reasons God may have had for any instance of evil, pain, and suffering. In support of their position, they quote verses such as:

---

[1] Spykman, *Reformational Theology*, 303.

- "For my thoughts are not your thoughts, and your ways are not my ways. . . . For as the heavens are higher than the earth, so are my ways higher than your ways and my thoughts than your thoughts" (Isa. 55:8-9).
- "The secret things belong to the LORD our God." Unfortunately, many stop quoting halfway through this verse. The second half goes on to proclaim: "but the things revealed belong to us and to our children forever, that we may follow all the words of this law" (Duet. 29:29).
- "Oh, the depth of the riches of the wisdom and knowledge of God! How unsearchable his judgments, and his paths beyond tracing out!" (Rom. 11:33).
- Also see the entire Book of Job. Hence, Keller admonishes that when Job called on God to explain why such evils had come upon him and his family, "God confronts Job with his own finitude, his inability to understand God's counsels and purposes even if they were revealed."[2]

Another disclaiming example is Boice. In his textbook on systematic theology, he attempts to address the issue of the existence of evil without ever addressing the origin of evil. Nevertheless, he does address the fact that "God uses it [evil] in accomplishing his good purposes in the world" and correctly cites several biblical examples.[3] Yet he later admits that "why God permits evil to exist even temporarily as he obviously does is also beyond our full comprehension."[4]

Even more ironical, Yancey, whose book is singularly subtitled "Why," concedes that "in sum, I avoid trying to answer the *Why?* question because any attempt will inevitably fall short." To make matters worse, he fears that doing so "may even rub salt in an open wound."[4] Anderson merely chimes in with a broad-brush assertion that "the mystery of suffering . . . is finally unanswered in the Bible as a whole,"[5]

---

[2] Keller, *Walking with God through Pain and Suffering*, 119.
[3] Boice, *Foundations of the Christian Faith*, 181.
[4] Ibid, 195.
[4] Yancey, *The Question That Never Goes Away*, 63.
[5] Anderson, *Understanding the Old Testament*, 560.

In spite of these above disclaimers (and more), the purpose of this chapter will be to prove these writers significantly wrong. I say "significantly" because this is still an arena of mystery (2 Thess. 2:7; Deut. 29:29). And no human being, this side of heaven, can have all the answers or be absolutely certain and dogmatic about something as veiled and mysterious as what we are pursuing herein. But pursue we shall.

Fortunately for us, the Book of Job, as Keller rightly recognizes, "is not the Bible's last word on suffering. . . . the New Testament gives us more with which to face the terrors of life."[6] In this vein, Ganssle and Lee both understand and disclaim that:

> In many cases we may be able to discern that there are reasons to permit evil. For example, God may allow some evils to help develop the character of the people involved. Some he may allow so people will turn to him and experience answers to prayer. Some evil may contribute to the good of others. It is also reasonable that some evil may allow for free choices. . . . So, it is not the case that we can never discern that there are good reasons available that might justify God in permitting evil. But given the gulf between God's knowledge and our knowledge, it seems unreasonable to expect that we could know the God-justifying reason for every case of evil.[7]

Admittedly, discerning God's purposes for evil, pain, and suffering, even in general, is not easy. For example, Job's sufferings were quite mysterious and hidden from Job. Similarly, who back then could have discerned God's purposes during arguably the greatest act of suffering in history—Jesus' crucifixion? All of this prompts Keller to further and correctly surmise that "though God's purposes are often every bit as hidden and obscure [to us] as they were to Job and to the observers at the foot of the cross, we—who have the teaching of the Bible and have grasped the message of the Bible—know that the way up is down. The way to power, freedom, and joy is through suffering, loss, and sorrow. . . . suffering is actually at the heart of the Christian story. . . . suffering can be redemptive, a way of serving others, and a way of glorifying God."[8]

---

[6] Keller, *Walking with God through Pain and Suffering*, 119, 121.
[7] Gregory E. Ganssle and Yena Lee, "Evidential Problems of Evil" in Meister and Dew, Jr., eds., *God and Evil*, 18.
[8] Keller, *Walking with God through Pain and Suffering*, 52, 77, 79.

Indeed, in the past and as we have been seeing in this book, we have been hamstrung by widely held but deficient concepts of the ordained origin of evil and finite and defective concepts of the purposes of evil. Consequently, one can hardly dispute that what is being presented in this book represents a departure from many of the traditional conceptions of God, evil, and our world.

But if God is indeed the first-cause Creator of evil and continues to create evil (Isa. 45:7), then it is not our prerogative to shield or absolve God from responsibility. Rather, our challenge and duty is to try and understand his grand purposes for placing this opposition in our world in the first place and sustaining it.

Thus, Sproul Jr. appropriately admonishes that "without an understanding of God's sovereignty over our suffering, we cannot understand the meaning of our suffering. And no suffering is worse than suffering which seems to be pointless."[9]

Four Planned Purpose Areas

Obviously, we humans have a limited ability to understand many things about God. For one, He is God and we aren't. And on this side of heaven we will never be able to account for all evil, pain, and suffering with a single model, as I've previously conceded. But when we properly recognize and biblically realize Who was the first-cause origin and Creator of evil, we shall be in a much better position to re-explore and understand some of the great sovereign purposes of God in creating evil, and for responding more appropriately (the subject of our last chapter).

Of course, some suffering is avoidable. But much isn't. Either way, we must accept that we are called to resist it, to overcome it, to reduce and eliminate it wherever possible. But we must also understand that sometimes God sends evil, pain, and suffering into our lives. And that we simply must not seek to divert or distance Him away from that responsibility.

---

[9] Sproul Jr., *Almighty Over All*, 140.

Critical Objection: "If you believe that the world was made for our benefit by God, then horrendous suffering and evil will shake your understanding of life."[10]

My Response: Plainly and simply, as John Sanders grants, "the evils in the world are here because God specifically wants them to exist. Though this may sound ghastly to many readers, there is a well-known, and historical Christian tradition that affirms this point of view. It is called the 'soul-making theodicy.'"[11] (See again Chapter 2, pp. 59-60.)

Consequently, in this chapter we shall be reexamining the Scriptures to see if they will support this historic Christian tradition of soul-making and the three other planned purpose areas of evil as well. And even though God has never given humankind a full explanation of the operation and purposes of the evil forces in this world, you will see a number of ways that this earth is, as Dembski points out, "an arena of purpose" and "a way of purpose" making "life on this earth no longer hellish but a wondrous place of duty" with "everything . . . luminous with purpose."[12] Hence, as we go forth, may God's Word cast much light upon these purposes, give us divine insights, and liberate and enhance our vision so that we may better fulfill his purposes for and in each of us.

The four planned purpose areas we shall address herein are:

Fear of the Lord
Preparation for the next life
Soul making
To glorify God

Fear of the Lord

Make no mistake. This is the first and foremost planned purpose, which the Bible emphatically and repeatedly proclaims:

---

[10] Keller, *Walking with God through Pain and Suffering*, 56.
[11] John Sanders, "A Freewill Theist's Response to Talbott's Universalism" in Robin A. Parry & Christopher H. Partridge, *Universal Salvation? The Current Debate* (Grand Rapids, MI: Eerdmans, 2003), 182.
[12] Dembski, *The End of Christianity*, 187-188, 191.

- "The fear of the Lord is the beginning of wisdom" (Prov. 9:10a; Psa. 111:10a).
- "The fear of the Lord is the beginning of knowledge" (Prov. 1:7a).
- "The fear of the Lord – that is wisdom" (Job 28:28a).
- "And now, O Israel, what does the LORD your God ask of you but to fear the LORD your God, to walk in all his ways, to love him, to serve the LORD your God with all your heart and with all your soul, . . . Fear the LORD your God and serve him. Hold fast to him and take your oaths in his name. He is your praise; he is your God, who performed for you those great and awesome wonders you saw with your own eyes" (Deut. 10:12, 20-21).
- "It is a dreadful/fearful thing to fall into the hands of the living God" (Heb. 10:31 NIV, KJV).
- Work out your salvation with fear and trembling (Phil. 2:12).
- "Then the church . . . . grew in numbers, living in the fear of the Lord" (Acts 9:31).
- And so, the psalmist David laments in the Old Testament and is quoted by the Apostle Paul in the New that "there is no fear of God before their eyes" (Rom. 3:18; from Psa. 36:1).

The fact is, many Christians still today view God, mostly if not exclusively, in terms of love, grace, and mercy, which He is, of course. But God has other attributes. Galli thusly ties in this fear of the Lord with fearful instances recorded in the Bible:

I can hardly count the number of times in the Bible that 'the fear of the Lord' is extolled as a virtue, or when people meet God almighty and are left stammering. At the foot of Mount Sinai, 'there were thunders and lightnings and a thick cloud on the mountain and a very loud trumpet blast, so that all the people in the camp trembled (Exod. 19:16, ESV). . . . When people witnessed the power and glory of almighty God, they are terrified. They think they are going to die. When we blithely sing to God to 'show us your glory, Lord,' we might as well be making a death wish. Or maybe we just want to get close to something that scares us to death.[13]

---

[13] Galli, "The Fear That Draws Us," 46-49.

Many wonder: What does this phrase "fear of the Lord" mean? Why does God command us to fear Him? And why does He present this fear as the beginning of wisdom and knowledge? Some fear that this fear literally means to be terrified and paralyzed by Him. Others redefine fear to mean merely "respecting" Him. And being terrified and respecting God are definitely included in this concept of fearing God. Then there is a fear of God that does not produce good results, such as when people flee from Him because of fear. Most certainly, this phrase has troubled and confused many people. But I believe there is more to this fear than all that.

According to *W.E. Vine: An Expository Dictionary of Biblical Words*, the main Hebrew and Greek words used in the Bible and translated as "fear" have different nuances of meaning. For instance, the Hebrew verb *yare* can mean "to fear, to be afraid, to respect, to stand in awe, to reverence." Similarly, the Hebrew noun *yirah* can mean "fear; reverence . . . of men, things, situations, and of God" and *mora* "fear" like "the fear of being before a superior kind of being." The Greek noun *phobos* can mean "first . . . the meaning of flight, that which is caused by being scared; then . . . . fear, dread, terror . . . . reverential fear of God." Likewise, the Greek verb *phobeo* can mean "to fear, be afraid . . . to show reverential fear."

Positively, I believe all of these definitional nuances of a fear of the Lord convey a continuum of meaning—starting with being scared and afraid, but then progressing into an attitude of respect, and on to wonder, awe, reverence, and a greater understanding of how much God hates sin. Then, negatively, I believe it progresses into a healthy fear of disobedience and of coming under his discipline and judgment in this life and the next (Heb. 12:5-12). For the believer, all this transpires under the umbrella of love and as a loving father disciplining a son. But it is still a fearful thing (Heb. 10:31).

The goal is for us to grow from being scared of God into reverence. However, the full spectrum of these meanings should continue motivating us throughout our lives to live and behave in ways that please Him, and onward into love, trust, obedience, submitting to his discipline, and worshipping Him in awe. This, I believe is the full meaning of a reverential fear of the Lord. It is should be the first and foremost element in changing our lives. It gives us the proper and humble attitude toward our awesome God. It helps us in times of temptation as we remember the serious consequences of sin and disobedience. And it motivates us to grow, spiritually and morally. It's this spiritual and moral growth that removes the need to be terrified by the prospects of his wrath and judgment in this life and the next. Thus, the benefits of fearing the Lord are both here and now and eternal, as more scriptures clearly say:

- "Do not let your heart envy sinners, but be zealous for the fear of the LORD all the day; for surely there is a hereafter, and your hope will not be cut off" (Prov. 23:17-18).
- "The fear of the LORD is a fountain of life, to turn one away from the snares of death" (Prov. 14:27).
- "The fear of the LORD leads to life, and he who has it will abide in satisfaction; he will not be visited with evil" (Prov. 19:23).

Preparation for the Next Life

"For what is your life?" poignantly asks James. "You are a mist/vapour that appears for a little while and then vanishes" (Jas. 4:14b NIV/KJV). But many are earthly myopic—near- or short-sighted. We live as though this life is all there is. But our earthly life is not just about the here and now or meaningless. It's the preparation and proving grounds for all eternity.

Clearly and distinctly, Jesus laid out this prime, if not primary, and planned purpose for our earthly existence when He instructed his followers: "Do not store up for yourselves treasures on earth, where moth and rust destroy, and where thieves break in and steal. But store up for yourselves treasures in heaven, where moth and rust do not destroy, and where thieves do not break in and steal. For where your treasure is, there your heart will be also" (Matt. 6:19-20).

Seriously, how we spend our time, talents, and resources on Earth during our temporary lives here prepares us for our next life in a different world and for all eternity. Notably, this time of preparation directly corresponds with the nine months we spent in our mother's womb. That time of floating about in the placenta, was also a time of preparation for our next life on the surface of a pale blue dot in the immense darkness of physical space. But during that gestation period, the world of the womb was the only world we knew. We just did not know its purpose. In contrast, the preparatory purpose for this life on the surface of planet Earth can be known. However, this purposeful significance, in an environment where good is mixed with evil, is a greatly ignored, overlooked and/or, under-emphasized in most churches.

Please be assured, this life is preparatory. And we need to better understand what kind of a world we inhabit and know this prime planned purpose. How can we know? Simply, the Bible tells us so. Rick Warren, the pastor of Saddleback Church in California and author of the mega-bestselling book, *The Purpose Driven Life*, also tells us so. When asked, What is the purpose of life?, he immediately responded:

> In a nutshell, life is preparation for eternity. . . . in Heaven. . . . I may live 60 to 100 years on earth, but I am going to spend trillions of years in eternity. This is the warm-up act – the dress rehearsal. God wants us to practice on earth what we will do forever in eternity. We were made by God and for God, and until you figure that out, life isn't going to make sense. Life is a series of problems: Either you are in one now, you're just coming out of one, or you're getting ready to go into another one. The reason for this is that God is more interested in your character than your comfort. God is more interested in making your life holy than He is in making your life happy. . . . the goal of life . . . is to grow in character, in Christ likeness. This past year has been the greatest year of my life but also the toughest, with my wife, Kay, getting cancer.[14] (Six years after Rick Warren made these comments, Matthew Warren, his son, committed suicide.)

Obvious to everyone is the fact that life on earth is finite and ends in death. In the interim, it's filled with both good and evil, joy and sorrow, successes and failures, gains and losses. Yet many think life's chief purpose is to "live the good life," be happy, be safe, be comfortable, and certainly escape tragedies and be spared from sufferings. But another fact is, this life is the womb and death is the birthing canal into the next life. That's why death is our "last enemy" (1 Cor. 15:26). It is not only our ticket out of one realty (again) but also our entrance into a greater and grander reality for all eternity.

---

[14] From an interview by Paul Bradshaw with Rich Warren, "Purpose Driven Life," email, 9/20/07.

Yes, this life is terminal. But the next life is not. Thus, this life "prepares us for eternal joy. . . for eternity"[15] So where do you think our prime focus in this life should be? Without hesitancy Alcorn responds, it's to "focus on the eternal." He cites 2 Corinthians 4:18: "So we fix our eyes not on what is seen, but on what is unseen. For what is seen is temporary, but what is unseen is eternal"[16] Keller concurs and remarks: "when we die . . . we don't cease to exist. Death is a transformation from one state into another."[17]

Seriously, how we do or don't spend our time, talents, and resources on Earth during our temporary lives here prepares us for our next life in a different world and for all eternity.

One day this world will end for each of us. On that day, we will be forced out and introduced into a totally different world. And we've all been given different lots during our temporary life in this world. How we handle our lot—what we do and don't do with it—will determine how and how well we spend all eternity. Why is this so? It's because in heaven there are different degrees of glory, rewards, blessings, punishment and loss; different levels of existence, enjoyment, and knowledge; and inequalities of opportunities. In other words, heaven gives eternal meaning and purpose to our temporary and short lives on earth. Again, how do we know. The Bible tells us so. Sadly, little is preached, taught, or understood in most churches about this eventuality. It's termed the doctrine of eternal rewards, loss, and punishment for believers.[18]

Regrettably, however, most of us have grown up thinking more about and pursuing earthly things, such as: playing with friends, kindergarten, grade school, high school, college, job, marriage, career,

---

[15] Alcorn, *If God Is Good*, 419-420.

[16] Ibid., 433.

[17] Keller, *Walking with God through Pain and Suffering*, 39.

[18] I have address the likely after life scenarios for both believers and unbelievers in my chapter titled "The Postmortem Experience" in my book, *Hell Yes / Hell No*, 329-363.

children, sports, shopping, vacations, etc. As we grow older, some of us begin to realize that's not all there is. Gradually, we find ourselves beginning to think more and more about and longing for our final destination. Some of us also begin to realize how much we've squandered our time, talent, and resources and wasted our humanity in this important regard. But now is the time to wake up. After all, would you like to know about this eventuality now while you can do something about it? Or would you rather wait until later when you can't? But so many of us long for retirement years and plan, save, and invest for it instead of investing in heaven, sad to say.

Critical Objection: "I grew up among Christians who placed too much emphasis on the afterlife, as if this life were a kind of pre-death state that we must get through en route to Beulah Land. Thankfully, theologians such as Jürgen Moltmann and N.T. Wright have helped correct that imbalance by underscoring the linkage between our present state and the next."[19]

My Response: Indeed, there is a linkage. Awareness of that linkage is exactly what is needed. It's a longer view of life, not just from birth to death, but from birth to birth into eternity. Certainly, otherworldliness that renders one so heavenly minded so as to be of little or no earthly good is to be avoided. What is needed is a pilgrim attitude that effectively realizes the preparatory significance of our time here on earth for the next life. Most assuredly, our citizenship is in heaven (Phil. 3:20), and not on earth or on a so-called "new earth" someday.

Critical Objection: So where is the hope in always having to struggle with evil? Where is the peace in knowing that you will always be fighting with the sin, pain, and sufferings of life?

My Response: The fulfillment of that hope lies not on Earth, where some live in the worst of conditions and oppression now. Heaven is the only place evil, pain, and suffering don't exist. These hardships and injustices must be confronted and contended with mainly during our brief mortal lives on Earth. And God has shown us ways to endure and overcome them. But they will not be finally overcome until our next life to come in heaven.[20]

---

[19] Yancey, *The Question That Never Goes Away*, 139-140.
[20] Again, see footnote 18 above.

190 THE CREATION OF EVIL

Additionally, as Bill Wiese points out in an apropos article titled "Are You Investing in Heaven?", "the Bible states there are many rewards given in heaven to those who were obedient on the earth." In support he lists these verses: "Psa. 19:11; 62:12; Prov. 11:18; 13:13; Jer. 31:16; Hos. 4:9; Matt. 5:11-12; 6:1, 4; 16:27; Mark 9:41; Luke 14:13-14; 1 Cor. 3:8; Col. 3:24; Heb. 11:6; Rev. 11:18; 22:12; also possibly Gal. 6:7."[21]

I would add to Wiese's list, rewards for suffering (see Heb. 19:32-36; Luke 6:22f, Matt. 5:11-12; Rom. 5:3; 8:17) and the following verses bulleted below for the reason that Keller discloses: "We need something more than knowing God is with us in our difficulties. We also need hope that our suffering is 'not in vain.'"[22] As you are about to see, "this is the ultimate defeat of evil and suffering."[23] It is the perspective and pathway to the greatest joy of all, both here and now, and there and then.

- "For our light and momentary troubles are achieving for us an eternal glory that far outweighs them all" (2 Cor. 4:17).
- "And we know that in all things [including evil] God works for the good of those who love him, who have been called according to his purpose" (Rom. 8:28). Hendriksen includes in "all things" the following: "slaughter and poverty, war, famine, and pestilence. . . . Yet, in a broader sense . . . are the martyrs. They suffer poverty and hardship. . . . But this form of persecution is also an instrument in the hand of Christ for the furtherance of His kingdom. The hard-pressed individual feels his dependence on God."[24] Admittedly, however, these evil realities of life seem like a paradox or foreign territory for most Christians today from western countries who are arguably but basically "at ease in Zion" (Amos 6:1a KJV – "Woe to them that are at ease in Zion.").

  Sproul explains that "this verse [Rom. 8:28] is not merely a biblical expression of comfort for those who suffer affliction. It

---

[21] Bill Wiese, "Are You Investing in Heaven?" (*Charisma*, November 2013), 61-66.
[22] Timothy Keller, *The Reason for God* (New York, NY: Dutton, 2008), 31.
[23] Ibid., 34.
[24] Hendriksen, *More than Conquerors*, 85, 102.

is far more than that. . . . It represents the absolute triumph of divine purpose over all alleged acts of chaos. It erases 'misfortune' from the vocabulary of the Christian."[25]

In a similar manner, Alcorn adds that "Romans 8:28 isn't about God *trying*, it's about God actually working together *all* things for our good"[26]—whether we realize it now or not. Alcorn further advises that "those who believe in a God who knows 'the end from the beginning' (Isaiah 46:10), however, can relax because even though *they* don't know what lies ahead, their sovereign God does."[27]

Sittser, on the other hand, offers this caveat: "Well-meaning people often quote this passage at the most inopportune times, usually to comfort people who have recently experienced a loss, as if it is a kind of spiritual pain medication. However true the passage, it does not promise to medicate or eliminate sorrow. Paul did not write it to diminish the severity of suffering and pain it causes. If anyone knew how bad suffering is, surely Paul was that person."[28]

- "Blessed are you when men hate you, when they exclude you and insult you and reject your name as evil, because of the Son of Man. Rejoice in that day and leap for joy, because great is your reward in heaven" (Luke 6:22-23a; also Matt. 5:11-12).

- "Now if we are children, then we are heirs – heirs of God and co-heirs with Christ, if indeed we share in his sufferings in order that we may also share in his glory" (Rom. 8:17). Please notice the relevance of the words "if" and "may" in this verse.

- "I consider that our present sufferings are not worth comparing with the glory that will be revealed in us" (Rom. 8:18). That's quite a purpose!

- "Beloved, do not be surprised at the fiery ordeal among you, which comes upon you for your testing, as though some strange thing were happening to you; but to the degree that you share the sufferings of Christ, keep on rejoicing, so that also at the

---

[25] Sproul, *When Worlds Collide*, 43.

[26] Alcorn, *If God Is Good*, 155.

[27] Ibid., 158.

[28] Sittser, *A Grace Revealed*, 83.

revelation of His glory you may rejoice with exultation" (1 Pet. 4:12-13 NAS). I'm saying that this takes place in heaven, and not on earth at a so-called "second coming."[29]

- "I have fought the good fight, I have finished the race, I have kept the faith. Now there is in store for me the crown of righteousness, which the Lord, the righteous Judge, will award to me on that day—and not only to me, but also to all who have longed for his appearing" (2 Tim. 4:7-8).

- Blessed is the man who perseveres under trial, because when he has stood the test, he will receive the crown of life that God has promised to those who love Him (Jas. 1:12).

- "Therefore, my dear brothers and sisters, stand firm. Let nothing move you. Always give yourselves fully to the work of the Lord, because you know that your labor in the Lord is not in vain" (1 Cor. 15:58).

- "If any man builds on this foundation using gold, silver, costly stones, wood, hay or straw, his work will be shown for what it is, because the Day will bring it to light. It will be revealed with fire, and the fire will test the quality of each man's work. If what he has built survives, he will receive his reward. If it is burned up, he will suffer loss; he himself will be saved, but only as one escaping through the flames" (1 Cor. 3:12-15).

- "That servant who knows his master's will and does not get ready or does not do what his master wants will be beaten with many blows. But the one who does not know and does things deserving punishment will be beaten with few blows. From everyone who has been given much, much will be demanded; and from the one who has been entrusted with much, much more will be asked" (Luke 12:47-48).

- The believer receives his or her eternal rewards or losses when he or she stands before Christ in judgment (Heb. 9:27; 2 Cor. 5:10; 2 John 8; Rev. 20:11-13).

- For a more extensive treatment of the doctrine of eternal rewards, loss, and punishment for believers, which is so greatly ignored and/or under taught, see: "God's Incentive Plan –A

---

[29] See Noē, *Unraveling the End*, 249-260. Noē, *The Greater Jesus*, 21-56.

Hierarchical View of Heaven" (pp. 354-363) and "Appendix A – A Scriptural Recap of God's Incentive Plan" (pp. 371-374) in my book *Hell Yes / Hell No.*

But so many today are living, mostly or totally, for this present world with all of its problems and uncertainties. Thus, their lives lack ultimate meaning or eternal purpose. But you and I were made for eternity. Our time on this earth is short. However, when you and I surrender our lives to Jesus and follow Him as Lord, we can then live our best life possible both here and now and in the hereafter. Yes, this world serves as a preparation and proving grounds for a system of eternal rewards and punishment. And there are many scriptures that support this eventual and critical reality.

So wake up now. Sadly, many of us are investing too much in the wrong place and not enough in the right place.

Special Summary Insights of Scholars

Robert Jeffress: He hits the proverbial nail squarely on the head when he writes that: "God will always seem unfair to a person trapped in time. Because of our limited perspective and our propensity toward premature judgments, we often arrive at the wrong conclusion regarding God's goodness and wisdom. Every dart of adversity that stings us and every push from the Hunter that plunges us further into the jaws of suffering convince us that God must be up to no good."

He offers these "three insights about God's plan for our lives that give us a different perspective about suffering. . . . God's purpose for our lives is 1) good . . . to reshape your attitudes, actions, and affections to perfectly mirror those of His Son, Jesus Christ, 2) [this] requires discomfort . . . some serious 'hammering,' resulting in temporary, but nevertheless real pain, 3) will be ultimately realized . . . One day, at long last, that renovation project is completed, and you deem the final product well worth the temporary inconveniences. . . . one day, the Bible promises, from the vantage point of eternity, Christians will be able to look back, and we will smile as we see how God turned tragedy into triumph."[30]

---

[30] Jeffress, *Hell Yes!*, 63-66.

David Chilton: "We are not to see salvation as a magic formula for trouble-avoidance. As the white-robed army of Christ, we are more than conquerors. Our calling is to endure and overcome."[31] And for those who do, there will be great reward. But still, I have questions about the degree of hate, sin, pain, suffering, and evil in our world and how God can use temporary (short-term) suffering to accomplish eternal (long-term) good. Likewise, I certainly cannot grasp the length, breadth, or depth or explain sufficiently what I've presented above in this positive and hopeful section.

John Hick: This warning from Hick is well worth a pause: "It is certainly a great mistake to underestimate the extent of human suffering, which indeed exceeds the wide scope of our imagination."[32] But I believe it is a greater mistake to underestimate the extent of human happiness, joy, and contentment, and reward in the afterlife and fail to prepare for eternity while we still can and as we've been strongly instructed to do.

Bernhard W. Anderson: "The problem of life [for many] is that Man, with his limited wisdom, cannot discern any overall purpose running consistently through life's experiences . . . . he is overwhelmed with the meaninglessness of human existence as he sees it." He further believes that "the tragedy of life is heightened by the intense realization that the problem of existence must be answered within the brief span between birth and death . . . . [and] "the problem of death . . . hangs like a dark shadow. . ."[33]

In other words, and once again, the problem of life is a lack of an eternal perspective and preparatory meaning for our earthly life. Certainly it is better to suffer evil than to inflict it. But if we truly believed there is nothing beyond this short temporary cameo we call life on Earth, what then? Yet there are spiritual beings and powers, which have penetrated heaven itself (see Job), and are at work throughout our world, seeking to thwart God's purposes in this world. But God's desire for his human creation is for us to overcome and triumph over these adversaries and through these adversities.

---

[31] Chilton, *The Days of Vengeance*, 221.
[32] John Hick, "Soul-Making and Suffering" in Adams and Adams, *The Problem of Evil,* 176.
[33] Anderson, *Understanding the Old Testament*, 545.

F.F. Bruce: "Faith in God carries with it no guarantee of comfort in this world . . . . But it does carry with it great reward in the only world that ultimately matters."[34] That next world is our true homeland. It's "a better country—a heavenly one" (Heb. 11:16).

Joni Eareckson Tada: As a quadriplegic resulting from a diving accident, she volunteers that "the Bible calls suffering a mystery for good reason. Our thoughts are not God's thoughts. We can't see the big picture."[35] Or can we?

"Amazing Grace:" This longing for an evil-less existence is a longing for heaven not for earth. Perhaps, in the words of the classic hymn, "Amazing Grace," "when we've been there ten thousand years,"[36] and then forevermore, we will greatly appreciate the fact that we were told about this back when we were still able to do something about it, rather than finding out "In the Sweet by and by"[37] when it was too late.

Rabbi David Aaron: He concludes that "when we will look back and see the whole picture, we will realize that every bad thing that happened to us contributed to God's plan, which is to bring upon us ultimate goodness. This is also true about every bad thing we *did*."[38] And yet, his conclusion is far from obvious and quite difficult for some to grasp in the here and now. Why is this so? It's because it demands revelational knowledge along with the exercise of faith in accordance with and trust in God's word.

Randy Alcorn: "No wonder Scripture makes clear that the one central business of this life is to prepare for the next. . . . Your life on earth is a dot. From that dot extends a line that goes on for all eternity. Right now you're living *in* the dot. But what are you living *for*? Are you living for the dot or for the line? Are you living for earth or for heaven? Are you living for the short today or the long tomorrow?"[39] The bottom

---

[34] F.F. Bruce, *The Epistle to the Hebrews* (Grand Rapids, MI: Eerdmans, 1990), 329.
[35] Marvin Olasky, "Choosing to sing," interview with Joni Eareckson Tada, *World* 26 January 2013, 27.
[36] From a stanza written by an anonymous author and added to the lyrics of "Amazing Grace" by John Newton (1725-1807).
[37] A Christian hymn, lyrics by S. Fillmore Bennett and music by Joseph P. Webster, 1868.
[38] Aaron, *Inviting God In*, 103.
[39] Randy Alcorn, *In Light of Eternity* (Colorado Springs, Co: WaterBrook Press,

line, as Alcorn expresses is: "We were made for another world, not this one."[40] Accordingly, he compares two great historical figures: "Nero . . . lived for prosperity on Earth." But the Apostle Paul "now lives in prosperity in Heaven."[41] This comparative eventuality is why the Psalmist Moses prays to God: "Teach us to number our days aright, that we may gain a heart of wisdom (Psa. 90:12).

R.C. Sproul: "Things may appear to be without purpose or meaning. Their ultimate purpose might elude us for the present. Yet if we fail to see purpose in what happens, we must remember that our view of things is limited by our earthly perspective. An important slogan in theology is *finitum non capax.* This means that 'the finite cannot grasp the infinite.'"[42]

A.E. Knoch: concludes: "Our afflictions will lead to an overwhelming glory, for which these sufferings are essential. . . . There is a blessed future for which all our trials are a preparation."[43]

Jeremy A. Evans: In answer to these two tough and perennial questions: "Why do the wicked prosper, and why do the righteous suffer?," Evans responds that "implicit in such questions is a principle of justice, presumably conjoined with the belief that the wicked should be punished and the righteous rewarded. If this is correct, then intense suffering that results from human sin is a live option in theodicy—the only detail is discerning its place of application."[44]

Norman L. Geisler: "As to why God could not make this ultimate condition of being freed from all sin up front: Heaven is the end, and earth is the means. One cannot get to the Promised Land without going through the wilderness. Earth is the testing ground; heaven is our final home. We cannot reach home without the proving grounds. Allowing the choice of good and evil is necessary in achieving the highest good. . . . the highest freedom is *from* sin (heaven), not *of* sin. One is not fit for the freedom from sin unless he has exercised the freedom to sin, for unless he has had the choice of good over evil, he is not ready for a place where

---

1999), 142-143.

[40] Alcorn, *If God Is Good*, 492.

[41] Ibid., 384.

[42] Sproul, *When Worlds Collide*, 38-39.

[43] Knoch, *The Problem of Evil and the Judgments of God*, 11, 143.

[44] Evans, *The Problem of Evil*, 8.

good dominates and evil is defeated."[45] Thus, and as a free will advocate, Geisler concludes that "God is not producing or promoting evil . . . [but] allows evil to produce the greater good."[46]

Gregory A. Boyd: "I refer to life in this epoch as a 'probationary period.' We are now deciding the kind of eternal being we will become. In this period we make choices, though in time our choices make us. . . . It is the gestation period of our eternal life, the courtship of the heavenly groom and his earthly bride . . . the temporal time of choice that eventually forms our eternal being."[47] Yes, God in his sovereignty created a world and redemptive system in which good is eventually rewarded and evil eventually punished. But this eventuality mostly takes shape and form in the next life, not in this life.

John Greenleaf Whittier: These sad and often quoted words from this influential American Quaker poet and ardent advocate of the abolition of slavery (1807-1892) certainly apply to the preparatory purpose we've been discussing and appropriately bring us into our next purpose area:

> Of all sad words of tongue or pen, the saddest are these,
> 'It might have been.'[48]

Soul Making

Scripture abounds with verses befitting this soul-making process and planned purpose. Its bottom line is the development of spiritual and moral character in this life. All these verses are easy to read, write, and proclaim, but not easy to live out, especially when you are going through an attack of evil or walking through "the valley of the shadow of death" itself (Psa. 23:4b).

While it is true that in this life we shall never completely understand evil or know all the reasons why evil, hard times, pain, and suffering come to us and are allowed by God, still this one fact remains. Jesus told

---

[45] Geisler, *If God, Why Evil?*, 63-64.
[46] Ibid., 69.
[47] Boyd, *Satan and the Problem of Evil*, 188-189, 320.
[48] John Greenleaf Whittier, *Maud Muller* – Pamphlet.

his followers some two thousand years ago, and us today as well, that "in this world you will have trouble/tribulation." Then He encouragingly added: "But take heart I have overcome the world" (John 16:33 NIV/KJV). But why should we take heart over trouble and tribulation that we face in this world? It's because one of God's purposes and goal for creating the type of world in which we live was to bring many souls to glory (Heb. 2:10). Nevertheless, many object to this purpose.

Critical Objection: Yancey's view is: "I resist those who assume that God *sends* the suffering to accomplish good. No, in the Gospels I have yet to find Jesus saying to the afflicted, 'The reason you suffer from hemorrhage (or paralysis or leprosy) is that God is working to build your character.' Jesus did not lecture such people, he healed them." But Yancey also admits, "nonetheless, nearly every New Testament passage on suffering explores how even a 'bad' thing can be redeemed for good."[49]

My Response: Yancey's admission is the essence of the "soul-making" theodicy, as God has purposed that we humans be rational creatures and Godlike, "knowing [both] good and evil" (Gen. 3:22).

Highlighting Hick –A Systematic Overview of John Hick's Irenaean Soul-Making Theodicy

As we discussed in Chapter 2, "soul-making" was one of the first theodicies ever formally presented. Its influence throughout Church history has been considerable. It was first formulated by the second-century theologian Irenaeus (A.D. 120 – 202) and has been promoted in contemporary form by author John Hick (1922 – 2012). Arguably, "this period" of A.D. 100-300 was "the age of extraordinary expansion before Christianity moved from the catacombs to the imperial courts."[50] After this time, Christianity was drastically changed by Constantine (A.D. 272 – 337) and Augustine (354 – 430), who pushed out Irenaeus' "soul-making" theodicy with a "free will" theodicy.[51]

---

[49] Yancey, *The Question That Never Goes Away*, 96.

[50] Bruce L. Shelley, *Church History in Plan Language*, (Dallas, TX: Word Publishing, 1982), 51

[51] For more about the first six hundred years of Church history see: Noē, *Hell Yes / Hell No*, 105-125.

According to some, John Hick was one of the most important and influential philosophers of religion of the second half of the twentieth century. As a British philosopher in the Anglo-analytic tradition, Hick did groundbreaking work in religious epistemology, philosophical theology, and religious pluralism.[52]

Below is a succession of excerpts from Hick's "soul-making" book, *Evil and the Love of God*, followed by critical objections thereto:

- In the wisdom and sight of God all things He created, including evil and consequential sin, pain, and suffering, "combine to form a wonderful harmony which is not only good but 'very good'"[53] (Gen. 1:31).

- We humans exit in God's created world to respond "to tasks and challenges . . . being summoned to serve God as He reveals Himself to human faith in the midst of life's mingled meanings and mysteries."[54]

- "God willed to create finite beings who should be capable of personal relationship with Himself, and that He created our enigmatic world as an environment whose apparently arbitrary character provides the concrete occasions and opportunities for free and faithful obedience to Him. But this is to move in a different direction from that of the medieval tradition, and towards an alternative type of theodicy."[55]

- "The universe is wholly good; for even the evil within it is made to contribute to the complex perfection of the whole."[56]

- "God so overrules human affairs as to use sinners, including the devil himself, for the furtherance of His own good purposes. . . . and eventually brings good out of evil, and indeed brings an eternal and therefore infinite good out of a temporal and therefore finite evil, is a thought of great promise for Christian theodicy."[57]

---

[52] Internet Encyclopedia of Philosophy, http://www.iep.utm.edu/hick/, 9/24/14.
[53] Hick, *Evil and the Love of God*, 38.
[54] Ibid., 72.
[55] Ibid., 77.
[56] Ibid., 82.
[57] Ibid., 88-89.

- "The redeemed state is worth a hundred times more than that of innocence."[58]
- "On such a view the good purpose for which evil . . . 'exists' is to make possible the supreme good of redemption. Starting from . . . the death and resurrection of Christ . . . . If the whole creation centres upon this great event, is it not implied that man's need for salvation was envisaged in God's creative plan, the presence of evil being a necessary precondition of redemption, and the fall accordingly serving ultimately the high purpose of setting God as Saviour at the centre of His creation?"[59]
- "This is the positive meaning of human existence and all existence. But this elevation presupposes a wretchedness of human and all existence which His own Son will share and bear. This is the negative meaning of creation. Since everything is created for Jesus Christ and His death and resurrection, from the very outset everything must stand under this twofold and contradictory determination."[60]
- "Since God is good it would be inconsistent with His own nature to have chosen any other world than the best: for 'supreme wisdom, united to a goodness that is no less infinite, cannot but have chosen the best.' . . . His original decision to create a dependent universe was a decision of the absolute divine freedom . . . . [that] arose from an inner necessity of His own nature. . . . The infinite mind of the Creator has surveyed the infinite realm of world-possibilities and has selected the best."[61]
- Hence, God has created "The 'Best Possible World' . . . . a dependent universe. . . . [that] world is a 'vale of soul-making,' designed as an environment in which finite persons may develop the more valuable qualities of moral personality."[62]
- "This line of thought points towards an alternative type of theodicy which, instead of seeking a solution by looking to the past and finding its clue to the meaning of evil in a heinous

---

[58] Ibid., 110 – in quotation of Journet and St. Francis de Sales.
[59] Ibid., 139.
[60] Ibid., 140 – in quotation of Carl Barth.
[61] Ibid., 159, 162 – in summary of Leibniz's central thesis.
[62] Ibid., 160, 168 – in summary of Leibniz's central thesis.

original crime, seeks for light by looking in faith to the future, to an eventual triumphant bringing of good out of evil."[63]

- "Speculative and daring as this statement may seem, it represents a position that is almost inevitably reached when one contemplates the sovereignty of God in its relation to the fact of evil."[64]

- "Within God's providence man is being taught by his contrasting experience of good and evil to value the one for himself and to shun the other. Hence the mixture of good and evil in our world."[65]

- "To lead him [man] forward by God's help through their growth and development to the realization of his life's destiny, which is to come into the likeness of God."[66]

- To lead us "towards higher states of God-consciousness, and thereby constituting our present situation as one of sin and guilt and of need of salvation, God is ultimately responsible for sin as the precondition of our reception of His redeeming grace."[67]

- In sum: "The world exists to be an environment for man's life, and its imperfections are integral to its fitness as a place of soul-making."[68]

- "The final end-product of the human story will justify the evil within that story [and] points to an eschatological understanding of the divine purpose which gives meaning to human life."[69]

- "Man is in process of becoming the perfected being whom God is seeking to create. . . . However . . . . this is a pilgrimage within the life of each individual, rather than a racial evolution." Hence, "the progressive fulfillment of God's purpose does not entail any corresponding progressive improvement in the moral state of the world. There is no doubt a development in man's ethical

---

[63] Ibid., 174.

[64] Ibid., 176.

[65] Ibid., 214.

[66] Ibid., 218 – in quotation of Bratsiotis.

[67] Ibid., 231 – in quotation of Schleiermacher.

[68] Ibid., 237 – in interaction with Augustinian tradition.

[69] Ibid., 239 – in interaction with both Augustinian and Irenaean theodicy traditions.

situation from generation to generation through the building of individual choices into public institutions, but this involves an accumulation of evil as well as of good."[70]

- "This, then, is the starting-point from which we propose to try to relate the realities of sin and suffering to the perfect love of an omnipotent Creator."[71]

- "At this point a further, eschatological, dimension of Christian belief becomes importantly relevant, and must be brought into the discussion . . . ."[72]

- "a life after death . . . . If there is any eventual resolution of the interplay between good and evil, any decisive bringing of good out of evil, it must lie beyond this world and beyond the enigma of death."[73]

- "The Irenaean approach, which sees moral evil as an inevitable result of God's creation of man as an immature creature, at the beginning of a long process of moral and spiritual development. . . . it offers a theodicy in respect of natural as well as moral evil. For the harsh features of the world, which we call natural evil, are integral to its being an environment in which a morally and spiritually immature creature can begin to grow towards his perfection. . . . [and] that the person-making process continues far beyond this earthly life."[74]

- Therefore, "we have to affirm God's ultimate responsibility for the existence of both moral and natural evil. I wish to add . . . even this ultimate omni-responsibility of the Creator does not take away each human individual's accountability for his own deliberate actions."[75]

- Lastly, "the experience of participating in the final heavenly state, and of seeing from that vantage point that the way in which

---

[70] Ibid., 256.

[71] Ibid., 261.

[72] Ibid., 336.

[73] Ibid., 338-339.

[74] Ibid., 369, 376.

[75] Ibid., 381.

one has come to it, however long and difficult, is justified by the supreme value of the end-state itself."[76]

Critical Objection: "The mere fact that evils give rise to goods cannot serve as a morally sufficient reason for an omnipotent and omniscient being to permit suffering. . . . an omnipotent and omniscient being could devise a law-governed world which would not include suffering . . . . Having a morally sufficient reason for permitting suffering *entails* having some lack of knowledge or power."[77]

Critical Objection: "The theist may point out that some suffering leads to moral and spiritual development impossible without suffering. But it's reasonably clear that suffering often occurs in a degree far beyond what is required for character development. . . . much suffering occurs not as a result of human free choices."[78]

Critical Objection: "Note, my view does not make participation in horrors necessary for the individual's incommensurate good. A horror-free life that ended in beatific intimacy with God would also be one in which the individual enjoyed incommensurate good. . . . Nor is participation in horrors merely instrumentally related to the beatific end, as God's necessary or chosen means for educating one into beatitude. . . . Particularly noxious are putative justifications of God, which—like the 'consolations' of Job's friends—fail to respect the depth of suffering by domesticating it under some overarching scheme. . . . Talk that does not aim at action implicitly sanctions what goes on. . . . rather than analyzing the causes of suffering with a view to stopping it."[79]

My Response: Adams and Adams answer their own raised objections as follows:

> The general difficulty with this direct attack . . . is twofold. First, it cannot succeed, for the theist does not know what greater goods might be served, or evils prevented, by each instance of intense human or animal suffering.

---

[76] Ibid., 384.

[77] Nelson Pike, "Hume on Evil" in Adams and Adams, *The Problem of Evil*, 44-45.

[78] William L. Rowe, "The Problem of Evil and Varieties of Atheism," in Adams and Adams, *The Problem of Evil*, 133.

[79] Marilyn McCord Adams, *Horrendous Evil and the Goodness of God* (Ithaca, NY: and London, Cornell University Press, 1999), 167, 185-186.

Second, the theist's own religious tradition usually maintains that in this life it is not given to us to know God's purpose in allowing particular instances of suffering.[80]

To which I arguably add that Jesus' suffering, Paul's, Peter's, and many others by God's ordination also went, as Rowe in his objection above mentioned, "far beyond what is required for character development."

Detailing Many Soul-Making Purposes

Dualistically, Adams maintains that "the Bible is short on explanations of why God permits evils and relatively long on how God makes good on them."[81] But is this really true? Obviously, it's not possible for any human to provide an explanation, reason, or purpose for every evil occurrence. That provision must await the afterlife. But let's try. Here's my compiled "short" list (not so "short"). I believe it contains many nuggets well worth pondering.

To help guide our passage through these many soul-making purposes, we shall format them in a bulleted manner and arbitrarily organize them under these four categories: Personal Transformation, Draw Us unto God, Outreach to Others, and Weaning Us from Earth onto Heaven. But many of them are obviously interconnected and interwoven. All, however, can be placed under the overarching banner of "soul-making." In this manner, therefore, "And we, who with unveiled faces all reflect the Lord's glory, are being transformed into his likeness with ever-increasing glory, which comes from the Lord, who is the Spirit" (2 Cor. 3:18).

Perhaps you can think of more divinely ordained purposes for evil, pain, and suffering. Or, you may simply not agree with some of them. But my hope in providing this compilation is that it will bless you as much as it continues to bless me every time I read through and ponder these purposes and added insights:

---

[80] Rowe, "The Problem of Evil and Varieties of Atheism" in Adams and Adams, *The Problem of Evil*, 133.

[81] Adams, *Horrendous Evils and the Goodness of God*, 137.

Personal Transformation

To come to the end of our self complacency

- To know that we are not sufficient unto ourselves (autonomous)
- To humble stubborn and rebellious people
- To remove our self-sufficient swagger of having everything under control
- To become aware of our innate poverty and our next-breath dependence
- To remind us that we are not in control
- To learn "bit by bit—the lesson of our material vulnerability"[82]
- To keep us from self-destruction
- "To find a source of love outside of this world and ourselves. That source is God."[83]
- To reflect on the kind of person I want to be and what I really want to be doing
- To take inventory of our life, reconsider priorities, and set a new direction
- To initiate self-examination
- To force us to face our weaknesses, failures, and regrets and search for a new life beyond ourselves
- To strip us of the present self-focused life and force us to ask and seek answers for life's basic questions
- To lead into a profound spiritual awakening and transformation
- "Suffering can get our attention and lead us to repentance and transformation."[84]
- "Suffering reminds us to stop taking life for granted and to contemplate the larger picture. God intends that it draw our attention to life-and-death realities far greater than ourselves."[85]

---

[82] Diogenes Allen, "Natural Evil and the Love of God" in Adams and Adams, *The Problem of Evil*, 197.

[83] Sittser, *A Grace Disguised*, 185.

[84] Alcorn, *If God Is Good*, 417.

[85] Ibid., 43.

- "Loss strips us of the props we rely on for our well-being. It knocks us off our feet and puts us on our backs. In the experience of loss, we come to the end of ourselves."[86]
- "Suffering draws independent people to faith and teaches them dependence on Christ."[87]

To Grow

- To facilitate our growth from self-centeredness to God- and other-centeredness
- To strengthen our spiritual muscles and grow stronger (we rarely grow during good times)
- To develop morally and theologically
- To develop virtues like truthfulness, compassion, and faithfulness there apparently must be polar opposition. Otherwise, there would be no meaningful choice, challenge, or differentiating and distinguishing element.
- To produce authentic moral and spiritual growth and maturity
- To gain wisdom and find contentment
- To make us better aware and appreciative of the wonder of life itself
- ". . . sin is crouching at your door; it desires to have you, but you must master it" (Gen. 4:7b)
- "God made him who had no sin to be sin for us, so that in him we might become the righteousness of God" (2 Cor. 5:21). But some might not.

To Be Tested

- To test, purify, and mature our faith and help us grow
- To refine, cleanse as by fire, purge away the dross of sin (1 Pet. 1:7)
- To "be counted worthy of the kingdom" (2 Thess. 1:3-5)

---

[86] Sittser, *A Grace Disguised*, 89.
[87] Alcorn, *If God Is Good*, 418.

- To develop genuine faith, strength of character, and righteousness
- To train – "Training [is] preferable to testing, largely because it depends less on chance and more on choice."[88]
- "Untested faith is not valid faith and never amounts to much"[89] (see 1 Pet. 1:6-7; Jas. 1:2-4).
- "The trials of Christians are not ordained ultimately by Satan, but by God; and the outcome is not destruction, but purity."[90]
- "God uses adversity as well as prosperity to shape our lives; forming character in us, calling us to fruitful service, enabling us to love and trust him."[91]
- Pain, suffering, tragedy, illness, and disaster provide a powerful path to redemption and character development (Rom. 5:3-4).
- After a season of pain and suffering most of us look and act very different.

To Learn

- To persevere through hardships, which builds character
- To share in Jesus' sufferings (1 Pet. 4:13; Col. 1:24; Heb. 5:8)
- To turn from sin and live in obedience
- To provide occasions for repentance and faith
- How to handle adversity
- Why to be persecuted for Christ's sake (see Matt. 5:11-12; 10:17-22)
- To become a more effective instrument of sovereign purpose and use
- **Critical Objection:** "God's heart is drawn to the suffering; God's desire is to see our pain ended, our hearts comforted, and our relationships healed" (from a local pastor's sermon).

---

[88] Sittser, *A Grace Revealed*, 186.
[89] Myles Munroe, *Rediscovering Faith* (Shippensburg, PA: Destiny Image, 2009), 31.
[90] Chilton, *The Days of Vengeance*, 103.
[91] Sittser, *A Grace Revealed*, 82.

- **My Response:** Oh? He didn't do so for Jesus, Paul, or many other Christians in their earthly lives. God allowed them to suffer greatly as they were severely mistreated, tortured, and killed for their faith. And yet why someone gets cancer and another not; or why someone is healed and another not, is—from our limited, human perspective—simply unanswerable.
- "Not only so, but we also rejoice in our sufferings, because we know that suffering produces perseverance; perseverance, character; and character, hope. And hope does not disappoint us. . ." (Rom. 5:3-5).
- "Suffering produces in us qualities that otherwise would never develop."[92]
- "Before I was afflicted I went astray, but now I obey your word . . . . It was good for me to be afflicted so that I might learn your decrees. . . . in faithfulness you have afflicted me" (Psa. 119:67, 71, 75b).
- "Although he [Jesus] was a son, he learned obedience [how?] from what he suffered" and by this suffering had been "made perfect" (Heb. 5:8-9; 2:10).
- "To this you were called, because Christ suffered for you, leaving you an example, that you should follow in his steps" (1 Pet. 2:21; 4:1).
- "The purpose of pain is to teach us some important lessons. Pain is in fact nature's most efficacious instructor."[93]
- " Suffering, as sin's consequence, points us back to sin's ugliness."[94]
- "Sometimes bad things do happen to us because we've chosen to disobey God and do things that are clearly harmful. For example, someone who deliberately ignores God's moral laws and becomes wildly promiscuous may pay a terrible price by contracting a sexually transmitted disease."[95]

---

[92] Alcorn, *If God Is Good*, 407.
[93] D'Souza, *Godforsaken*, 154.
[94] Alcorn, *If God Is Good*, 405.
[95] Billy Graham, "My Answer," *The Indianapolis Star* (Indianapolis, IN), 18 October 2013, E-4.

- "Suffering is the condition of developing many virtues—unselfishness, good faith, courage, commitment, truthfulness. The capacity for love is deepened by trials and so on."[96]

To Endure

- "My son, do not make light of the Lord's discipline, and do not lose heart when he rebukes you, because the Lord disciplines those he loves, and he punishes everyone he accepts as a son. Endure hardship as discipline; God is treating you as sons . . . . God disciplines us for our good, that we may share in his holiness. No discipline seems pleasant at the time, but painful. Later on, however, it produces a harvest of righteousness and peace for those who have been trained by it" (Heb. 12:5-11; also Prov. 3:12). Alcorn terms this "God's parenting method."[97]
- To punish misdeeds – "Judaism teaches that parents who do not discipline their children hate their children. Punishment gives children an opportunity to discover their personal boundaries. It confirms to them that they are powerful, that there are consequences to their actions and their choices matter."[98] The purpose of these sufferings is like discipline of a wayward child from a loving parent. The bottom line is, disobey God and discipline hardships will come. Thus, those who embrace God are not immune from the misfortunes of sin and evil.
- To chastise and correct a person for wrongful patterns of life, as in the case of Jonah
- To prevent future wrongs, as in the case of Paul's thorn in the side to keep him from becoming conceited (2 Cor. 12:7)
- To triumph over trials, as in the case of Joseph, who endured as God tested him. "Joseph, sold as a slave. They bruised his feet with shackles, his neck was put in irons, till what he foretold came to pass, till the word of the Lord proved him true" (Psa. 105:17-19).

---

[96] Adams, *Horrendous Evils and the Goodness of God*, 52.
[97] Alcorn, *If God Is Good*, 422.
[98] Aaron, *Inviting God In*, 83.

- Many more examples could be cited. But the lesson of biblical history should be evident. Evil, pain, and suffering are tools God uses—from Adam to Job through Christ, from Paul to us.
- To give us greater perspectives, ability, and confidence to endure
- To achieve self-discipline
- To struggle, compete, and work hard is essential for producing desirable results that take commitment, energy, and determination (see 1 Cor. 9:27)
- To refine and strengthen our character (see Rom. 5:3-4)
- To enter the kingdom of God (Acts 14:22)
- Like a sculptor, God uses some of the harsh conditions of life to form and shape us into the person He always intended us to be— something beautiful for all eternity.
- Hence, "In this world you shall have tribulation" (John 16:33).
- Throughout the Bible, God often initiated suffering by sending evil, as He disciplined those He loves and led his children to repentance and back to Him (Gen. 32:25; Exod. 4:24; 32:35; Isa. 30:26; Acts 5:5, 10).
- God instructed believers by afflictions (Deut. 28:59-63; Isa. 38:15; 2 Cor. 12:7-9; Rev. 2:23). He likewise judged people in this manner (Gen. 12:17; 20:7; 38:7, 10; Exod. 9:9; 11:1; 19:22; 15:26; 22:24; 32:14, 34-35; 1 Sam. 16:14; 2 Sam. 24:15; Acts 12:23; 13:11; Rom. 12:19; 1 Cor. 10:10; 11:27-30).
- Why, then, shouldn't we Christians today also expect to experience evil, pain, suffering, and destruction in this life?
- "Hardship often cultivates Christlikeness in us and prepares us for greatness."[99]

To Mature

- Suffering is an instrument of God for the humbling, strengthening, purification, and maturing of his people (see Rom. 5:3; 12:12; 2 Thess. 1:4; 2 Tim. 3:10-11; Jas. 1:3; 5:10; Rev. 1:9; 13:10).

---

[99] Alcorn, *If God Is Good*, 168.

- "But solid food is for the mature, who by constant use have trained themselves to distinguish good from evil" (Heb. 5:14).
- To make us more like Him, Who knows both good and evil, like the Godhead did and does (Gen. 3:22)
- To develop our character attributes akin to God's
- To triumph through our suffering
- To "fight the good fight of faith" (1 Tim. 6:12)
- To conform to the image of Christ
- "for it is God who works in you to will and to act according to his good purpose" (Phil. 2:13).
- "He who overcomes [the evil listed in the next verse] will inherit all this, and I will be his God and he will be my son" (Rev. 21:7; 12:11). Isn't this the goal of training in righteousness, in enduring, and in maturing?
- "Now if we are children, then we are heirs – heirs of God and co-heirs with Christ, if indeed we share in his sufferings in order that we may also share in his glory" (Rom. 8:17).
- "Consider it pure joy, my brothers, whenever you face trails of many kinds, because you know that the testing of your faith develops perseverance. Perseverance must finish its work so that you may be mature and complete, not lacking anything" (Jas. 1:2-4).
- "Suffering reminds us of our inability to control life."[100]
- "This is the unceasing struggle of a lifetime. It is the long and painful process of becoming like Christ in the way I choose to think, speak, and live each day."[101]

Draw Us unto God

- "God whispers to us in our pleasure, speaks in our conscience, but shouts in our pains; it is His megaphone to rouse a deaf world."[102]

---

[100] Ibid., 418.
[101] Brennan Manning, *Abba's Child* (Colorado Springs, CO: NavPress, 2002, 1994), 72.
[102] C.S. Lewis, *The Problem of Pain* (London, 1940), 81.

- "Troubles . . . God can use them to make our faith stronger and draw us closer to himself."[103]
- To turn us to God and invite Him into our lives
- To force us to cry out, "Lord have mercy on me a sinner."
- To acknowledge our constant dependence upon God, especially in difficulties
- To produce a surrendered attitude and call on Him as "our weakness provides a platform for showing his strength"[104] (see 2 Cor. 12:7-10)
- To grow our intimacy with, trust in, and love for God
- To move us beyond our self, goals, aspirations, and problems so we can perceive and hear God
- "To lead a person to love God . . . [and] discover the ultimate peace and freedom (as in the case of Job)"[105]
- To "empty us of our pride and lead us to find our true joy and only security in Christ"[106]
- To "drive you more into God"[107]
- To enlarge your life with God
- To force us to address the issue of God's sovereignty over our life
- To seek forgiveness of God
- To enable God to become a living reality in and at the center of our life
- To learn simply to be, regardless what has happened to us, as a creature loved by God and made in his image and likeness
- To remind us that God is greater than our understanding and that He works in ways beyond our understanding
- To develop confidence that God will care for you and reward your fidelity when we experience persecutions (2 Tim. 3:12; 4:8)

---

[103] Billy Graham, "My Answer," *The Indianapolis Star* (Indianapolis, IN), 7 February 2013, E-4.
[104] Alcorn, *If God Is Good*, 172.
[105] Keller, *Walking with God through Pain and Suffering*, 47.
[106] Ibid., 49.
[107] Ibid., 253.

Outreach to Others

- To prepare us to comfort others who are afflicted
- To draw us closer to others by being able to relate to their sufferings
- To make us more sensitive persons and more effective sympathizers, comforters, and counselors (2 Cor. 1:3-4)
- To give us greater love for others
- To seek the forgiveness of others
- To become more generous people
- To see that suffering is not unique to you and does not have the final say
- To help turn suffering into something that results in good
- To enlarge the soul for feeling more of the world's pain and anguish
- To give and receive love and support from each other
- To be citizens of his kingdom, agents of moral change, confronters of evil, fighters for justice, and bearers of divine healing throughout our world
- To drive us into "a life of other-directed, self-giving love toward God and neighbor. [because] Our ultimate joy and fulfillment as creatures is found in this experience, for it is the end for which we were made."[108]
- "It [evil] creates special conditions in which virtue can flourish." And yet, "the thought that God decided to permit Auschwitz because some heroes would emerge is hardly a solution to the problem . . . . often such 'solutions' simply make the problem worse."[109]
- But without suffering, there would be no reason for compassion.

---

[108] Blanchette and Walls, "God and Hell Reconciled" in Meister and Dew, Jr., eds., *God and Evil*, 252-253.
[109] Wright, *Evil and the Justice of God*, 28.

Weaning Us from Earth onto Heaven

- "We come into this world needy, and we leave it the same way. Without suffering we would forget our neediness."[110]
- To help us come to terms with our mortality via a radical change in perspectives
- To long for heaven (2 Cor. 5:1-8), God, gradually or suddenly, weans us away from the attachments of this world and life (2 Cor. 4:16 – "Therefore we do not lose heart. Though outwardly we are wasting away, yet inwardly we are being renewed day by day.")
- To bring us into the concrete knowledge of our own mortality verses it only being an abstract idea
- To realize that we cannot regain what we have lost or are losing and drive our focus onto anticipating the next life, more and more
- To look heavenward and toward Jesus as we are weaned off worldly desires and the impulse to cling to this life and into the willingness to accept and meet death with dignity
- Gradually or suddenly, God takes earthly things away from us—our physical capabilities, our goods, and eventually our life through adversity, pain, and suffering. And in the end we all suffer and die (Heb. 9:27).
- Yes, "we are all dying, relinquishing little bits of life every day, and while medical technologies can win us a short delay, they cannot prevent us from moving steadily, inexorably to our graves."[111]
- "The pain of disease . . . the decay of old age, the imminence of death—takes away a person's satisfaction with himself. It tends to humble him, show him his frailty, make him reflect on the transience of temporal goods, and turn his affections towards other-worldly things, away from the things of this world."[112]

---

[110] Alcorn, *If God Is Good*, 418.

[111] D'Souza, *What's So Great About Christianity*, 278-279.

[112] Swinburne, *Providence and the Problem of Evil*, 202 – in quotation of Eleonore Stump, *The Problem of Evil*.

- ". . . our bones start weakening as we get older, we lose virility and fertility, there is diminished vision and reaction time, and even the brain atrophies. Certainly, all of this seems normal to us, but it is the very norm that we are questioning here. If God is an omnipotent engineer, why would he design such defective and deteriorating creatures?"[113]

- We become "totally uninterested in . . . conversations about material things" or "on possessions, but always of Christ and people." A friend told him, "I consider it a privilege to live each day knowing I'll die soon. What a difference it makes!"[114]

- "Those who do reach old age usually suffer many losses along the way."[115]

- "We live suspended between the familiar past and the expected future. The scenery we enjoy today gradually fades into the background, finally receding from sight. But what looms ahead comes nearer and gets clearer, until it becomes the scenery of the present moment that fills our vision"[116] (see Phil. 3:13-14).

- But even though death is the victor in this life. It does not have the final word. God does as we inch, hesitantly but steadily, closer and closer, to see death as the door to resurrection and the birth into our new next life.

- "Our deepest longings point beyond this world as we know and experience it to something greater, to Heaven, where we will see Jesus and his kingdom in all its brilliance and perfection."[117]

- The "ultimate longing, which is the longing for Heaven."[118]

- "The object of our deepest longings."[119]

- Paul actually desired to suffer. He wrote, "I want to know Christ and the power of his resurrection and the fellowship of sharing in his sufferings, becoming like him in his death" (Phil. 3:10).

---

[113] D'Souza, *Godforsaken*, 140.
[114] Alcorn, *If God Is Good*, 480.
[115] Sittser, *A Grace Revealed*, 233.
[116] Sittser, *A Grace Disguised*, 31.
[117] Sittser, *A Grace Revealed*, 202.
[118] Ibid., 233.
[119] Ibid., 246.

- "Our experience of death completes our union with Christ . . . . that through death we imitate Christ in what he did and thereby experience closer union with him"[120] (see Rom. 8:17).
- "Our lack of a fear of death will provide a strong witness for Christians in an age that tries to avoid talking about death and has no answer for it"[121] (see Heb. 2:15).
- "We can look forward to our own death with a joyful expectation of being in Christ's presence" and "our attitude will be somewhat different when we experience the death of Christian friends and relatives."[122]

Special Summary Insights of Scholars

John Piper: "The Bible treats human life as something God has absolute rights over. He gives it and takes it, according to his will. We do not own it or have any absolute rights to it. It is a trust for as long as the owner wills for us to have it. To have life is a gift and to lose it is never an injustice from God, whether he takes it at age five or age ninety-five"[123] (see Job 1:21).

Nathan Day Wilson: It forces us "to focus on the important things in life. . . ." It gives us "opportunities to begin again. . . . [these] are necessary moments in the development of our souls. Sure of the absence of God, we become aware [or more aware] of the presence of God." Why is this so? He calls these times "a paradox: By losing everything, we come to the realization that everything is far less than we think and far more than we dreamed. In the end, everything is what cannot be taken away, what cannot be lost, what will not fail us in our hope."[124]

Basil Mitchell: ". . . the purpose of God's creation is that men should finally enjoy a communion with one another and with God which fully satisfies their hearts and minds, and the present world, with its suffering and its opportunities for moral evil, provides the only sort of environment in which men could develop the virtues needed to sustain

---

[120] Grudem, *Systematic Theology*, 812.
[121] Ibid., 814.
[122] ibid.
[123] Piper, "Is God Less Glorious Because He Ordained that Evil Be?"
[124] Nathan Day Wilson, "Faith Can Overcome Fear of Loss, Unknown," *The Indianapolis Star* (Indianapolis, IN), 6 September 2014, A-9.

and enjoy that status. Believing this and believing also, as Christians, that God has involved himself in the suffering of the world and, in so doing, shown how it may be transmuted, believers claim that they have been given some insight, however incomplete, into the mystery of evil. . . . It is in this characteristically human predicament that faith belongs. There would be no need of faith in a world where men had no tendency to lose heart and where circumstances were always clear, stable, and unambiguous; and faith would not be a virtue unless it were both difficult and necessary for men to pursue a steady course in the face of dangers, doubts and frustrations. . . . The temptation to apostasy is really a temptation . . . . A faith which could not cope with this predicament would be of little value.[125]

William Hendriksen: "The Church [too] needs these tribulations. It needs both the direct antagonism of the world and life as a result of sin. The Church, too, is sinful. It is in constant need of purification and sanctification. These tribulations, therefore, are employed by our Lord as an instrument for our own spiritual advancement. . . . to them that love God all things work together for good; but do we really believe it?"[126]

James Spiegel: "In a world devoid both of dangers to be avoided and rewards to be won, we may assume that virtually no development of human intellect and imagination would have taken place, and hence no development of the sciences, the arts, human civilization, or culture."[127] He concludes that the "soul-making theodicy has many strengths. For one thing, it appeals to the generally observable facts that we build character as we experience adversity and that many moral virtues can only be developed as we struggle against evil, whether in the form of sin or suffering. . . . [and] is directly endorsed in many biblical passages. Finally, this perspective has many benefits when it comes to Christian spiritual formation. . . ."[128]

Donald Guthrie: "Much confusion arises from the fact that it is generally assumed that all suffering should be avoided. The notion that God could use suffering does not come naturally. But the NT approach to

---

[125] Mitchell, *The Justification of Religious Belief*, 10, 138, 140.
[126] Hendriksen, *More than Conquerors*, 81.
[127] Spiegel, "The Irenaean Soul-Making Theodicy" in Meister and Dew, Jr., eds., *God and Evil*, 84.
[128] Ibid., 93.

suffering constantly takes it into the sphere of God's purpose. Although it is true that suffering is nowhere explained . . . ."[129] Or is it?

Philip Yancey: Yancey reports from a survey on spiritual formation once conducted by John Ortberg that "asked thousands of people when they grew most spiritually and what contributed to that growth. The number one contributor surprised him. It was not pastoral teaching, or small group fellowship, or worship services, or books of theology— rather they mentioned suffering. 'People said they grew more during seasons of loss, pain, and crisis than they did at any other time.'"[130]

Arthur W. Pink: "The secret of development of Christian character is the realization of our own powerlessness, acknowledged powerlessness, and the consequent turning unto the Lord for help. . . . 'In nothing be anxious.'"[131]

Timothy Keller: "The Bible does not promise that suffering will issue in full resolution or a 'happy ending' in this life."[132]

Randy Alcorn: "If you tell God he should not have allowed evil and suffering, then you are saying he should not have allowed us to experience compassion, mercy, and sacrificial love. In order for those characteristics to develop and become part of us, God had to permit evil and suffering. Can we fault God for ordaining the kind of world in which we could experience such great good?"[133]

A.E. Knoch: "Were God to let mankind live in sin until they learn its lessons, it would take a long and weary life, and might never reach the desired result. Hence, He also introduced the death state . . . . Can we not see the marvelous wisdom that provided that evil should make men mortal? Evil that results in death is sufficient to teach the lesson. Death . . . . is the divine method of impressing upon the sinner the sinfulness of sin, and is the necessary prelude to resurrection, which introduces the sinner into an actual experience of God's power and justice. . . . Indeed, this is the climax of evil."[134] . . . . "It is God's intention to draw His

---

[129] Donald Guthrie, *New Testament Theology* (Downers Grove, IL: Inter-Varsity Press, 1981), 98.
[130] Yancey, *The Question That Never Goes Away*, 102-103.
[131] Pink, *The Sovereignty of God*, 189.
[132] Keller, *Walking with God through Pain and Suffering*, 9.
[133] Alcorn, *If God Is Good*, 194.
[134] Knoch, *The Problem of Evil and the Judgments of God*, 59, 61.

creatures into loving intimacy with Himself through sin and a Saviour. . . . the delicious depths of love . . . could not be displayed by any other device, or appreciated by any other plan."[135]

Norman L. Geisler: "The unexplained is not necessarily the unexplainable. Likewise, that we don't know a good purpose for some suffering does not mean there is none. . . . 'The secret things belong to the Lord our God' (Duet. 29:29)."[136]

God is "more interested in our character than our comfort; more concerned about our holiness than our happiness. And given that pain is such an effective means in developing character (Rom. 5:2-4; Jas. 1:2-3; 2 Cor. 4:17), it should be no surprise that God has provided a suitable training ground conducive to our moral development. In fact . . . it is surprising that there is not more pain. . . . 'No pain, no gain' is not just a popular slogan, it is a moral postulate (Gen. 50:20)."[137]

"But some things cannot be created directly; some things can be produced only through a process. Again, patience is produced through the process of tribulation (Rom. 5:3 KJV). Trial forms character (Jas. 1:2), and there can be no sense of forgiveness without sin."[138]

Kenneth L. Gentry, Jr.: "Christianity is an historical faith designed for the long run. The faithful are to be diligently laboring now amidst trials and tribulations with an eye to the future. . . . We as Christians are to learn through our trials and tribulations, through our affliction and suffering."[139]

Jeremy A. Evans: "It is logically impossible for humans to be created already in this perfect state because in its spiritual aspect it involves coming freely to an uncoerced consciousness of God . . . . The messy and time-consuming nature of this endeavor in soul-making will likely not be fulfilled on this side of heaven."[140]

Critical Objection: On the other hand, Evans cites the rape and murder of a little girl and a deer, Bambi, trapped under a fallen timber

---

[135] Ibid., 191-192.

[136] Geisler, *If God, Why Evil?*, 48.

[137] Ibid., 55.

[138] Ibid., 62.

[139] Kenneth L. Gentry, Jr., *He Shall Have Dominion* (Tyler, TX: Institute for Christian Economics, 1992), 534.

[140] Evans, *The Problem of Evil*, 14.

that is burning as a result of a lightning strike and surmises that "the suffering involved in each circumstance is unnecessary. There either is (1) no morally sufficient reason for which these evils are permitted, or (2) even if there is a morally sufficient reason for permitting these evils, God could attain those ends without the requisite suffering supposedly necessary to bring about those ends. . . . [such] instances of gratuitous evil . . . [are] not necessary for the attainment of a greater good, or for which no greater good ever obtains."[141]

Critical Objection: "The earth as a place for soul-making . . . leaves much to be desired. The metaphor here is that of a school that attempts to train us to become great souls. But rigors of a curriculum are one thing; Lisbon earthquakes and Asian tsunamis, not to mention Auschwitz and the Killing Fields, are another. Do we really need a curriculum that grinds so many of its pupils to powder? If the earth is indeed a place for soul making, how many great souls does it produce? Is it not a tiny, tiny minority? How many flunk out of Hick's school of soul-making? How many do not merely flunk out but end up in the gutter . . . . Hick's view of the world as a school for soul-making, . . . I previously dismissed as inadequate."[142]

My Response: Dembski is right, of course. A soul-making theodicy by itself is inadequate. Evans' criticism above is also partially correct. We creatures, confined by space and time to the surface of this planet, are certainly inadequate to understand it because (as he says) it "will likely not be fulfilled on this side of heaven." Likewise, as Boyd well notes, "the insight of the psalmist that the wicked often prosper and the righteous suffer is at least as true today as it was when first written (e.g., Psa. 10:2-11; 73:2-14).[143]

Critical Objection: "Horrendous evils don't merely deform people; they crush and degrade them. Far from making people better, such evils produce self-loathing and defilement. While in some cases such evils may turn people to God, this seems like a very sadistic way to win them over. . . . [It's] just as likely to turn people away from God."[144]

---

[141] Ibid., 24-25,.
[142] Dembski, *The End of Christianity*, 31, 45.
[143] Boyd, *Satan and the Problem of Evil*, 253.
[144] D'Souza, *Godforsaken*, 53.

My Response: These critical objections illustrate is why soul-making is only one of our four purpose areas and bring us to our final purpose. But I also agree with Spiegel's assessment as he wisely counsels and concludes that the "soul-making perspective is directly endorsed in many biblical passages." Therefore, "it seems clear that the soul-making theodicy should at least be *part* of a Christian [perspective and] response to the problem of evil."[145]

To Glorify God

Warning: This purpose for the presence and persistence of evil, pain, and suffering in our world may be the most difficult for some to grasp and accept—perhaps even an anathema. But as Keller rightly acknowledges, "according to all branches of Christian theology, the ultimate purpose of life is to glorify God." This realization also means that the paramount purpose for our suffering is to glorify God. Hence, "the words *suffering* and *glory* are linked in a surprising number of biblical passages."[146] Properly understood, this linkage should be both enlightening and comforting. Alcorn further explains that "God wondrously displays his greatness when he brings good out of bad. . . . So it is with the drama of redemption. . . . The greater the obstacles, the greater the glory to God."[147]

To help guide our passage through this final purpose of maximizing God's own glory, we shall once again utilize a bulleted format:

- When Jesus' disciples questioned Him about a man born blind and the relationship between sin and suffering, Jesus responded, "Neither this man nor his parents sinned, said Jesus, but this happened so that the work of God might be displayed in his life" (John 9:3). Sproul expounds that this happened "so that, on this particular day, God's kingdom could be manifested through his

---

[145] Spiegel, "The Irenaean Soul-Making Theodicy" in Meister and Dew, Jr., eds., *God and Evil*, 93.

[146] Keller, *Walking with God through Pain and Suffering*, 167 – he cites Rom. 8:17-18; 2 Cor. 4:17; Eph. 3:13 1 Pet. 1:6-7; 4:13

[147] Alcorn, *If God Is Good*, 290.

healing. God's purpose here was to demonstrate who Jesus was. And to this day, 2,000 years later, that blind man, who presumably is in heaven today . . . sits . . . and talks about how God used his blindness to demonstrate the identity of Christ. . . . [Thus] his tragic condition was by no means senseless."[148]

- In a similar instance, after Jesus healed a paralytic, "the multitudes . . . marvelled, and gloried God, which had given such power unto men" (Matt. 9:8 KJV).

- "What if God, choosing to show his wrath and make his power known, bore with great patience the objects of this wrath – prepared for destruction? What if he did this to make the riches of his glory known to the objects of his mercy, whom he prepared in advance for glory?" (Rom. 9:22-23). After all, how is God going to demonstrate grace, mercy, love, and wrath and anger if there are no sinners and those who hate Him?

- God has absolute rights over all created things. Of the same lump of clay he can make "one vessel for honour, and another for dishonour." The clay has no claims on the potter (see Rom. 9:10-21 KJV). Likewise, how could God ever reveal his love, mercy, long-suffering, compassion, and forgiveness had not evil put humans and Him a position to call for the exercise of these attributes in our behalf?

- Romans 9:17 tells us: "For the Scripture says to Pharaoh: 'I raised you up for this very purpose, that I might display my power in you and that my name might be proclaimed in all the earth" (Rom. 9:17; Exod. 9:16). Once again, how could God have put his power and nature on display if there was no opportunity?

- God purposed good in all the evil choice's of Joseph's brothers in getting rid of him and selling him into slavery. "And as for you, you meant evil against me, but God meant it for good in order to bring about this present result, to preserve many people alive" (see Gen. 50:20 NAS). How is God going to show his love if there are no enemies?

- "Let your light so shine before men, that they may see your good works, and glorify your Father which is in heaven" (Matt. 5:16

---

[148] Sproul, *When Worlds Collide*, 50.

KJV). Aren't we followers of Christ to be dedicated to reflecting the glory of God in our lives, words, and works?

- The classic example is the death of Jesus. Here, God's sovereignty ordained horrendous evil acts to be carried out for this greater good. Therefore, Jesus exclaimed, "No, it was for this very reason I came to this hour. Father, glorify your name!" (John 12:27b-28a). Alcorn extrapolates that "if God can use the horror of Christ's crucifixion for good, then surely he can use our suffering for good."[149]

- Hence, Christ's crucifixion, arguably "the worst event in history" came in concert with "the best event"—"his resurrection."[150]

- Re: Isaiah 48:10 – "See, I have refined you, though not as silver; I have tested you in the furnace of affliction. For my own sake, I do this." Again, Alcorn spot on points out that "if you don't understand that the universe is about God and his glory—and that whatever exalts God's glory also works for your ultimate good—then you will misunderstand this passage and countless others." But he also concedes that "some consider God egotistical or cruel to test us for his sake. But the testing he does for *his* sake accrues to *our* eternal benefit."[151]

- "According to R.C. Sproul Jr., the reason God wanted Adam and Eve to fall into sin was because of God's eternal attribute of wrath. . . . So . . . God must necessarily create objects of judgment—'something on which I can exhibit the glory of my wrath.' If God had not created human beings and angelic creatures who would necessarily fall into sin, God would not have had the opportunity to display his glory in this way. So Sproul Jr., asserts something rather startling: 'It was [God's] desire to make his wrath known. He needed, then, something on which to be wrathful. He needed to have sinful creatures.'"[152]

- "But the Lord said to Ananias, 'Go! This man is my chosen instrument to carry my name before the Gentiles and their kings

---

[149] Alcorn, *If God Is Good*, 216.

[150] Ibid., 280.

[151] Ibid., 392.

[152] Copan, "Evil and Primeval Sin" in Meister and Dew, Jr., eds., *God and Evil*, 114. Quotations from Sproul Jr., *Almighty Over All*, 52-53, 57.

and before the people of Israel. I will show him how much he must suffer for my name." (Acts 9:15-16). For listings of Paul's sufferings, (see Rom. 8:35; 1 Cor. 4:9-13; 2 Cor. 4:8-9; 6:4-5; 11:23-30; 12:10).

- "In him we were also chosen, having been predestined according to the plan of him who works out everything in conformity with the purpose of his will, in order that we, who were the first to hope in Christ, might be for the praise of his glory" (Eph. 1:11-12). Yes, you and I are not exempt.

- "And, we, who with unveiled faces all reflect the Lord's glory, are being transformed into his likeness with ever-increasing glory, which comes from the Lord, who is the Spirit" (2 Cor. 3:18).

- "Praise be to his glorious name forever; may the whole earth be filled with his glory. Amen and Amen" (Psa. 72:19).

- "I say to the north, 'Give them up!' and to the south, 'Do not hold them back.' Bring my sons from afar and my daughters from the ends of the earth – everyone who is called by my name, whom I created for my glory, whom I formed and made" (Isa. 43:6-7).

Special Summary Insights of Scholars

John Piper: "Thus it is necessary, that God's awful majesty, his authority and dreadful greatness, justice, and holiness should be manifested. But this could not be, unless sin and punishment had been decreed; so that the shining forth of God's glory . . . . the glory of his goodness, love, and holiness would be faint without them; nay, they could scarcely shine forth at all. . . . There would be no manifestation of God's grace or true goodness, if there was no sin to be pardoned, no misery to be saved from. . . . So evil is necessary . . . ."[153]

Arthur W. Pink: "Had sin never been permitted, how could the justice of God have been displayed in punishing it? How could the wisdom of God have been manifested in so wondrously over-ruling [sic] it? How could the grace of God have been exhibited in pardoning it? How could the power of God have been exercised in subduing it? . . . .

[153] Piper, "Is God Less Glorious . . ." 7/19/14.

Should it be asked why God does this, the answer must be, To promote His own glory, i.e., the glory of His justice, power, and wrath."[154]

Pink then emphasizes that God designed man "chiefly to manifest His glory. But how?" Pink answers, "not . . . by continuing in a state of innocency. . . . [rather] From all eternity God designed that our world should be the stage on which He would display His manifold grace and wisdom in the redemption of lost sinners . . . (Eph. 3:11). . . . For the accomplishment of this glorious design God has governed the world from the beginning, and will continue it to the end. . . . The end and object of all is the glory of God."[155]

Timothy Keller: "And apart from sin and evil, we would never have seen the courage of God, or the astonishing extent of his love, or the glory of a deity who lays aside his glory and goes to the cross."[156]

Gordon J. Spykman: "We should remember that there are things that are *right* for God to do but *wrong* for us to do: He requires others to worship him, and he accepts worship from them. He seeks glory for himself. . . . He also uses evil to bring about good purposes, but he does not allow us to do so. Calvin quotes a statement of Augustine with approval: 'There is a great difference between what is fitting for man to will and what is fitting for God. . . . For through the bad wills of evil men God fulfills what he righteously wills.'"[157]

R.C. Sproul, Jr.: "God has a different role than we do. We are not to seek after our own glory precisely because it is his glory which we are to seek. . . . To suggest that God may not seek his own glory is akin to suggesting that because God forbids us to worship other gods, we many not worship him. We make the mistake of trying to mold God in our image when we try to make him be anything other than consumed with his glory."[158]

Randy Alcorn: "If we come to see the purpose of the universe as God's long-term glory rather than our short-term happiness, then we will undergo a critical paradigm shift in tackling the problem of evil and suffering. . . . I'm part of something great, far bigger than myself. . . .

---

[154] Pink, *The Sovereignty of God*, 203, 77.

[155] Ibid., 89, 192.

[156] Keller, *Walking with God through Pain and Suffering*, 117.

[157] Spykman, *Reformational Theology*, 329.

[158] Sproul Jr., *Almighty Over All*, 106.

then why not affirm by faith, even in the midst of suffering that it's worth it now? . . . The God of love is also the God of wrath (see Romans 1:18). Evil angers God. He hates evil, despises it, and will punish it. . . . But we err in judging God by our standards."[159]

Westminster Catechism: The "chief end of man is to glorify God and enjoy him forever"— Once we understand and accept that our main purpose for existing on this planet is to glorify God, then whatever befalls our lot in life will be easier to accept and understand in the form of self-sacrifice, the final one being our acceptance of death itself. After all, isn't this what faith and trust are all about?

Myles Munroe: These tests "give God a reason to put you on display."[160] Hence, it's not what we escape, but what and how we endure and overcome that gives God glory and gains us respect.

David Chilton: "God has ordained all things for His glory and for our ultimate good. This means that our sufferings are part of a consistent Plan. . . . God is completely sovereign, and uses both demons and the heathen to accomplish His holy purposes (1 Kings 22:20-22; Job 1:12-21); of course, He then punishes the heathen for their wicked motives and goals which led them to fulfill His decree: cf. Isa. 10:5-14)."[161] And, of course, we may not understand or agree with this. But according to the revelation of Scripture, this is how this world works.

A.E. Knoch: "Man needs trial and testing. Hence evil is used by God. But it is only unbelief and disloyalty to do anything which calls *His* power or beneficence into question. *We should not do evil, for we are not able to bring good out of it as God can.*"[162]

"The great glory of God's wisdom is displayed in the way He works out His will by means of the ignorance and opposition of His enemies. Christ crucified shows the utter futility of opposing God, for He . . . has planned accordingly. Let us always keep God's purpose distinct from the process used in its accomplishment."[163]

"But we forget the divine *purpose* behind of it all. Israel's liberation and exodus and Pharaoh's defeat were not the end in view. They were

---

[159] Alcorn, *If God Is Good*, 60, 199, 202, 183, 165.
[160] Munroe, *Re-discovering Faith*, 85.
[161] Chilton, *The Days of Vengeance*, 251.
[162] Knoch, *The Problem of Evil and the Judgments of God*, 49.
[163] Ibid., 68.

merely the means. The immediate purpose was the revelation of God's power. The ultimate purpose is the complete revelation of Himself."[164]

"But once we see that sin and sufferings are parts of the divine process, not the goal, and that all will contribute to the full revelation of Himself and the utmost blessing of His creatures, we have a destiny which does not demand His dethronement at the beginning. We do not need to fabricate another god to take the blame from His shoulders. . . . O, that I had known these things long ago!"[165]

O, That We Had Known These Things Long Ago

Most assuredly, God created and sustains the type of world that best suits his sovereign purposes. But He has not fully answered the question of "Why He allows so much evil, pain, and suffering in our world to persist?" And yet "one of the main teachings of the Bible," as Keller maintains, "is that almost no one grows into greatness or finds God without suffering, without pain coming into our lives like smelling salts to wake us up to all sorts of facts about life and our hearts to which we were blind."[166] One day, of course, we'll see all this from God's vantage point. Until that time, if we are troubled by evil, pain, and suffering in the world and are not involved in doing something about it, in our spheres of influence, then we are not being faithful to our calling and will pay an eternal price for our disobedience.

Admittedly, this chapter may have contained some uncomfortable truths. But the lives of Jesus, Paul, Peter, the other disciples, the New Testament church, and so many others ever since bear out these truths. And we moderns are not exempt. How then shall we respond when, not if, evil, pain, and suffering come across our path in this life?

It's to this task and challenge of our response to evil, pain, and suffering that we next turn as we re-explore how we can become better prepared than most of us have been in the past, and do so in advance of need. It's one of the greatest freedoms and privileges God has given us.

---

[164] Ibid., 196.
[165] Ibid., 205, 264.
[166] Keller, *Walking with God through Pain and Suffering*, 80.

One day, of course, we'll see all this from God's
vantage point. Until that time, if we are troubled by
evil, pain, and suffering in the world and are not
involved in doing something about it, in our spheres
of influence, then we are not being faithful
to our calling and will pay an eternal price
for our disobedience.

Chapter 7

Our Rehearsed Responses to Evil

It's the common language of the human soul. It's prominent throughout the Bible and at the very center of the Christian gospel. No effort is made to deny it, cover it up, or avoid it. Notably, "even before the cross, Jesus had been rejected by his family members who thought that he was mentally disturbed (Mark 3:20-21)."[1] Someday we will all speak that language when that moment hits and we find our lives suddenly altered with pain, loss, and suffering.

The only question will be: How will you respond?

Theoretically and pastorally, we could both begin and end this last chapter with this one-sentence recommendation. Please read Jerry Sittser's book, *A Grace Disguise: How the soul grows through loss*, for a modeled example of how to respond, endure, grow, overcome, and recover when evil, even horrendous evil, crosses your path in life. Yes, Sittser's book is that good (more on it later).

Someday we will all speak that language . . .

---

[1] Gary Habermas, "Evil, the Resurrection and the Example of Jesus" in Meister and Dew, Jr., eds., *God and Evil*, 169.

Our Greatest Freedom

During the 80s and 90s, when I was traveling about as a motivational speaker,[2] I often utilized this popular story to illustrate what I termed our greatest freedom in life. It's the story of identical twin girls raised in the family of an alcoholic father. The twins grow up. One becomes an alcoholic; the other becomes a total abstainer. Each is interviewed separately by a psychologist.

"Why did you become an alcoholic?" the psychologist asks the first twin.

"What do you expect from the daughter of an alcoholic?" she responds.

The other twin is asked a similar question, "Why did you become a total abstainer?"

She responds, "What do you expect from the daughter of an alcoholic?"

"Isn't that interesting," I would suggest to my audience. "Here we have about as identical of a situation as you can have from both a genetic and environment standpoint. Yet these twin girls chose two, diametrically opposed courses of response. Why do you think they made totally different choices?" I would rhetorically ask, pause, and then answer.

"It's because our greatest freedom in life is the freedom to decide how we will respond to any person, situation, or circumstance that crosses our path in life—and we have the freedom to do this in advance.[3] How so? By mentally rehearsing our response, over and over again, etching it deeper and deeper into our minds and spirits through mental role playing. Then, if and when something of this nature happens, we are already prepared on how to respond because we've rehearsed it over and over." Nowadays, I would also add the spiritual disciplines of prayer and

---

[2] See John Noē, *Peak Performance Principles for High Achievers* (Hollywood, FL: Frederick Fell, 2006, 1984).

[3] At least, we think we have this "freedom." That is debatable. But as I mentioned in Chapter 1 – Entering into a lengthy discussion of human free will verses the sovereignty of God is beyond the scope and purposes of this book. For more, see again, pp. 29-30 of Chapter 1.

biblical study to that practice. In short, we don't have to wait for adversity to strike and be forced to respond in an unprepared, knee-jerk, spur-of-the-moment manner.

Let's you and I play this out. What are some of the worst things that could happen to you and how would you respond? For instance, how would you respond if your spouse or a child died suddenly or was terribly hurt in an accident? If someone close or dear betrayed you? If you received a bad health report from the doctor? If you lost your job or a major part of your possessions or wealth? The fact is, Job, the patron saint of tragedy and loss, had to deal with most all of this at the same time. For sure, evil adversity will strike each one of us someday. When it happens, you and I need to be as well prepared and equipped as possible by our rehearsals (plural) in order to respond in a godly, humble, effective, and glorifying manner.

No question, this chapter will be the hardest and most challenging to implement when the time comes. Again, that's why it's so important to rehearse in advance. So what should be the proper Christian attitude and response toward evil, pain, and suffering?

Critical Objection: "Two years ago I met a teenage girl who is hideously crippled. She crawls on the floor like a crab. She cannot hold her head up to talk to you. Her head keeps jerking backward. The condition is painful. She must wear a diaper, if she's not diapered she would be crawling around in her own excrement.

If God is all powerful, God did this cruel thing to a child.

Why would anyone believe in such a God? Indeed, how could anyone worship Him?

Please don't quote Job to me. I've read it and there's no answer there.

We are told to call on God for help. We are told God will even move a mountain in response to our supplication. But when we are facing real pain and terrible needs, the preachers and priests and rabbis have nothing to offer except, 'Oh, dear child, you are suffering for a reason, just trust in God.'"[4]

My Response: Any number of painful and seemingly pointless situations, atrocities, or injustices could be substituted in place of the one

---

[4] From a private email I received after speaking at a conference on the topic of "The Origin of Evil," 2/11/03.

just described above. And from a human perspective, we Americans (especially) live with an entitlement mentality in an entitlement culture. Many of us believe that we ought not suffer, die of hunger, or be incapacitated or killed by any evil menace. But on what basis? Therefore, let's get intensely practical and honest. This arena of responding to evil is rationally inexplicable by human account. Moreover, as Wright points out, "evil has a hidden dimension; there is more to it than meets the eye."[5] Of course, one day we'll see this from God's vantage point. But until that time, we live in a tri-dimensional and polarized world filled with both good and evil. And, once again, if we are Christians and troubled by evil, pain, and suffering and are not involved in doing something about them in our spheres of influence, then we are not being faithful to our calling, and will pay a big price for this later.

Biblically, our tasks, here and now, are to endure, overcome, comfort, encourage, forgive, and reign on Earth over evil (Rev. 5:9-10) by seeking to deliver people from its subjugation and triumph through and over opposition no matter what happens to us, to those we love, or to those we meet, and no matter how senseless things may seem at the time. Hence, according to the Bible, we are not here to be merely under goers and stop there; we are here to be overcomers (Rev. 12:11; 21:7)!

Critical Objection: "If we think God caused this or that bad thing to happen for some big reason . . . play that out: That would mean God tipped the ferry over. God directed the tornado into the path of specific people. God gives a person cancer. You know you don't believe that. So what does Romans 8:28 mean then ['And we know that in all things God works for the good of those who love him, who have been called according to his purpose']? The key is the word 'works.'" It means "cooperates with . . . works in synergy with us and the tragedy to bring something good out of it. There may not have been a reason *for* it but there can be a purpose that emerges *from* it."[6]

My Response: I like Alcorn's plain and simple response about the use and misuse of this one verse. "Darrell Scott told me that after his daughter Rachel was murdered at Columbine, people often quoted Romans 8:28 to him. He wasn't ready to hear it. How sad that such a powerful verse, cited carelessly or prematurely, becomes a source of pain

---

[5] Wright, *Evil and the Justice of God*, 107.
[6] From a sermon of a local pastor, 5/4/14.

when it should offer great comfort." He then adds this piece of pastoral advice: "Don't use a hammer when you need a wrench. And don't use either when you need to give someone a hug, a blanket, or a meal—or just weep with them."[7] Sanders is more blunt: Don't "attempt to comfort those suffering with such explanations regarding God's intentions for the sufferer."[8]

Cautious Insights of Scholars

N.T. Wright: "This theme" of *"reigning on earth* . . . so frequent in the New Testament [is] so widely ignored in Christian theology. . . . [i.e.,] to bring his [God's] wise and healing order to the world, putting the world to rights under his just and gentle rule. . . . to be a kingdom and priest to serve God and to reign on the earth." Wright further claims that our "talk merely of 'going to heaven,' has combined to rob us of this central biblical theme. But until we put it back where it belongs we won't see how the New Testament ultimately offers a solution to the problem of evil."[9] (My next book will address this issue—see pp. 277-278 at the end of this book.)

And since we usually don't know the reason that God creates, allows, permits, and uses any particular situation of evil, pain, and suffering, we must be very careful about our responses because, as Wright elaborates, "we can't explain them and we can't eradicate them."[10] Wright compares this ignorance and inability to "the same way that a baby in the womb would lack the categories to think about the outside world."[11]

Timothy Keller: "Just because you can't see or imagine a good reason why God might allow something to happen doesn't mean there can't be one. . . . If our minds can't plumb the depths of the universe for good answers to suffering," and we conclude that "well, then, there can't

---

[7] Alcorn, *If God Is Good*, 471.

[8] Sanders, "A Freewill Theist's Response to Talbott's Universalism" in Parry &Partridge, *Universal Salvation?*, 183.

[9] Ibid., 139.

[10] N.T. Wright, *Surprised by Hope* (New York, NY: HarperOne, 2008), 85.

[11] Wright, *Evil and the Justice of God*, 164.

be any!" is to use reasoning that is 'fallacious' and 'blind faith of a high order.'"[12]

Wm. Paul Young: This non-scholar but mega-best-selling novelist suggests that this conundrum is perhaps like what Papa (God) explains to Mackenzie, whose young daughter was brutally murdered, in the bestselling novel *The Shack*. "There are millions of reasons to allow pain and hurt and suffering rather than to eradicate them, but most of those reasons can only be understood within each person's story. . . . If you could only see how all of this ends and what we will achieve without the violation of one human will—then you would understand. One day you will." To which Mackenzie objects, "But the cost! . . . Look at the cost— all the pain, all the suffering, everything that is so terrible and evil. . . . Is it worth it? . . . It all sounds like the end justifies the means, that to get what you want you will go to any length, even if it costs the lives of billions of people." To which Papa calmly replies, "you try to make sense of the world in which you live based on a very small and incomplete picture of reality. . . . The real underlying flaw in your life, Mackenzie, is that you don't think that I am good. . . . This world is not a playground where I keep all my children free from evil."[13]

The fact is, once again, we live in a world created by God that includes both good and evil. And we have been instructed how to respond. Trusting in God's sovereignty, omnipotence, and goodness we can be secure, regardless of what befalls us—predestined or not.

In this regard, a friend of mine shared with me that he was always worried about his business turning south and that he might turn away from God if that happened. He wisely sought the counsel of an older gentleman who offered this sage piece of advice. "Be much more concerned about your turning away from God if your business continues being successful."

How then should we respond when evil strikes?

---

[12] Keller, *The Reason for God*, 23.
[13] Wm. Paul Young, *The Shack* (Newbury Park, CA: Windblown Media, 2007), 125-126, 190.

Top Twelve Biblical Responses and Attitudes

Throughout the Bible, God directly or through inspiration has emphatically and repeatedly exhorted us how to respond and the proper attitudes to maintain. "The problem is," according to Spiegel, "our own stubborn resistance."[14] Hence, how we respond to both the good and evil situations we confront in life will define us and determine two things: 1) Whether or not we experience our best life possible here on this earth. 2) How well we will spend eternity.

Below is my "top twelve" list that I've compiled from Scripture. I have forced ranked them. But I'm not dogmatic about the order. You may or may not agree with either my ranking or inclusions. You might also find other verses you like better.

1. "Though he slay me, yet will I trust in him" (Job 13:15a KJV). Job is speaking of God here. And Job remained faithful in the face of adversity, as did Jesus, as did Paul, as did so many others in face of evil, pain, suffering, and death in the Bible (see Heb. 11:1-38 for instance – "These were all commended for their faith" – Heb. 11:39a).

2. "My Father, if it is possible, may this cup be taken from me. Yet not as I will, but as you will" (Matt. 26:39b, 42, 44). Thrice, Jesus prayed this to his Father in heaven, the night he was betrayed.

3. "Naked I came from my mother's womb, and naked I will depart. The LORD gave and the LORD has taken away; may the name of the LORD be praised. In all this, Job did not sin by charging God with wrongdoing / in what he said" (Job 1:21-22; 2:10b). Wilson terms this response the "telltale sign of whether your love for God is ultimately rooted in his loveliness . . . . When you are able to endure suffering like Job, without cursing God, you know you have come to love God. You love him, not because he's your sugar daddy, but because he has become beautiful to you. If God can wound you deeply yet still have your heart, then you have come to love him for his sake, not simply for your own."[15]

---

[14] Spiegel, "The Irenaean Soul-Making Theodicy" in Meister and Dew, Jr., eds., *God and Evil*, 88.

[15] Wilson, *Real Christian*, 155.

4. "I will extol the LORD at all times; his praise will always be on my lips. My soul will boast in the Lord; let the afflicted hear and rejoice. Glorify the LORD with me; and let us exalt his name together!" (Psa. 34:1-3). Keller makes special note of how "we almost completely ignored the words at the center of the passage . . . that 'the afflicted hear and be glad.'" He relates that "many people *find* God through affliction and suffering. They find that adversity moves them toward God rather than away." Also, adversity pulls "those who already believed into a deeper experience of God's reality, love, and grace." He characterizes this avenue as being "one of the main ways we move from abstract knowledge about God to a personal encounter with him as a living reality is through the furnace of affliction [Isa. 48:10]." He further claims that he, like many of us, "always knew, in principle, that 'Jesus is all you need' to get through. But you don't really know Jesus is all you need until Jesus is all you have."[16]

Keller terms the biblical metaphor of the furnace of affliction "a rich one," cites several verses (Isa. 48:10; also see: Isa. 43:2; 1 Pet. 1:6-7; 4:12), and then stresses that "if used properly, it does not destroy. Things put into the furnace properly can be shaped, refined, purified, and even beautified." He concludes that "this is a remarkable view of suffering, that if faced and endured with faith, it can in the end only make us better, stronger, and more filled with greatness and joy. Suffering, then, actually can use evil against itself. It can thwart the destructive purposes of evil and bring light and life out of darkness and death."[17]

5.   **"Show me, O LORD, my life's end**
                    and the number of my days;
             let me know how fleeing is my life.
       You have made my days a mere handbreadth;
       the span of my years is as nothing before you.
             Each man's life is but a breath.
       Man is a mere phantom as he goes to and fro:
             He bustles about, but only in vain;
       he heaps up wealth, not knowing who will get it.
    But now, LORD, what do I look for? My hope is in you"
                    (Psa. 39:4-7; also see Psa. 90:10, 12).

---

[16] Keller, *Walking with God through Pain and Suffering*, 4-5.
[17] Ibid., 8.

6. "Humble yourselves, therefore, under God's mighty hand, that he may lift you up in due time. Cast all your anxiety on him because he cares for you . . . . standing firm in the faith, because you know that your brothers throughout the world are undergoing the same kind of sufferings" (1 Pet. 5:6-7, 9).

7. "Forgetting what is behind and straining toward what is ahead, I press on toward the goal to win the prize for which God has called me heavenward in Christ Jesus" (Phil. 3:13b-14).

8. "Fight the good fight of the faith. Take hold of the eternal life to which you were called when you made your good confession in the presence of many witnesses" (1 Tim. 6:12a; also see 2 Tim. 4:7).

9. "No, in all these things we are more than conquerors through him who loved us. For I am convinced that neither death nor life, neither angels nor demons, neither the present nor the future, nor any powers, neither height nor depth, nor anything else in all creation, will be able to separate us from the love of God that is in Christ Jesus our Lord" (Rom. 8:37-39).

10. "I can do all things through Him who strengthens me" (Phil. 4:13 NAS). Including dying in the Lord. More on this later.

11. "For our light and momentary troubles are achieving for us an eternal glory that far outweighs them all. So we fix our eyes not on what is seen, but on what is unseen. For what is seen is temporary, but what is unseen is eternal" (2 Cor. 4:17-18). Do we really believe this? If we do, shouldn't this perspective make our "light and momentary troubles" (2 Cor. 4:17) more bearable as we look up fixing our eyes on Jesus? This response reorients us from looking upon ourselves and our pain and suffering into seeing how great and powerful He is. But there is another problem.

12. "But I tell you: Love your enemies and pray for those who persecute you" (Matt. 5:44). This command was never issued by any other religious leader or religion, including biblical Judaism. This also means, as Wilson factually points out, that "retaliation is out of the question, as is revenge—what the Bible calls repaying evil for evil: 'Repay no one evil for evil, but give thought to do what is honorable in the sight of all' (Romans 12:17). So, too, is harboring grudges or boiling in bitterness for days, weeks, or even months."[18]

---

[18] Wilson, *Real Christian*, 83.

Other Candidates for Responses and Attitudes

- "The Lord gives, and the Lord takes away, blessed be the name of the Lord" (Job 1:21).
- "I have set the LORD always before me. Because he is at my right hand, I will not be shaken" (Psa. 16:8).
- "For none of us lives to himself alone and none of us dies to himself alone. If we live, we live to the Lord and if we die, we die to the Lord. So whether we live or die, we belong to the Lord. For this very reason, Christ died and returned to life so that he might be the Lord of both the dead and the living" (Rom. 14:7-9).
- "Consider it pure joy, my brothers, whenever you face trials of many kinds, because you know that the testing of your faith develops perseverance. Perseverance must finish its work so that you may be mature and complete, not lacking anything" (Jas. 1:2-4).
- "Dear friends, do not be surprised at the painful trial you are suffering, as though something strange were happening to you. But rejoice that you participate in the sufferings of Christ, so that you may be overjoyed when his glory is revealed" (1 Pet. 4:12-13). We need to learn to cooperate with God and allow Him to refine, cleanse, test, and purify us. Yes, God is more interested in changing us than in changing our circumstances. Remember, nothing happens *to* me; it happens *for* me.
- "Do everything without complaining or arguing" (Phil. 2:14)— especially against God.
- "Be joyful always; pray continually; give thanks in all circumstances, for this is God's will for you in Christ Jesus" (1 Thess. 5:16-18; also Eph. 5:20).
- "I have learned to be content whatever the circumstances. I know what it is to be in need, and I know what it is to have plenty. I have learned the secret of being content in any and every situation, whether well fed or hungry, whether living in plenty or in want. I can do everything through him who gives me strength" (Phil. 4:11b-13).

- "Shall we indeed accept good from God and not accept adversity" (Job 2:10).
- "If anyone would come after me, he must deny himself and take up his cross and follow me" (Matt. 16:24b).
- "Who shall separate us from the love of Christ? Shall trouble, or hardship, or persecution, or famine, or nakedness, or danger, or sword? As it is written: 'For your sake we face death all day long; we are considered as sheep to be slaughtered'" (Rom. 8:35-36; from Psa. 44:22).
- "Jesus Christ, who died – more than that, who was raised to life – is at the right hand of God and is also interceding for us" (Rom. 8:34b; Heb. 7:25). At this very moment in the midst of your adversities, pains, and sorrows, Jesus is interceding for you.
- "Rejoice in the Lord always. I will say it again: Rejoice! Let your gentleness be evident to all. The Lord is near. Do not be anxious about anything, but in everything, by prayer and petition, with thanksgiving, present your requests to God. And the peace of God, which transcends all understanding, will guard your hearts and your minds in Christ Jesus" (Phil. 4:4-7).
- "Be joyful always; pray continually; give thanks in all circumstances, for this is God's will for you in Christ Jesus. . . . Avoid every kind of evil" (1 Thess. 5:16-18, 22).
- "Love must be sincere. Hate what is evil; cling to what is good" (Rom. 12:9).
- "Do not repay anyone evil for evil. Be careful to do what is right in the eyes of everybody. . . . Do not be overcome by evil, but overcome evil with good" (Rom. 12:17, 21).
- "A fool gives full vent to his anger, but a wise man keeps himself under control" (Prov. 29:11).
- "My son, do not make light of the Lord's discipline, and do not lose heart when he rebukes you, because the Lord disciplines those he loves, and he punishes everyone he accepts as a son" (Heb. 12:5b-6; Prov. 3:11-12).
- "Whatever happens, conduct yourselves in a manner worthy of the gospel of Christ. . . . For it has been granted to you on behalf of Christ not only to believe on him, but also to suffer for him,

since you are going through the same struggle you saw I had, and now hear that I still have." (Phil. 1:27a, 29-30).

The Hiddenness of God

Long ago, the psalmist cried out in response to God's seeming absence "Awake, O Lord! Why do you sleep? Rouse yourself! Do not reject us forever. Why do you hide your face and forget our misery and oppression?" (Psa. 44:23-24).

Today, as Keller reports, this familiar lament and so-frequent response throughout the Bible has not appreciably changed. He writes: "Probably the most common issue I hear today has to do broadly with believers who are bothered by the subject of God's silence. . . . In short, we are starved for divine attention . . . such as unanswered prayers or broken promises. . . . emotional suffering, quite unconnected with physical pain, can grip us more inwardly and encroach more inexorably upon the centre of our personal being."[19]

D'Souza terms this seeming absence, the "hiddenness of God." But he defends this aspect of God's distanced dealing with humanity this way:

God largely hides himself. The reason is that, if God made his presence obvious, then humans would be, in a sense forced to believe in him. God's presence would be so overwhelming and controlling that agnosticism, let alone atheism, would not even be an option. Even those who didn't want to submit to God would, as a practical matter, be forced to do so. Clearly God didn't want this. He gave freedom, and he wanted this freedom to count for something. So God made himself invisible in the world so that his presence would be obvious only to those who desired to meet him. God wanted to ensure that if we seek him, we will indeed find him; but if we don't, we will have plenty of excuses for ignoring or rejecting him.[20]

---

[19] Habermas, "Evil, the Resurrection and the Example of Jesus" in Meister and Dew, Jr., eds., *God and Evil*, 166-167.
[20] D'Souza, *Godforsaken*, 111.

In continuing support of God's hiddenness, D'Souza quotes Blaise Pascal. "There is enough light for those who desire to see, and enough darkness for those of a contrary disposition."[21] He further discloses that: "we are learning through science that lawful worlds are a package deal. Everything is woven together by a set of elaborate rules and dependencies; . . . Evils they may be, but they are necessary evils in order for us to be here to deplore them."[22]

In concluding, he rightly asks: "So is it really true that there is no other way for God to have made a universe containing human beings?" He responds that "the burden of proof" lies upon "those who say that God should have done something other than he did. . . . No such burden has ever been met; no such project has ever been attempted. We cannot argue based on fantasy about luxurious life . . . . Therefore, we can safely conclude . . . . in order to produce creatures like us, the pain and violence we witness in the world . . . are 'simply an inevitable tariff for achieving the desired end.'"[23]

So given that our world is plagued by hunger, war, sickness, loneliness, and brokenness; and if you find yourself or someone you love being beaten up, robbed, raped, infected with AIDS, or diagnosed with a debilitating or terminal illness, how can you find solace in knowing that it's all a part of God's plan? The continuing question many are asking remains: "Where is God in all this?"

My pastor asks this question in this manner. "Where is God when there is no happy ending? He is present in the people of God (as He was with Jesus). He is present in the lives of the people He sent to care for you. He is there in the community of the church. . . . Carrying each other's burdens, and in this way you will fulfill the law of Christ (Gal. 6:2)." Hence for my pastor, "the final answer to the question (at least the final answer for now) [for] Where is God when there's no happy ending?" is this. "God shows up . . . we are God with skin on. . . . He's working to redeem your life. Re-deem [defined as] to make something that is bad better or more acceptable; to rescue from loss; to buy back. . .

---

[21] Blaise Pascal, *Pensées and Other Writings* (New York, NY: Oxford University Press, 1995), 57.
[22] D'Souza, *Godforsaken*, 134.
[23] Ibid., 147-148.

. redemption is the concept that answers if anything good can come out of tragedy!"[24]

The Bible provides these further revelations about God's closeness (among others):

- "The Lord is close to the brokenhearted and saves those who are crushed in spirit" (Psa. 34:18). Keller terms this verse, "perhaps the single most concrete and practical thing sufferers can learn."[25]
- "He upholds all who fall, and lifts up all who are bowed down (Psa. 145:14)" Keller adds that these "are universals—God is near and cares about all sufferers. . . . And he says to believers in Christ 'I will never leave you; I will never forsake you' (Heb. 13:5)."[26]
- "Even though I walk through the valley of the shadow of death, I will fear no evil, for you are with me; your rod and your staff, they comfort me" (Psa. 23:4).
- "The eyes of the Lord are in every place, beholding the evil and the good" (Prov. 15:3 KJV).

Without the assuredness of our connectedness with our Creator and confidence of his unconditional love, Eben Alexander maintains, "we will always feel lost here on earth."[27] And that this lack of connectedness "is the root of every form of anxiety."[28] Anderson terms this sense of separation, "the anxiety of meaninglessness."[29] But Alexander insists that the revealed knowledge of God's connectedness and closeness with us is "the cure for it."[30] D'Souza agrees and explains that: "God is not interested in our merely knowing about him; he wants us to relate to him.

---

[24] Dave Rodriguez, sermon, Grace Church, Noblesville, IN. 5/11/14.

[25] Keller, *Walking with God through Pain and Suffering*, 228.

[26] ibid.

[27] Eben Alexander, *Proof of Heaven: A Neurosurgeon's Journey into the Afterlife* (New York, NY: Simon & Schuster Paperbacks, 2012), 171.

[28] Ibid., 76

[29] Anderson, *Understanding the Old Testament*, 555.

[30] Alexander, *Proof of Heaven*, 76.

[But] Divine concealment is a necessary strategy to seek out those who are open to a filial relationship with God."[31]

To top it all off, Alcorn adds that "whatever others do to his [God's] people, positively or negatively, he [Jesus] regards it as being done to him (see Matthew 25:40, 45)." Hence, "Christ no longer suffers on the cross, but he suffers with his suffering people."[32]

A Theodicy of Victory

Leon Morris in his book, *Revelation*, reminds us that "in the early church the day of a person's martyrdom was often called the day of his victory. Barclay comments, 'The real victory is not to live in safety, to evade trouble, cautiously and prudently to preserve life; the real victory is to face the worst that evil can do, and if need be to be faithful unto death."[33]

As an example, Keller cites "Shadrach, Meshach, and Abendnego . . . . Their greatest joy was to honor God, not to use God to get what they wanted in life. And as a result, they were fearless. Nothing could overthrow them."[34]

And, of course, it is better to suffer evil than to inflict it. But with the realization that God cannot be relieved of the responsibility for creating both good and evil, along with the long trail of failures to find an adequate theodicy, our challenge becomes to make better sense of our God-created world filled with evil, pain, and suffering, as well as with goodness, pleasure, and joyfulness.

This is why the Bible calls Christians to take responsibility to "turn away from wickedness" (2 Tim. 2:19), to expect to be persecuted (2 Tim. 3:12), to make decisions to "hate what is evil; cling to what is good (Rom. 12:9), to "not repay anyone evil for evil" (Rom. 12:17), to "overcome evil with good" (Rom. 12:21), to participate in the ongoing, dynamic victory over evil by being "a kingdom and priest to serve our God" and "reign on earth" (Rev. 5:10-11), to "do your best to present

---

[31] D'Souza, *Godforsaken*, 112.

[32] Alcorn, *If God Is Good*, 217.

[33] Leon Morris, *Revelation* (Grand Rapids, MI: Eerdmans, 1987), 182.

[34] Keller, *Walking with God through Pain and Suffering*, 231.

yourself to God as one approved, a workman who does not need to be ashamed and who correctly handles the word of truth" (2 Tim. 2:15), to "rule in the midst of your [our] enemies" (Psa. 110:2) as He prepares "a table before me [us] in the presence of my [our] enemies (Psa. 23:5), to be "patient in affliction," (Rom. 12:12), and yet to fight "the good fight" (2 Tim. 4:7). Somehow, and in some way or ways known fully only to God, all this is part of the purposes for evil. Certainly, all this is much easier to say than to do. But we have been assured that "your labor in the Lord is not in vain" (1 Cor. 15:58b).

I therefore suggest that we call this theodicy a "theodicy of victory." After all, we only live in this world once and for such a brief time, and our immortal spirits are contained in vulnerable and perishing physical bodies. But . . .

> Who shall separate us from the love of Christ? Shall trouble or hardship or persecution or famine or nakedness or danger or sword? As it is written: "For your sake we face death all day long; we are considered as sheep to be slaughtered." No, in all these things we are more than conquerors through him who loved us. For I am convinced that neither death nor life, neither angels nor demons, neither the present nor the future, nor any powers, neither height nor depth, nor anything else in all creation, will be able to separate us from the love of God that is in Christ Jesus our Lord. (Rom. 8:35-39).

Do we really believe this? If so, why shouldn't we "Consider it pure joy whenever you face trails of many kinds" (Jas. 1:2)? Doesn't it build character (Jas. 1:3-4) and bring "praise, glory, and honor" to Christ (1 Pet. 1:6-9)? Isn't it "commendable" and helpful in making us "conscious of God" (1 Pet. 2:19)? Moreover, aren't we "called" to suffering as Christ is our "example" (1 Pet. 2:20-21; 4:1, 12-16; 5:6-10)? Rather than being downcast, why shouldn't we focus on the positive value and attestation that we are being accepted and trained "as a son?" (Heb. 12:5-6). Is this too hard to believe? But doesn't this higher, greater, and often-revealed perspective make our "light and momentary troubles" (2 Cor. 4:17) more bearable?

The biblical fact is, faith in God does not guarantee an evil-free existence in this world, nor a life of comfort and easy. Nor does every problem or pain bring some good end or personal or moral development, as far as our earthly perspective is concerned. But if we truly believe "that in all things [including evil] God works for the good of those who love him, who have been called according to his purpose" (Rom. 8:28), then to face opposition and to struggle is truly for our betterment. Moreover, He has promised to be with us through all these experiences.

Furthermore, our reaction to evil holds out a great reward in the next world, the afterlife. And that's the world of eternity that ultimately matters the most. Therefore, shouldn't our knowing of this ultimate end-goal help free us from feeling resentful or rebellious? And shouldn't our proper response to the will of God and whatever evil befalls our path in this life be one of an obedient and faithful heart?

As we adopt this biblically sound "theodicy of victory" (it's also a worldview), let's likewise accept the world as God chosen to create it and chose for us to face. We shall never be able to answer all the questions and remove all the doubts. That would be to remove all need for faith. Instead, let's take on the primary attitude of Job, "Though he slay me, yet will I trust him" (Job 13:15).

Do we really believe this? If so, why shouldn't we "Consider it pure joy whenever you face trails of many kinds" (Jas. 1:2)?

Let's also stop hoping for and teaching a future, evil-less earthly world coming at some unscriptural "end of time," or at any time. Knowingly and intentionally, God set up a world in which both good and evil exist. It's also a world that is without end (Eph. 3:21 KJV; also see Eccl. 1:4; Psa. 78:69; 89:36-37; 93:1; 96:10; 104:5; 119:90; 148:4, 6).[35] He is the One solely responsible for it. Obviously, He could have arranged things differently, so that Adam and Eve would not have been tempted or would not have succumbed to that temptation. But He didn't.

Naturally, questions remain. But who are we to complain? We must simply trust God, recognize his purposes, and accept the things that come our way. In other words, we must stop struggling against them and start trusting and overcoming, no matter what happens to us or to those we love, and no matter how senseless things may seem at the time . . . because they aren't.

---

[35] See Noē *The Perfect Ending for the World*, 81-106

Showcasing Sittser—a Discerning Response

I know of no better example of a discerning response to evil, pain, and suffering from my various readings and research than those contained in Jerry Sittser's book, *A Grace Disguised: How the soul grows through loss*. Therefore, below is a succession of excerpts taken by chapter. I believe they beautifully showcase, in a chronological manner, both his human and godly responses to a horrendous evil that drastically changed his life. My hope is that this overview will peak your interest to read his book and more of his compelling, comforting, and encouraging story.

In one night of terror, Jerry Sittser lost three generations of women in his family when their car was struck by a drunk driver. His wife Lynda, his four-year-old daughter Diana Jane, and his mother Grace were killed. He, his daughter Catherine (then eight), sons David (seven) and John (two) were hurt but survived. He pulled them from the car, but watched as the other three died "before my eyes."[36]

A Grace Disguise (Inside Front Flap)
"The experience of loss does not have to be the defining moment of our lives . . . the defining moment can be our response to the loss. It is not what happens to us that matters so much as what happens in us."[37]

The End and the Beginning (Chapter 1)
"By some strange twist of fate or mysterious manifestation of divine providence I had been suddenly thrust into circumstances I had not chosen and could never have imagined. I had become the victim of a terrible tragedy. . . . I could not avoid it or escape it. There was no way out but ahead, into the abyss."[38]

Whose Loss Is Worse? (Chapter 2)
"Every week I hear stories about people's pain. I have probably always heard these stories, but until I experienced loss myself, I did not listen intently to them or let those stories penetrate the protective shell

---

[36] Sittser, *A Grace Disguise*, 26.
[37] Ibid., inside front flap.
[38] Ibid., 29.

around my heart. I am more sensitive to the pain now, not as oblivious and selfish as I used to be."[39]

Darkness Closes In (Chapter 3)
"Sudden and tragic loss leads to terrible darkness. It is as inescapable as nightmares during a high fever. . . . and we must face it alone. . . . and . . . descend into it. . . . The accident kept replaying itself in my mind like a horror movie repeating its most gruesome scene. . . I felt I was on the edge of insanity. . . . Never have I experienced such anguish and emptiness. It was my first encounter with existential darkness."[40]

"I chose to turn toward the pain, however falteringly, and to yield to the loss, though I had no idea at the time what that would mean. . . . I did not know the depths of suffering to which I would descend. For months I kept staring at the accident and reliving its trauma."[41]

"We can run from the darkness, or we can enter into the darkness and face the pain of loss. We can indulge ourselves in self-pity, or we can empathize with others and embrace their pain as our own. . . . We can return evil for evil, or we can overcome evil with good. It is this power to choose that adds dignity to our humanity and gives us the ability to transcend our circumstances, thus releasing us from living as mere victims. These choices are *never easy*."[42]

"Suffering is an ineradicable part of life, even as fate and death. Without suffering and death human life cannot be complete. . . . tragedy can increase the soul's capacity for darkness and light, for pleasure as well as pain, for hope as well as for dejection."[43]

"It is therefore not true that we become less through loss—unless we allow loss to make us less, grinding our soul down until there is nothing left but an external self entirely under the control of

---

[39] Ibid., 37.
[40] Ibid., 40-41.
[41] Ibid., 42-43.
[42] Ibid., 46.
[43] Ibid., 48.

circumstances. Loss can also make us more. In the darkness we can still find light. In death we can also find life. It depends on the choices we make."[44]

"I knew that running from darkness would only lead to greater darkness later on. I also knew that my soul had the capacity to grow—to absorb evil and good, to die and live again, to suffer abandonment and find God. In choosing to face the night, I took my first steps toward the sunrise."[45]

The Silent Scream of Pain (Chapter 4)
"for I knew that anger can turn easily into bitterness. I did not want to exacerbate that problem . . . . I see now that my faith was becoming an ally rather than an enemy because I could vent anger freely, even toward God, without fearing retribution."[46]

"In the end I was forced to address the problem of life's mortality— *my* mortality—which for a time made me profoundly depressed."[47]

Sailing on a Sea of Nothingness (Chapter 5)
"These memories were, and are, beautiful to me. I cling to them as a man clings to a plank of wood while lost in the middle of the sea. But they are also troubling . . . . They involve people I will never again see. I cannot live with the memories, and I cannot live without them."[48]

"Recovery is a misleading and empty expectation. We recover from broken limbs, not amputations. Catastrophic loss by definition precludes recovery. It will transform us or destroy us, but it will never leave us the same."[49]

---

[44] Ibid., 49.
[45] Ibid., 52.
[46] Ibid., 59.
[47] Ibid., 60.
[48] Ibid., 70.
[49] Ibid., 73.

"I have lost, but I have also gained. I lost the world I loved, but I gained a deeper awareness of grace. That grace has enabled me to clarify my purpose in life and rediscover the wonder of the present moment."[50]

The Amputation of the Familiar Self (Chapter 6)
"This crisis of identity, however, can lead to the formation of a new identity that integrates the loss into it. Loss creates a new set of circumstances in which we must live."[51]

"Finally, we reach the point where we begin to search for a new life, one that depends less on circumstances and more on the depth of our souls."[52]

"My loss has revealed how small my life is and how limited my resources are. But it has also enabled me to see how privileged I am to be alive and how meaningful are the opportunities afforded me to serve as a parent and a teacher."[53]

A Sudden Halt to Business As Usual (Chapter 7)
"Many people are destroyed by loss because . . . they choose to wallow in guilt and regret, to become bitter in spirit, or to fall into despair. . . . That causes gradual destruction of the soul."[54]

"Regret can also lead to transformation if we view loss as an opportunity to take inventory of our lives. Loss forces us to see ourselves for what we are. . . . This period of reflection proved to be liberating for me. I am more free from the past now than I would otherwise have been."[55]

"Still, a problem remained. . . . I wondered if I could trust a God who allowed, or caused, suffering in the first place. . . . Was it even possible

---

[50] Ibid., 79.
[51] Ibid., 85.
[52] Ibid., 90.
[53] Ibid., 91.
[54] Ibid., 99.
[55] Ibid., 102.

to believe in God, considering what had happened? . . . that question haunted me for a long time."[56]

The Terror of Randomness (Chapter 8)
"Suffering may be at its fiercest when it is random."[57]

"I do not know. Yet I choose to believe that God is working toward some ultimate purpose, even using my loss to that end. . . . It may fit into a scheme that surpasses even what our imaginations dare to think."[58]

Why Not Me? (Chapter 9)
"No one *is* safe . . . . There is often no rhyme or reason to the misery of some and to the happiness of others. . . . "So why not me? Can I expect to live an entire lifetime free of disappointment and suffering? Free of loss and pain? The very expectation strikes me as not only unrealistic but also arrogant."[59]

Forgive and Remember (Chapter 10)
"There is no going back. But there can be going ahead. Victims can choose life instead of death. . . . Forgiveness is simply choosing to do the right thing. It heals instead of hurts . . . . But forgiveness is costly. Forgiving people must give up the right to get even . . . ."[60]

"Unforgiveness makes a person sick by projecting the same scene of pain into the soul day after day, as if it were a video-tape that never stops. Every time the scene is replayed, he or she relives the pain and becomes angry and bitter all over again. That repetition pollutes the soul."[61]

---

[56] Ibid., 106.
[57] Ibid., 111.
[58] Ibid., 119.
[59] Ibid., 121, 124.
[60] Ibid., 141-142.
[61] Ibid., 144.

"In the end, I wonder whether it is really possible to forgive wrongdoers if we do not trust God first. Faith enables us to face wrongdoing in the light of God's sovereignty."[62]

"But it did focus my attention less on people, however terrible their wrongdoing, and more on God. I held God responsible for my circumstances. I placed my confidence in him; I also argued with him. In any case, God played the key role."[63]

<u>The Absence of God (Chapter 11)</u>
"But I have found comfort knowing that the sovereign God, who is in control of everything, is the same God who has experienced the pain I live with every day. . . . He is not aloof from my suffering but draws near to me when I suffer."[64]

"In the end, however, I do not think that I will ever be able to comprehend God's sovereignty. . . . Still, I have come to a partial resolution. I have made peace with his sovereignty and have found comfort in it. It is no longer odious to me. . . . From that point on I began, in small ways at least, to believe that God's sovereignty was a blessing and not a curse. . . . it gives me security and fills me with awe."[65]

<u>Life Has the Final Word (Chapter 12)</u>
"We do not happily and willingly accept life's mortality, which is an affront to everything we cherish. We want to control how life will turn out and claim the good life for ourselves . . . . Loss reminds us that we do not have the final word. Death does, whether it be the death of a spouse, a friendship, a marriage, a job, or our health. In the end death conquers all. It is inevitable, then, that loss of any kind forces us to look hard and long at the reality of death."[66]

---

[62] Ibid., 146-147.
[63] Ibid., 147.
[64] Ibid., 158.
[65] Ibid., 160-161.
[66] Ibid., 163, 164.

"Death does not have the final word; life does. Jesus' death and resurrection made it possible. He now has the authority and desire to give life to those who want and need it. . . . we inch hesitantly toward death, yet see death as the door to resurrection."[67]

A Community of Brokenness (Chapter 13)
"If people want their souls to grow through loss, whatever the loss is, they must eventually decide to love even more deeply than they did before. . . . If loss increases our capacity for love, then an increased capacity for love will only make us feel greater sorrow when suffering strikes again. There is no simple solution for this dilemma. Choosing to withdraw from people and to protect the self diminishes the soul; . . . the choice to love requires the courage to grieve."[68]

The Cloud of Witnesses (Chapter 14)
"The Bible tells the stories of the great 'cloud of witnesses' [Heb. 12:1] some of whom endured losses similar to the ones we face today and who have gone to the grave before us. They trusted God in their afflictions, loved him with their whole being, and obeyed him, even when obedience required sacrifice and led to death . . . . Because of them I see that I am only one of millions of people who in suffering believe nevertheless that God is still God."[69]

". . . life on earth is transitory and full of sorrow and that true life awaits the faithful in heaven."[70]

"[But] pain and death do not have the final word; God does. That final word involves more than life on earth; it involves life in heaven as well, the final destination of this great cloud of witnesses. . . . life here is not the end. Reality is more than we think it to be."[71]

---

[67] Ibid., 167, 168.
[68] Ibid., 183-184.
[69] Ibid., 187-188.
[70] Ibid., 190.
[71] Ibid., 193.

Heritage in a Graveyard (Chapter 15)

"God is growing my soul, making it bigger, and filling it with himself. . . .Though I have endured pain, I believe that the outcome is going to be wonderful. Lynda, Diana Jane, and my mother Grace have gone to death before me. Someday I too will die. . . . As long as I remain alive, I want to live as joyfully, serenely, and productively as I can. My heritage has set a standard for me, and I feel honored to uphold it."[72]

Responsive Insights of Scholars

When that time comes for you and me, these further insights may be easier to read than to implement. Once again, this is why rehearsal is so important. It prepares and conditions us in advance for how we will respond, as opposed to being a spur-of-the-moment reaction, which we may later regret.

F.F. Bruce: Writes that Jesus did not escape through supernatural means but, "Jesus has been qualified for his high-priestly service by his agony and tears, his supplication and suffering, throughout which his trust in God never failed."[73] He is our example when we are faced with trials, evil, pain, suffering, and death. Bruce concludes: "So the sufferings which Jesus endured were the necessary price of his obedience, the very means by which he fulfilled the will of God . . . . One can clearly recognize the motif of humiliation and suffering followed by exaltation in glory . . . ."[74] Should we his servants expect an easier or different path through this world? Or, should we take comfort in painful experiences as a mark that we are being treated "as a son" and "trained?"

Billy Graham: "We don't always know why God allows hard times to come to us, but we all experience them, and when we do, our response should be one of faith and trust. Remember: Jesus knows what it is to suffer – for he endured the suffering of the cross."[75] "I've often said that

---

[72] Ibid., 199-200.

[73] Bruce, *The Epistle to the Hebrews*, 129.

[74] Ibid, 131-132.

[75] Billy Graham, "My Answer," *The Indianapolis Star* (Indianapolis, IN), 10 February 2012, E-6.

hard times in life will do one of two things to us: they'll either drive us away from God or turn us toward Him. Which is better? The answer is clear: It's far better to put our lives into God's hands than to try living without Him. The Bible says, 'God is our refuge and strength, an ever-present help in trouble' (Psalm 46:1)."[76]

Heidelberg Catechism of 1563: Has a great first question and answer.

"Q. What is your only comfort in life and in death?

A. That I am not my own, but belong—body and soul, in life and death— to my faithful Savior, Jesus Christ. He has fully paid for all my sins with his precious blood, and has set me free from the tyranny of the devil. He also watches over me in such a way that not a hair can fall from my head without the will of my Father in heaven; in fact, all things must work together for my salvation. Because I belong to him, Christ, by his Holy Spirit, assures me of eternal life and makes me wholeheartedly willing and ready from now on to live for Him."

Martin Luther: "For the Christian's chief and only comfort in adversity lies in knowing that God does not lie, but brings all things to pass immutably, and that His will cannot be resisted, altered, or impeded."[77]

Dinesh D'Souza: "Rather than reply directly to Job, God asks what gives the creature the right to question its creator. Did Job make the universe? Did he give himself life? God seems to be pulling rank on Job here, and Job finally acquiesces, surrendering to God without having his questions fully answered. Thus Job becomes a biblical hero not of understanding, but of faith."[78]

". . . on the sufferings of people outside the West, the people of Asia, Africa, and South America . . . . it is a simple fact that people in those countries don't interpret their suffering as evidence that there is no God. . . . in third-world countries . . . suffering turns people to God, not away from him."[79]

---

[76] Billy Graham, "My Answer," *The Indianapolis Star* (Indianapolis, IN), 24 September 2013, E-4.

[77] Martin Luther, *The Bondage of the Will* , J.I. Pacer and O.R. Johnston, trans. (Old Tappan, NJ: Fleming H. Revell Co., 1957), 84.

[78] D'Souza, *What's So Great about Christianity?*, 277.

[79] D'Souza, *Godforsaken*, 11.

"There is something a little off key about Western academics saying, 'I have lost my faith because of the suffering of the Rwandans,' while Rwandans are saying, 'Our faith draws us closer to the only one who can console and protect us, which is God.'"[80]

Rabbi David Aaron: "To be fully alive means to open ourselves up to the spectrum of life's experiences and to embrace the dance of pain and pleasure, joy and sadness, laughter and tears. . . . to immerse yourself in the complete drama of being alive and human. . . . What in your life is worth crying over? What is worth being pained about? What is really missing, and what do you really want? When each one of us answers these questions, we will . . . . discover that what is really missing and all that we truly want is love—love for God and each other."[81]

Amazing Grace:

"Through many dangers, toils, and snares
I have already come;
'Tis Grace that brought me safe thus far
and Grace will lead me home."

Yea, when this flesh and heart shall fail,
And mortal life shall cease,
I shall possess within the veil,
A life of joy and peace."[82]

Rick Warren: "One of the easiest ways to get rid of pain is to get your focus off yourself and onto God and others."[83] (Rick Warren's son, Matthew, committed suicide in 2013.)

Myles Munroe: "The fight between faith and fear is the only fight we really have in life. . . . People will let you down. Systems will fail. Jobs will go away. Put your faith in God. His kingdom will never fail. God will never fail you. He is steady. He is stable. God is forever. . . . Learn to welcome tough circumstances as dear friends that have arrived

---

[80] Ibid., 12.

[81] Aaron, *Inviting God In*, 71.

[82] John Newton, "Amazing Grace," lyrics.

[83] From an interview by Paul Bradshaw with Rich Warren, "Purpose Driven Life," email, 9/20/07.

to make you better and prepare you for your award. . . . [But] How can we rejoice in suffering? It is impossible from a human perspective. Only the heavenly perspective, seen though the eyes of faith, makes it possible. . . . Have you reached that place in your faith? Could your faith handle losing everything?"[84] (Myles Munroe, his wife, and others were killed in a private airplane crash in 2014.)

Timothy Keller: "Suffering can refine us rather than destroy us because God himself walks with us in the fire . . . . to know the God who says 'when you pass through the waters . . . when you walk through the fire . . . I will be with you' (Isa. 43:2)."[85]

"Nothing is more important than to learn how to maintain a life of purpose in the midst of painful adversity."[86]

"Sociologists and anthropologists have analyzed and compared the various ways that cultures train its [sic] members for grief, pain, and loss. And when this comparison is done, it is often noted that our own contemporary secular, Western culture is one of the weakest and worst in history at doing so. . . . [It] gives its members no explanation for suffering and very little guidance as to how to deal with it."[87]

". . . death and all its consequences is an enormous human problem—perhaps *the* problem . . . . The answer is that we can do that only if we locate our meaning in things that can't be touched by death. . . . in things that suffering cannot destroy."[88]

"We must rest in the sufficiency of Christ's sufferings for us before we can even begin to suffer like him."[89]

". . . the main response of the secular person to evil and suffering is not to find meaning in it, nor to prepare to triumph over it in some future life, but to make the world better, to slowly but surely eliminate suffering right here. . . . But that is impossible."[90]

"Virtually every kind of evil was thrown at Jesus at the end of his life. He was abandoned, betrayed, and denied by friends. He was handed

---

[84] Munroe, *Rediscovering Faith*, 68, 70, 88, 113, 169.
[85] Keller, *Walking with God through Pain and Suffering*, 9.
[86] Ibid., 13.
[87] Ibid., 14-15.
[88] Ibid., 36-37.
[89] Ibid., 52.
[90] Ibid., 74.

over by a fickle mob. He was given a sham trial and was tortured and killed, a victim of injustice

"There is no way to know who you really are until you are tested. There is no way to really empathize and sympathize with other suffering people unless you have suffered yourself. There is no way to really learn how to trust in God until you are drowning."[91]

Robert Jeffress: "Much of the suffering in the world is self-inflicted. . . . a direct result of what we do to others or what we do to ourselves. . . . they are the results of our wrong choices or the wrong choices of others. . . . Suffering is the price we continue paying for the freedom to choose between right and wrong."[92]

Nathan Wilson: "The loved one dies. The job fails. The illness strikes. The money disappears. The marriage dissolves. Any or all of those can leave us disoriented, lost, without sense of direction or purpose. What was is no more, and what is to come is unclear. . . . The ancients called these times the dark nights of the soul, moments of personal crucifixion when we finally wail along with the psalmist, along with Jesus, 'My God, my God, why have you forsaken me?' Our bodies may live on, but our souls – in those moments – seem lost in a darkness so thick that we cannot see through it."[93]

Mark Galli: "God is most deeply met not on the other side of suffering, but in the suffering itself."[94]

Paul Tillich: "It does not take a great deal of imagination or courage to believe that God is on your side when you are prospering or winning; it takes a great deal of courage and imagination to believe that God is on your side when you are suffering or losing. To believe in love in the face of hatred, life in the face of death, day in the dark of night, good in the face of evil—to some, all of these may seem to be hopelessly naive, wishful thinking, 'whistling in the dark' . . . but to Tillich, all of these are manifestations of enormous courage, the courage of confidence in more than the sovereignty of fact and appearance. . . . It is 'the character of

---

[91] Ibid., 234.

[92] Jeffress, *Hell? Yes!*, 61-62.

[93] Wilson, "Faith can overcome fear of loss, unknown," *The Indianapolis Star* (Indianapolis, IN), 6 September 2014, A-9.

[94] Mark Galli, "Pep Talks for Successful Living," *Christianity Today,* November 2013, 30.

accepting acceptance.' . . . It is faith that allows grace to do its work. . . . for Tillich, is the paradox of 'participation in something which transcends the self.' . . . I cannot imagine a more timely message for a more need people than that contained in *The Courage to Be.*"[95]

Brennan Manning: Whatever happened in the life of Jesus is in some way going to happen to us. Wounds are necessary. The soul has to be wounded as well as the body. To think that the natural and proper state is to be without wounds is an illusion. Those who wear bulletproof vests protecting themselves from failure, shipwreck, and heartbreak will never know what love is."[96]

William Barclay: "Christian joy is not dependent on things outside a man; its source is in our consciousness of the presence of living Lord, the certainty that nothing can separate us from the love of God in him. . . . Many are haunted by the chances and the changes of life. . . . The only end to that worry is the utter conviction that, whatever happens, God's hand will never cause his child a needless tear. Things will happen that we cannot understand, but if we are sure enough of God's love we can accept with serenity even those things which wound the heart and baffle the mind."[97]

Philip Yancey: "It seems to me that Christianity doesn't in any way lessen suffering. What is does is enable you to take it, to face it, to work through it, and eventually to convert it."[98]

"Bonhoeffer wrote this creed shortly before his execution by the Gestapo, which took place twenty-three days before Germany's surrender. Death, said Bonhoeffer, is the supreme festival on the road to freedom. If he's wrong, all is lost. If he's right, it's just begun."[99]

John Hick: "If we were fully conscious of God and of His universal purpose of good we should be able to accept our life in its entirety as God's gift and be free from anguish on account of it."[100]

---

[95] Peter J. Gomes in Introduction of Paul Tillich, *The Courage to Be*, 2nd ed. (New Haven & London: Yale University Press, 2000, 1952), *xxiii-xxiv, xxxii.*
[96] Manning, *Abba's Child*, 158.
[97] Barclay, *The Letter to the Romans*, 199-200.
[98] Yancey, *The Question that Never Goes Away*, 153.
[99] Ibid., 154.
[100] Hick, *Evil and the God of Love*, 319.

"Even death, that grim reminder of our utter vulnerability as creatures made out of dust of the earth, loses its sting. To believers, as Martin Luther wrote, death 'is already dead, and hath nothing terrible behind its grinning mask.'"[101]

Wayne Grudem: "However we understand God's relationship to evil, we must *never* come to the point where we think that we are not responsible for the evil that we do, or that God takes pleasure in evil or is to be blamed for it. Such a conclusion is clearly contrary to Scripture."[102]

William A. Dembski: "More than any other problem, people have used the problem of evil to distance God from themselves and even to rationalize that God doesn't exist. The problem of evil is part of a much larger problem, namely, how a benevolent God can restore a prodigal universe to himself. This is the problem of good, and it subsumes the problem of evil. . . . Redemption is God having the final word. . . . The good news of Christianity is that this great redemption is ours in Christ."[103]

Jennifer L. Bayne and Sarah E. Hinlicky: "But even more heinous to some is the thought that God wants evil in the world for his ultimate purposes and that we are just pawns in the game. People want to protect God. It is easier to accept a world spun out of control, with evil abounding, than a world ordered by God where evil has a chosen place."[104] Actually, those people are not contributing to our knowledge of God and our world. They are simply telling us something about themselves.

Randy Alcorn: "While people living in relative comfort reject faith in God due to the problem of evil, those subjected to the worst evil and suffering often turn *to* God. . . . This is one of the great paradoxes of suffering."[105]

---

[101] Ibid., 361.

[102] Grudem, *Systematic Theology*, 323.

[103] Dembski, *The End of Christianity*, 176, 185, 186..

[104] Jennifer L. Bayne and Sarah E. Hinlicky, "Free To Be Creatures," *Christianity Today*, 23 October 2000, 41.

[105] Alcorn, *If God Is Good*, 102.

"Your choice of whether you will trust God and worship him today. . .. has enormous implications for eternal rewards God promises us in the next life."[106]

"It's one thing to suffer terribly, another to *choose* to suffer terribly. Evil and suffering formed the crucible in which God demonstrates his love to mankind. . . . God's love comes to us soaked in divine blood. . . . What Jesus suffered, God suffered."[107]

"When we feel upset with God and tempted to blame him, we should look at the outstretched arms of Jesus and focus on his wounds, not ours. . . . Because once you see Jesus as he really is, your worldview, your goals, your affections, *everything*— including your view of evil and suffering—will change."[108]

"Hebrews 2:10 and 5:8 . . . speak of Christ learning obedience and being perfected through his sufferings . . . . 'If Christ had to suffer to be made complete, how can we expect not to have some form of suffering? . . . God tailors a package of suffering best suited for each of his own. We all have the opportunity to grow through these.'"[109]

"The sovereignty of God is the one impregnable rock to which the suffering human heart must cling. The circumstances surrounding our lives are no accident: they may be the work of evil, but that evil is held firmly within the mighty hand of our sovereign God. . . . All evil is subject to Him, and evil cannot touch His children unless He permits it."[110]

"We are puzzled sometimes because God could have shown his power by preventing tragedies and healing diseases, but chose not to. We would prefer that God crush and remove evil, not allow it to hurt us. But power isn't his sole attribute. He is also glorified in showing his wisdom. . . . one day in his presence, we will marvel at his wisdom in not preventing certain evils that he used, in ways we could never have imagined, for our ultimate good."[111]

---

[106] Ibid., 192.
[107] Ibid., 209.
[108] Ibid., 218-219.
[109] Ibid., 233-234 in quotation of David O'Brien who "has had a severe form of cerebral palsy since birth."
[110] Ibid., 272 in quotation of Margaret Clarkson.
[111] Ibid., 275.

"Everything that comes into your life—yes, even evil and suffering—is Father-filtered. Whether suffering brings us to Christlikeness depends, to some degree, upon our willingness to submit to God and trust him and draw our strength from him. Suffering will come whether we allow it to make us Christlike or not—but if we don't our suffering is wasted."[112]

"Every time we ask God to remove some obstacle in our lives, we should realize we may be asking him to forgo one more opportunity to declare his greatness. . . . But when he answers no, we should recognize that he desires to demonstrate his greater glory. May we then bend our knees and trust his sovereign grace."[113]

"Ironically, the problem of evil and suffering seems worse to us who live in affluent cultures precisely because we face less of it than many people have throughout history. . . . who have endured famine, genocide, and persecution, yet smile genuinely as they affirm God's goodness and grace."[114]

"We reveal a staggering arrogance in assuming God *owes* us an explanation for anything. God understands our curiosity but owes us nothing. To demand an explanation is to hold God accountable to us. What arrogance to say, 'If I cannot understand why a loving God would permit all this evil and suffering, then there cannot be a loving God!'"[115]

"Voice of the Martyrs reports that the twentieth century produced more Christian martyrs than the previous nineteen centuries combined. Nearly two hundred thousand believers in Christ are executed per year, while millions more languish in prisons and enforced servitude."[116]

"Worry is momentary atheism."[117]

"Sometimes God delivers us from suffering, and other times he sustains us through suffering. Sometimes God calms the storm, and sometimes he calms the heart. Both are acts of grace, and both should prompt us to praise him."[118]

---

[112] Ibid., 289.
[113] Ibid., 290.
[114] Ibid., 330.
[115] Ibid., 355.
[116] Ibid., 395.
[117] Ibid., 397.
[118] Ibid., 404.

"It seems counterintuitive to give thanks in suffering, but God commands it and countless people have benefited from it. Getting in touch every day with God's grace, learning to thank him for the small things, serves us well when we lose big things. It deepens our reservoir and gives us eyes to see God's faithfulness and blessings at a time when we most need clear vision."[119]

"Charles Spurgeon wrote: 'I venture to say that the greatest earthly blessing that God can give to any of us is health, with the possible exception of sickness. . . . if some men that I know of could only be favoured with a month of rheumatism, it would, by God's grace, mellow them marvelously."[120]

"It becomes easier to trust God when we understand that what he takes away belonged to him in the first place (see Job 1:21)."[121]

"How can we possibly obey this command to welcome difficulties instead of resenting them? By trusting that God tells us the truth when he says these make us better people, increase our endurance, expand our ministry, and prepare us for eternal joy. If learning to trust God is good for us and God loves us enough to act for our good, why are we surprised when difficulties come?"[122]

"What if the highest good in life is to draw close to Jesus? And what if suffering will help us achieve that good?"[123]

"When the day of crisis comes, we should pour out our hearts to God, who can handle our grief and even our anger. We should not turn from God and internalize our anger, allowing it to become bitterness. . . . We should not insist on taking control by demanding a rational explanation for the evils and suffering that befall us. We should look to God and ask Him to reveal himself to us; . . ."[124]

"Some people hold tenaciously to a faith that their child will not die, that their cancer will disappear, that their spouse will recover from a

---

[119] Ibid., 413.
[120] Ibid., 416.
[121] Ibid., 418.
[122] Ibid., 419.
[123] Ibid., 420.
[124] Ibid., 455.

stroke. Do they have faith in God or is their faith in what they desperately want God to do?"[125]

"When suffering comes, we should ask God to use it for his glory. . . . Blaming God and others keeps us from suffering's redemptive aspects. . . . Recognizing that suffering has meaning helps us learn not to waste it. . . . How you handle suffering tells your life story. . . . Learn to find your identity in God, not your illness. . . . We should view our God-permitted suffering as his specific calling to us, and not resent it if he calls others to suffer less. . . . God knows how much we can bear; he knows how to relieve suffering and how to strengthen us to endure it."[126]

"To suffer and die well, your eyes must lock on the invisible God. . . . In the end, Jesus Christ is the only satisfying answer to the problem of evil and suffering."[127]

How to Die Like a Christian

Our greatest opportunity in life to bring glory to the Lord may come at the end—i.e., your and my "day of victory"—as we are "being poured out like a drink offering, and the time has come for my [our] departure." This will only be true, however, if we "have fought the good fight," "finished the race," and "kept the faith" as the apostle Paul bore witness some nineteen hundred and fifty years ago (see 2 Tim. 4:6-7).

Munroe captures this possibility and grand occasion well. He writes: "Both the Bible and subsequent history are filled with the testimonies of believers who faced death fearlessly, confidently, and even with joyful anticipation because in faith they knew that death was not an ending but a beginning. . . . People generally aren't impressed by our faith during good times. . . . They are watching to see what we do when the going gets tough."[128]

Hence, Jesus assured us:

---

[125] Ibid., 466.
[126] Ibid., 473-477.
[127] Ibid., 491, 493.
[128] Munroe, *Re-discovering Faith*, 69, 79.

"I have told you these things, so that in me you may have peace.
In this world you will have trouble/tribulation.
But take heart! I have overcome the world"
(John 16:33 NIV / KJV).

Years ago, I heard a powerful story and have shared it many times with different groups. Whenever I do, it almost always brings a tear to my eye. It's about a ninety-year-old grandmother on her death bed with only a few days to live. She calls in her entire family (children, spouses, grandchildren, and great-grandchildren). They arrive and encircle her hospital bed for one last time, while she is still lucid. With a weakened voice, she tells them, "For ninety years I have been modeling for you how to live the Christian life. Now, I'm going to model for you how to die like one."[129]

Below, are two examples of modeling how to die well, like a Christian. One is Kara Trippetts. The other is my mother. For Christians living in some countries other than America, more radical stances may be appropriate and required.

Kara Tippetts

I met Kara Tippetts in November of 2014, during the time I was writing this book. She spoke at our church—bald head and all. Kara was in the process of modeling how to die like a Christian to her family and to many thousands more through her book and speaking engagements. Her book is appropriately titled by using lower case letters: *the hardest peace: expecting grace in the midst of life's hard.*

Kara has cancer. It has spread from her breasts to her bones, brains, and into her blood. She has only a short time left. Now, as I'm finishing the writing of this book (January 2015), Kara is in hospice care. By the time you read this, she may be in heaven. Below are six excerpts from her book about her difficulties in living through this time and modeling how to die like a Christian. She can be brutally honest and transparent.

"Cancer is a gift. There, I said it. I can say that cancer and suffering give the beautiful gift of perspective. It is the gift you never wanted, the

---

[129] Noē, *The Greater Jesus*, 355.

gift wrapped in confusion and brokenness and heartbreak. It's the gift that strips all your other ideas of living from your completely."[130]

"Brokenness is not to be feared, but humbly received. Maybe it is our culture that is wrong. . . . I have met many who have taken that diagnosis and slipped deeply into anger. I understand. It's an easy place to go. But I cannot go there. I have taken a path of seeking grace."[131]

"I never expected to be planning my funeral, counting my moments, and fighting for my next breath in my thirties. I never expected to be sitting on my daughter's bed with the sinking feeling her mama was going to die of cancer and not of old age, and not knowing the right words to love her well. Never. But those places, those raw, broken places, are the heart of life."[132]

"One of the highest callings in my life is shepherding the hearts of my children. . . . She and I will talk about searching for God's grace and naming it in this life and knowing grace in its fullest in the presence of Jesus in the next life. But in the tension between the two worlds, there is mercy for our lack of understanding, our pain in wanting to remain together, our holding on to this place so tightly."[133]

"I have confidence of my next life, but my vision of it is dim when I look upon the faces of my little ones. It's a gift and a challenge, living in the now and not in the fear of what is to come. I have no fear of death; I only fear seeing the effects of my suffering in the faces of my loves. Their struggle in the parting. I know my destination; I know I will be met with goodness and my ultimate life in God's grace."[134]

"Longevity is not the answer, but it is my soft heart's desire. But to give glory forever—yes, yes. That is my longevity in this place and in the next. . . . The veil between here and heaven is very thin."[135]

---

[130] Kara Tippetts, *the hardest peace: expecting grace in the midst of life's hard* (Colorado Springs, CO: David C. Cook, 2014), 114.

[131] Ibid., 118.

[132] Ibid., 139.

[133] Ibid., 140.

[134] Ibid., 151.

[135] Ibid., 153.

My Mother

Ten years ago, my mother, age 85, was dying of lung cancer. During her final weeks, our family traveled to Florida and surrounded her bed: my brother and I, our two spouses, her 5 grandchildren and one spouse, and 9 great grandchildren (at that time), but not all of us visited her at the same time. And she graciously received each one for the last time.

As her time on earth wound down she began seeing Jesus in the room and telling us about Him. No, we couldn't see Him, but whenever He appeared to her it seem to give her great comfort. More and more, she began pulling away from the attachments of this life, just as the lyrics of the refrain of this great old hymn proclaim:

> Turn your eyes upon Jesus,
> Look full in his wonderful face,
> And the things of earth will grow strangely dim,
> In the light of his glory and grace.[136]

My wife, Cindy, flew to Florida and spent three weeks attending to her during what would be her final month on earth. Here's how Cindy wonderfully reflects on their time together.

"I'll always be grateful to God and my mother-in-law, or just Mom as I called her, to have allowed me the time with her as she transitioned to her eternal home. It was three weeks of caring for her in a most personal way that cemented the wonders of that transition in my spirit, forever. The privilege of speaking into her life through the singing of hymns to her—especially "Turn Your Eyes Upon Jesus"—solidified 2 Corinthians 4:16-18 at my very core.

"There she was laying before me, her body wasting away while her spirit was being renewed daily. It was a revelation to find myself singing right past her wasting body to Eileen, the woman of God I knew, who was momentarily being held captive by her body, but being fully prepared for her entry into glory.

"Life is bookended. You enter this life at birth. It is a celebration. Those who love and surround you look with great expectation at the promise of your life to come. Then, life's path is walked. You look back

---

[136] "Turn Your Eyes Upon Jesus," Helen H. Lemmel, 1922.

and it all happened so quickly—the trials and tribulations, victories and triumphs, shortcomings, failures, surprises, disappointments, sweet times, healings, and scars—as you realize the challenges of knowing God, but knowing Him nonetheless, and seeing Him change you.

"Then your God ordained day arrives. There has been a loosening of those things you so cherished while here on earth as you focus on your coming eternal chapter. Those who had loved you surrounded you and looked with comfort and great expectation at the promise of your life to come. What a celebratory time that was! Amen and Amen."

On her last day, as she faced her "last enemy," only my brother Jim and I were by her side. Cindy had done her part and flown home. No, Reta Eileen Noe, Mom as we knew her, was not communicating with us any more or acknowledging our words.

"Just let go, Mom. It's okay. Go to heaven, go be with Jesus. Everything will be all right here. Dad is waiting for you." Endlessly, it seemed, we spoke these words to her in numerous ways and at various times during that day. Yes, there had come a point during her final weeks when we switched our prayers from requests for healing to requests for God to take her home.

Then when her strength was gone and her final moment of victory appeared nigh, she breathed her last, exhaled, and left this world for the next. So, too, will you and I one day.

That evening, during a beautiful sunset, my brother and I took a long walk on the beach, where she and Dad often walked, went to a fancy restaurant, and celebrated their lives. It was a great and memorable time together. Our father had died somewhat unexpectedly ten days prior. Unfortunately, neither my brother nor I were with him when he died. But within a one-month period, he and I conducted two funerals (in Indiana) and two memorial services (in Florida). All four were joyous and celebratory events. He and I made sure of that. Here is the opening part of my eulogy (notes) that I gave at the two, joint-memorial services:

Mom & Dad's Joint Eulogy (June 10, 12, 2005)

THANK YOU all for coming to this MEMORIAL SERVICE CELEBRATING the life of my and brother Jim's father and mother:
Dr. William R. Noe (Bob)
Reta Eileen Noe (Eileen)

LAST MONTH it was, indeed, a DUTY and an HONOR for a son . .
.

    —in this case TWO sons
    —to bury their two parents within 10 days of each other.

As it is written,
"For everything there is a season,
and a time for every matter under heaven:
a time to be born, and a time to die . . . .
a time to mourn, and a time to dance" (Eccl. 3:1-2, 4).

And so, AS I said at each funeral service – and it bears repeating –
In that hickory casket LAYS my dad's (later, my mom's) 85-year-
old body.
But he/she is NOT THERE.
He/she has RELOCATED.

Our SOLACE and COMFORT is in knowing
- that both of them have entered Heaven and are now with the
  Lord Jesus Christ.
- AND, both have traded in that old BODY for a new
  "spiritual body" which God "gives," according to (1 Cor.
  15:35-44).

HOW can we speak with so much CONFIDENCE and
ASSURANCE, you might ask?
- Because of the TESTIMONY and AUTHORITY of
  Scripture.
- It DOCUMENTS the GENERAL RESURRECTION of the
  DEAD
- As prophesied by the prophet DANIEL. . .
- 6 centuries before Christ, was UNDERWAY.
- As it is written (at Jesus' death): (Me – READ Matt. 27:51-53).

The REST of the righteous would be RESURRECTED from the
DEAD a few years LATER.

THIS IS WHY the Apostle John in the Book of Revelation WROTE – and it was FULFILLED:

"Then I heard a voice from heaven say,
'Write: Blessed are the dead who die in the Lord from now on.'
'Yes,' says the Spirit, 'they will rest from their labor, for their deeds will follow them.'" (Rev. 14:13)[137]

I completed my eulogy with a brief recap of their lives. Then my brother gave his eulogy.

He Who Calls You

In closing this last chapter, let's never forget; it's the sovereign God Who both gives and takes life. Modern medicine can sometimes delay it and provide some physical comfort during the process. But the prerogative of the when and how of birth and death is a sacred right and a line that belongs to God alone.

One day we shall all die. The key for responding when this time comes is to surrender to it with an open palm and not a closed fist. What's the difference? A closed fist signifies blaming, bitterness, and anxiety. An open palm signifies acceptance, patience, and perseverance.[138]

But that day of victory will be far better than our day of birth, which ushered us into this polarized world. For when we die, we will be born into the glorious presence of Christ, given our new "spiritual body," and enter a realm more stupendous than we could ever imagine. There, we will dwell forever.

Yes, and truly truly, "Christ in you, the *hope* of glory" (Col. 1:27b). But one hopes for something one does not have (Rom. 8:24-25). And what you are hoping for is that when you have it you will be better off

---

[137] Why do we believe resurrection is a fulfilled and ongoingly relevant reality? For scriptural and historical details, see Noë, *Unraveling the End,* Chapter 16, "Resurrection Reality," 379-414 and Noë, *The Greater Jesus*, Chapter 9, "He 'Raptures' a Remnant," 291-337.

[138] From a sermon by my pastor Dave Rodriguez, 1/12/14.

than when you don't, right? Well, you "in Christ," in both this life and death, *is* glory, here and now! If now you have it, you will show it and manifest it. There is a significant difference. For further insights on this, please compare John 15:1-11 with 1 John 2:5-6.[139]

And so, "we fix our eyes not on what is seen, but on what is unseen. For what is seen is temporary, but what is unseen is eternal" (2 Cor. 4:18). Do we really believe this?

Please be assured of this present and available reality. "Now we know that if the earthly tent [our physical body] we live in is destroyed, we have a building from God, an eternal house in heaven, not built by human hands [our new "spiritual body"]. Meanwhile we groan, longing to be clothed with our heavenly dwelling, because when we are clothed, we will not be found naked. For while we are in this tent, we groan and are burdened, because we do not wish to be unclothed but to be clothed with our heavenly dwelling, so that what is mortal may be swallowed up by life. Now it is God who has made us for this very purpose and has given us the Spirit as a deposit, guaranteeing what is to come" (2 Cor. 5:1-5).

Yes, this resurrection reality is all "now" stuff.[140] And if we so choose to enter, Scripture urges us "to live lives worthy of God, who calls you into his kingdom and glory" (1 Thess. 2:12b; also see Rom. 2:6-10). Do we really believe this? Will we model it in both this life and in our death?

I'll leave you with these three questions to ponder:

1) How now will you respond to Him Who calls you into his kingdom and glory, here and now?
2) Is the "last enemy" of death (1 Cor. 15:26) good or evil?
3) Which will it be for you when this time comes?

One day we shall all die. The key for responding when this time comes is to surrender to it with an open palm and not a closed fist.

---

[139] Also see: Noē, *The Greater Jesus*, 214-219, 320-321, 363, 370, 378.
[140] See again footnote 137 above.

Conclusion

Light at the End of the Darkness

In answer to the quintessential question: "If God is all-powerful, they why doesn't He stop all evil things that go on?", Dr. Billy Graham once again replies: ". . . I don't have a full answer. Someday in heaven, we will understand . . . . some day Satan will be defeated and all evil will be destroyed."[1] With due respect for Dr. Graham, that day of understanding has *now* arrived. This book has provide a *fuller* answer—at least as "full" as Scripture will allow us to make.

In conclusion, I make no apologies for utilizing the comments of so many others. I stand on their shoulders. They have enabled me to affirm—in a way I could never have done on my own—that the so-called problem of evil is not a problem at all. Rather, it's a God-ordained, created, allowed, permitted, utilized, purposed, and sustained reality. When we finally arrive at this realization and acceptance of this scripturally documented reality, "fantasy Christianity" of a someday evil-less earth and material world will be no more.[2]

---

[1] Billy Graham, "My Answer," *The Indianapolis Star* (Indianapolis, IN), 29 November 2014, E-4. But on and on it goes. In his 12/20/14 column titled, "All evil will be destroyed," Dr. Graham continues voices his popular mantra, once again: "for some day God will intervene and all evil will be destroyed." Who should we now believe—Dr. Graham's fantasy tradition that trumps the Bible or the Bible itself?

[2] Eschatology (the study of last things / the end times) is all about the change of covenants, not a future change of cosmos. I have consistently documented and

Certainly, this book will not be the last word. But I hope it has elevated your perspective. I am also aware that there is more to this topic that I have covered herein. But of this one thing I believe we can now be more confident. Our sovereign God is indeed the Lord of *all* creation.

My All-Time Favorite

Whenever I hear it, it always brings a tear to my eye, and writing about it just now was no exception. It may be my all-time favorite gospel song. It presents one of the greatest expressions of giving yourself over to a higher power—in our case to God—that I have ever heard. It's titled, "There's a Light at the End of the Darkness." Metaphorically, of course, "God is light" (1 John 1:5; also see John 1:9; 8:12; 1 Thess. 5:5; Isa. 9:2; Matt. 5:14-16). And this song's powerful message is totally relevant throughout our life's journey on this earth and beyond.

It was written my Larry Gatlin. But if you really want to be blessed, google Chris Christian (right now) and listen to him sing this song as you follow along with these lyrics:

> There's a light at the end of the darkness
> And it shines for all the world to see
> It will shine on your heart if you will let it
> I was blind when it finally shined on me.
>
> There is hope in that light for the hopeless
> And a soothing balm for pain and misery
> It's as near as your faith but sometimes seen fleeting
> I was blind when it finally shined on me.
>
> There's a light at the end of the darkness
> So look up when you are down and try to believe
> Sometimes we have to be knocked down to make us look upward
> I was looking up from the bottom when it finally shined on me.[3]

---

proclaimed this historic, timely, and precise fulfillment and its ongoing reality and benefits in my other books and on PRI's website (www.prophecyrefi.org.). I recommend them to your further attention.

[3] "There's a light at the End of the Darkness" by Larry Gatlin.

Please be assured that the peace, confidence, and contentment that the world cannot provide are only found in the light of a right relationship with our Creator God through Jesus Christ. Consequently, our attitudes and responses in times of evil, pain, and suffering will a good barometer of that relationship. He knows and wills what is best for us. Habermas is most observant of this truth as he submits "that changing [of] our thinking [from questioning to trusting] can actually cause the reduction of even significant amounts of pain in our lives. This is an incredible truth."[4]

Undeniably, the so-called problem of evil has been the most serious challenge to the Christian faith. And, unfortunately, the history of most orthodox Christian thought on this matter has been one of evasion, depreciation, or overt and uncalled for protection of God. As we have seen, these diversions have produced a confusing array of other problems and forced many to turn the so-called problem of evil into an "enigma" that is "hopelessly inconclusive," "unanswerable," and "insoluble." The burden, however, to construct a more responsible and viable solution must lie with us Christians who take a high view of the Bible.

Make no mistake; the bottom line boils down to this one basic question: Who is sovereign—i.e., in charge, in control of this world? Once again, here are our choices: God, human free will, Satan and his cohorts, pre-creation chaos, space aliens, other. Choose wisely.

The dualistic polar-opposite reality of good and evil in our world is both the human dilemma and opportunity. How we respond during our short stay on this planet will determine how well and under what conditions and situation we spend our next life for all eternity. This is why the presence of both good and evil in our world is not a problem to be solved or a dilemma to be escaped, but a God-ordained reality to be faced and overcome.

I leave you now with one final tidbit, which encapsulates the major message of this book. But you will need to turn the page.

---

[4] Habermas, "Evil, the Resurrection and the Example of Jesus" in Meister and Dew, Jr., eds., *God and Evil*, 174.

This is my Father's world,
and to my listening ears
all nature sings, and round me rings
the music of the spheres.

This is my Father's world:
I rest me in the thought
of rocks and trees, of skies and seas;
his hand the wonders wrought.[5]

Are you listening?

Recommending Further Reading

I heartily recommend these top ten books, from those upon which I've drawn herein, on this subject for your further attention:

Theological:

John Hick, *Evil and the God of Love*

A.E. Knoch, *The Problem of Evil and the Judgments of God*

Chad Meister and James K. Dew Jr., eds., *God and Evil: The Case for God in a World Filled with Pain*

John Noē, *Hell Yes / Hell No: What really is the extent of God's grace . . . and wrath?*

Arthur W. Pink, *The Sovereignty of God*

R.C. Sproul, Jr., *Almighty Over All: Understanding the Sovereignty of God*

---

[5] 1st stanza: "This Is My Father's World," hymn, **Text:** Maltbie D. Babcock, 1901 **Music:** Trad. English melody; adapt. by Franklin L. Sheppard, 1915.

William A. Dembski, *The End of Christianity: Finding a Good God in an Evil World**

* (I do not concur with Dembski's origin of evil as being human free will and sin at the Fall.)

Pastoral:

Timothy Keller, *Walking with God through Pain and Suffering*

Jerry Sittser, *A Grace Disguised: How the soul grows through loss*

Randy Alcorn, *If God Is Good: Faith in the Midst of Suffering and Evil***

** (I do not concur with Alcorn's eschatological position that the current heaven is temporary and our eventual eternal home and destiny is on a "new earth.")[6]

---

[6] See Noē, *The Perfect Ending for the World*, 279-319 and Noē, *Unraveling the End*, 155-169.

What's Next?

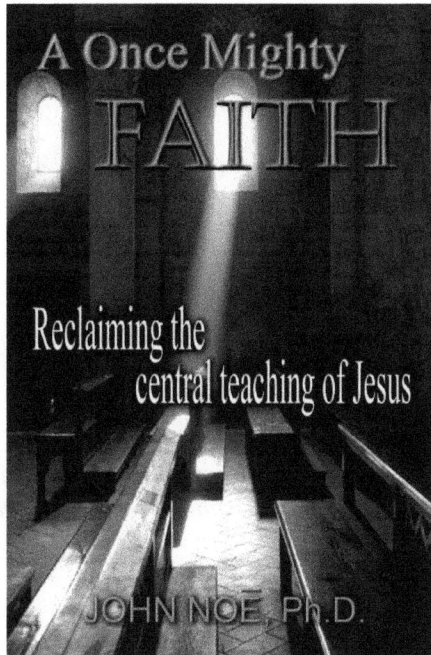

To combat and overcome evil, Jesus brought the everlasting form of the kingdom of God to this earth.

Hence, the kingdom was the central teaching of Jesus, at the heart of his ministry, and the very essence of New Testament Christianity. Sadly, today the kingdom is no longer the central teaching of most of his church, at the heart of its ministry, or its very essence.

My next book will address these three questions: What has happened? What has changed? What shall we do? It's tentatively titled and subtitled: *A Once Mighty Faith: Reclaiming the central teaching of Jesus*. Back cover heading: *Whatever Happened to Jesus' Almighty Kingdom?* (pub date 2016). Other subtitle options include: *Repossessing Jesus' almighty kingdom* or *Repossessing the almighty kingdom of Jesus*.

More pioneering and next-reformation titles are in development and forthcoming from John Noē and East2West Press. Tentatively titles and subtitles include:

GOD THE ULTIMATE COMPETITIVE EDGE
Transcending the limits of self / Why settle for anything less?

LIFE'S LAST GREAT ADVENTURE
What really happens today immediately after you die?—you may be surprised!

THE ISRAEL ILLUSION
Pulling back the curtain on the 'land of God' (Oz) / Major theological misconceptions about this modern-day nation

THE SCENE BEHIND THE SEEN
A Preterist-Idealist commentary of the Book of Revelation—unveiling its fulfillment and ongoing relevance—past, present & future

'TRAITOR WARRIOR'
The Days of Vengeance
The back story, theology, and script behind the movie

Books Out-of-Print

BEYOND THE END TIMES
SHATTERING THE 'LEFT BEHIND' DELUSION
DEAD IN THEIR TRACKS
**TOP TEN MISCONCEPTIONS ABOUT JESUS' SECOND
        COMING AND THE END TIMES**
PEOPLE POWER
THE APOCALYPSE CONSPIRACY

More Books from John Noē

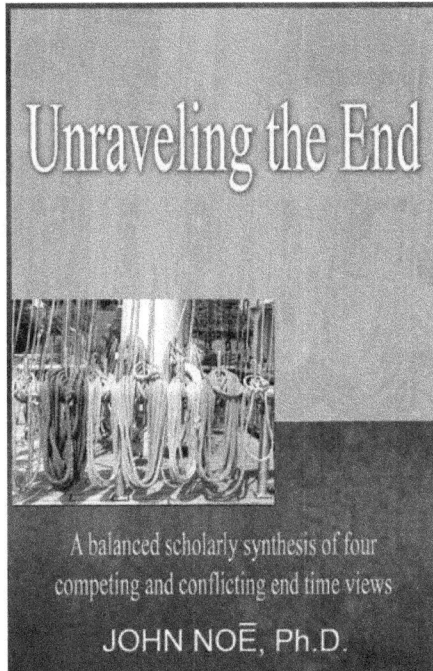

A Unifying Solution to the Divisive Stalemate

"There has been little attempt to synthesize the whole field of prophecy . . . and there is a great need . . . ." J. Dwight Pentecost

For nineteen centuries and counting, the Church has been made to look like a joke in the eyes of the world as predictions of Christ's Second Coming or Return and other related end-time events have supposedly come and gone without fulfillment. This book offers a unique solution. Herein, the author analyzes the strengths and weaknesses of the four major views, discards their weaknesses, and synthesizes their strengths into one meaningful, coherent, and cogent view that is more Christ-honoring, Scripture-authenticating, and faith-validating than any one view in and of itself.

The four views in order of their prominence today are: dispensational premillennialism, amillennialism, postmillennialism, and preterism. In this book, which is based on this author's doctoral dissertation and church seminar series, you will discover:

- 7 reasons your end-time view is so important.
- Why God is not the author of our confusion.
- The strengths and weaknesses of each view.
- A more comprehensive approach and disciplined methodology.
- Four false paradigms that force dichotomizing hermeneutics.
- God's divinely determined paradigm and timeline.
- A reconciliation of the divisive arena of eschatology.

'Synthesis Eschatology' on Nat'l TV

9 nationally televised TV programs featuring this book and introducing this unifying approach and synthesizing solution to the many problems of the end times aired twice weekly on TBN's "The Church Channel" (10/17 – 12/17/14). They are hosted by Dr. Lynn Hiles on his program is titled "That They Might Have Life."
To view or preview any of these nine programs, go to YouTube or PRI's website at http://www.prophecyrefi.org/tv-programs/.

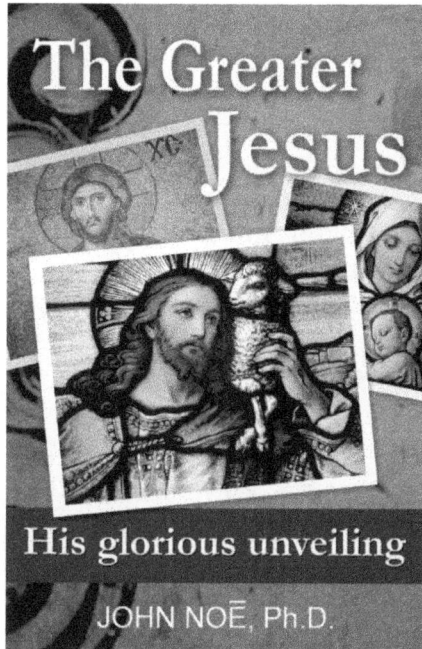

Which Jesus Is the Jesus You Follow?

No longer is Jesus the earth-bound, historical Jesus of Nazareth we have come to know and love in churches around the world every week. No longer is He the sleeping babe in a manger we celebrate every Christmas, or the boy who played in Galilee, or the man they hung at Calvary, or even the lamb who died for you and me. Those traditional views are simply out-of-date and inadequate. Why so? It's because *He's not like that anymore.*

Yes, the Jesus of the Gospels has changed since his birth and earthly ministry. Yet He's still the same Person. Most people today, however, remain unaware and uninformed about this same but more glorious, greater Jesus.

In this book you will discover:

- He looks different than the way we usually picture Him.
- He rides a horse on the clouds.
- He hosts a grand banquet.
- He's not sitting around (up in heaven) waiting to come back.
- He comes in many wondrous ways.
- He fights the battle of Armageddon.
- He plagues the great prostitute.
- He raptures a remnant.
- He wants you to live in the city.
- And much more.

". . . a terrific and timely read. I enjoyed the hell (whoops!) out of it. . . . This his fourth and longest book in a new series may just be Noē's most dynamic and challenging. — **John S. Evans, Ph.D., Amazon.com Review**

"This looks like a book that we have needed for a long time. I am excited to read it!" — **Edward J. Hassertt, JD**

"This book is of great interest to me, because I am developing a new course for Bible 10: 'Christ from Creation to Consummation.'" — **Robert Preston, M.A., M.Div., Bible Teacher at Liberty Christian School**

"This book is needed. I wish you well and much success in getting this out to thousands . . . hopefully millions." — **Jerry Bernard, BM, Ph.D., Phil.D., Litt.D.; Director of Research at Library in the Palms Research Center; VP of Scripture Research**

"It really and truly sounds very interesting and hopefully compelling . . . . Am looking forward to reading it." — **Miller Houghton, President, Houghton Oil Co.**

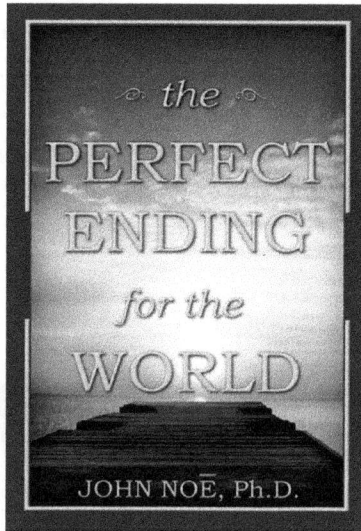

What are millions worldwide looking for today?

That's right! The perfect ending! Here it is!

Why All 'End-of-the-World' Prophets Will <u>Always</u> Be Wrong!

The perennial prophets of doom have failed to recognize that our world is without end and "the end" the Bible consistently proclaims *for* the world is behind us and not ahead of us; is past and not future. This is the perfect ending! It's also the climax of the rest of the greatest story ever foretold. In this book you'll discover:

~ WHY THE WORLD WILL NEVER END.
~ HOW THE PERFECT ENDING FOR THE WORLD CAME RIGHT ON TIME.
~ DIVINE PERFECTION IN GOD'S END-TIME PLAN.
~ A NEW & GREATER PARADIGM OF THOUGHT AND FAITH.
~ OUR GREATER RESPONSIBILITIES HEREIN.
~ WHY THE FUTURE IS BRIGHT AND PROMISING.
~ THE BASIS FOR THE NEXT REFORMATION OF CHRISTIANITY.

"Noē's book just could be the spark that ignites the next reformation of Christianity." – Dr. James Earl Massey, Former Sr. Editor, *Christianity Today* Dean Emeritus, School of Theology, Anderson University & Distinguished Professor-at-Large

*"Your treatment of the 'end of the world' is the best treatment of this idea . . .
. Your book could really open the eyes of a lot of people."* – Walter C.
Hibbard, Former Chairman, Great Christian Books

*"Noē . . . argues, with no little energy, against traditional views . . . [it] does
have an internal logic that makes for exegetically interesting reading."* – Mark
Galli, Book Review Editor, *Christianity Today*

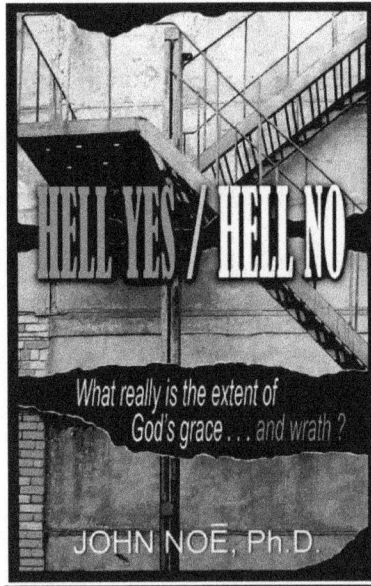

'Hell Yes / Hell No: What really is the extent of God's grace . . . and wrath?' –

This compelling and controversial book strikes at the heart of Christian theology
and Christianity itself. It presents a balanced and scholarly re-exploration of
"one of Christianity's most offensive doctrines"—Hell and the greater issue of
the extent of God's grace (mercy, love, compassion, justice) and wrath in the
eternal, afterlife destiny for all people. Inside, conflicting views are reevaluated,

their strengths and weaknesses reassessed, and all the demands of Scripture are reconciled into one coherent and consistent synthesized view. The author further suggests that our limited earthly view has been the problem, rediscovers the ultimate mystery of God's expressed desire, will, and purpose, and transcends troubling traditions as never before. The bottom line is, God's plan of salvation and condemnation may be far different and greater than we've been led to believe. In a clear and straightforward manner, this book lays out the historical and scriptural evidence as never before.

Can We Really Be So Sure Anymore?

Battle lines are drawn. Sides are fixed. Arguments are exhausted. The majority proclaim, "Hell yes!" But growing numbers are protesting, "Hell no!" After nineteen centuries of church history, no effective resolution or scriptural reconciliation has been offered—until now!

So what really is the true Christian doctrine on this matter of hell and the greater issue of the extent of God's grace (mercy, love, compassion, justice) and wrath in the eternal, afterlife destiny for all people? The answer goes to the heart of Christian theology and Christianity itself. Has our limited earthly view been the problem? Could God's plan of salvation be far different than and from what we've been led to believe?

In this book you'll discover:

- A balanced scholarly re-exploration of the mystery of God's desire, will, and purpose in the eternal afterlife destiny for all people.
- Reevaluation of conflicting views.
- Reassessment of the strengths and weaknesses of pro and con arguments.
- Synthesis of the strengths into one coherent and consistent view that meets all scriptural demands.
- Reconciliation of the greatest debate of 'all.'
- Transcending troubling traditions as never before!

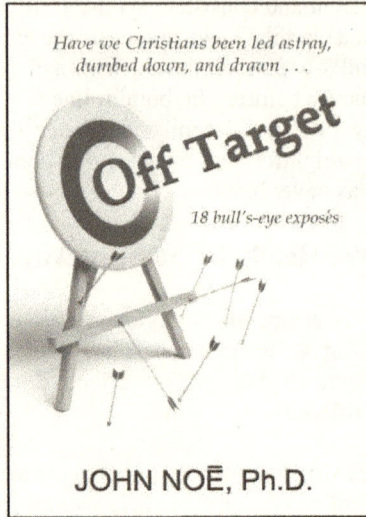

Have we Christians been led astray,
dumbed down, and drawn . . .

Off Target

18 bull's-eye exposés

JOHN NOĒ, Ph.D.

Today's Dumbed-down Dilemma

Truly, have we Christians been led astray by our own leaders; dumbed down in our theology by ideas, interpretations, teachings, doctrines of men, and traditions that will not stand up to an honest and sincere test of Scripture; and consequently drawn off target in the practice of our faith?

This on-target, bull's-eye-aimed book re-explores what authentic Christianity really is versus today's institutionalized and substandard versions that we've comfortably come to know and accept. As you'll discover, beliefs do have consequences. This is why our modern-day versions pale in comparison with vibrancy and effectiveness of the Christianity that was preached, practiced, and perceived in the 1st century and turned that hostile world "upside down" (Acts 17:6). They also pale in contrast with the faith that brought our forefathers to America to found this country and establish its great institutions—most of which we moderns have given away to the ungodly crowd and without a fight. Bottom line is, we Christians are paying an awful price for our self-inflicted deficiencies.

Inside these pages we will reassess today's dumbed-down dilemma in these key 18 exposé areas:

- Divine Perfection in Two Creations
- The Kingdom of God
- The Gospel
- Hell
- The 'Last Days'
- Second Coming / Return
- Rapture
- Antichrist
- The Contemporary Christ
- Book of Revelation
- Battle of Armageddon
- Israel
- Conflicting End-time Views
- Doing the Works of Jesus
- Doing Greater Works than Jesus
- Origin of Evil
- Eternal Rewards and Punishment for Believers
- Your Worldview

Revised edition – PEAK PERFORMANCE PRINICIPLES FOR HIGH ACHIEVERS *is a dynamic story of how one man transformed himself, sedentary and out-of-shape in his mid-thirties, into a dynamic leader – and how you can too.*

John R. Noē is using his mountain-climbing adventures as an allegory for the challenge of goal setting and the thrill of high achievement. He shows you how to choose accurate goals, how to reach them, how to remain committed to the accomplishment of a goal whether earthly or spiritual, and—in short—how to become a high achiever. To help you succeed, Noē offers a unique philosophy of reaching "beyond self-motivation" to the spiritual motivation that comes from God.

In this revised edition, Noē adds further insights and updates his reader on how these principles have fared in his life since the book's original writing in 1984— which was named one of Amway Corporation's "top ten recommended books."

Noē shows you how to learn the six essential attitudes
of a high achiever:

1. High Achievers make no small plans.
2. Are willing to do what they fear.
3. Are willing to prepare.
4. To risk failure.
5. To be taught.
6. And must have heart.

"After reading this marvelous book I realized how little I have accomplished with my life . . . compared to what I could have done. But, it's not too late."

> Og Mandino, Author of:
> *The Greatest Salesman in the World*

"So many Christians are going through life settling for mediocre, settling for second best, and choosing the path of least resistance. Not Dr. John R. Noē, author of this old (1984) and new (2006) book, *Peak Performance Principles for High Achievers – Revised Edition.* **He reminds us that the first mountain we need to conquer is that of ourselves and that God wants us to accomplish great things for His glory."**

> Dr. D. James Kennedy, Ph.D.
> Senior Minister
> Coral Ridge Presbyterian Church

Scripture Index

www.ingramcontent.com/pod-product-compliance
Lightning Source LLC
LaVergne TN
LVHW011344080426
835511LV00005B/124